COLLECTING, ANALYZING, AND REPORTING DATA

COLLECTING, ANALYZING, AND REPORTING DATA

AN OXFORD HANDBOOK OF QUALITATIVE RESEARCH IN AMERICAN MUSIC EDUCATION

Volume 2

Edited by
COLLEEN M. CONWAY

Oxford University Press is a department of the University of Oxford. It furthers
the University's objective of excellence in research, scholarship, and education
by publishing worldwide. Oxford is a registered trade mark of Oxford University
Press in the UK and certain other countries.

Published in the United States of America by Oxford University Press
198 Madison Avenue, New York, NY 10016, United States of America.

© Oxford University Press 2020

All rights reserved. No part of this publication may be reproduced, stored in
a retrieval system, or transmitted, in any form or by any means, without the
prior permission in writing of Oxford University Press, or as expressly permitted
by law, by license, or under terms agreed with the appropriate reproduction
rights organization. Inquiries concerning reproduction outside the scope of the
above should be sent to the Rights Department, Oxford University Press, at the
address above.

You must not circulate this work in any other form
and you must impose this same condition on any acquirer.

CIP data is on file at the Library of Congress
ISBN 978-0-19-092093-7

Contents

Preface	vii
COLLEEN M. CONWAY	
List of Contributors	xi
1. Ethics and Qualitative Research in Music Education	1
JUDITH M. BIRK AND CYNTHIA S. SHINDLEDECKER	
2. Generating and Analyzing Observation of Music Teaching and Learning Data	20
MARGARET SCHMIDT	
3. Generating and Analyzing Individual Interviews	43
KATHRYN ROULSTON	
4. Conducting and Analyzing Focus Group Data	63
JOHN EROS	
5. Generating and Analyzing Multimodal and Multimedia Data	80
EVAN S. TOBIAS	
6. Music-Making as Data: Collection and Analysis	99
KRISTEN PELLEGRINO	
7. Software to Interrogate Qualitative Data in Music Education	117
PETER R. WEBSTER	
8. Changing the Conversation: Considering Quality in Music Education Qualitative Research	130
MITCHELL ROBINSON	
9. The Politics of Publication: Voices, Venues, and Ethics	148
MITCHELL ROBINSON	
Index	165

Preface

Collecting, Analyzing, and Reporting Qualitative Data in American Music Education

Music education researchers doing qualitative studies finding themselves collecting, analyzing, and reporting on qualitative data. Decisions about the types of data to be gathered are guided by the research questions for a study. Music education qualitative researchers use a variety of strategies to collect information relevant to their research questions. The researcher has a responsibility to the reader to provide a thick description (Lincoln and Guba 1985) of data collection and analysis as well as findings.

Each of the qualitative traditions (e.g., narrative research) has a slightly different approach to collection and analysis of data. However, there are some common traits in all qualitative analysis. Authors in this text address data collection and analysis in relation to the type of data (observation, interview, focus group, multimedia and multimodal, and music-making). Researchers begin analysis with a review of all data. They create transcripts for interviews and may enter transcripts and field notes into software if the analysis is to be supported with technology. The first step in most analysis procedures is to begin to code the data. During coding, the researcher typically identifies and tentatively names the conceptual categories into which the events observed will be grouped. The goal is to create descriptive categories that form a preliminary framework for analysis. Words, phrases, or events that appear to be similar can be grouped into the same category. These categories may be gradually modified or replaced during the subsequent stages of analysis that follow. Once the data has been coded, the researcher can begin to combine codes to create larger categories. Next, categories are re-examined to determine if and how they are linked, comparing and combining them in new ways in an effort to develop an integrated understanding.

The results of qualitative studies are usually represented as findings or themes from the data. There is no template for the reporting of qualitative data. The story-like nature of the types of data collected can lead to any number of formats for reporting. The goal of the researcher is to provide a report that will be rich in detail and authentic. While the process of analysis has been described as a linear one, the individual steps may occur simultaneously and repeatedly. During the analysis, additional data may be collected if the researcher uncovers gaps in the data. In qualitative research, the analysis and data collection are really commingled, with one serving as a guide to the other.

CRITERIA FOR EVALUATING QUALITATIVE DATA AND ANALYSIS

In chapter 8 of this text, Robinson suggests:

> The establishment of criteria for quality in qualitative research in music education has existed as a problematic issue within our profession for many years. The range of opinions and beliefs concerning "goodness" criteria for qualitative research is vast, and encompasses multiple belief systems, paradigm orientations and research stances. (p. 130)

Robinson's chapter provides an extended discussion of these issues. For the purpose of considering key criteria of data collection and analysis in qualitative research, I touch on just a few of these issues in this Preface.

Quantitative researchers use research design, statistical techniques, and replication to demonstrate that their findings can be applied to other settings, that is, generalized. The idea of generalization is wedded to the philosophical foundation—understanding phenomena on a macro level that supersedes context and human perception. Qualitative researchers carefully discuss their conceptual frameworks and their interactions with research participants in order for readers to have enough information to consider the possible transferability of findings to other contexts. According to Lincoln and Guba (1985), transferability is defined as the "similarity between two contexts" or the "fittingness" or congruence between two contexts (124). The researcher is responsible for providing a thick, rich description of the phenomena and the contextual variables to allow the reader to determine transferability of the findings. Schwartz (1996) uses the idea of logical situational generalizability (7). If the reader can logically assume that participants in another population are in a situation similar to the one described in the study, it may be possible that results from the study are relevant in other contexts.

All of the studies referenced in this text were chosen to represent some aspect of the qualitative data collection and analysis process. Not all studies included are exemplary models. But all studies presented report on at least some of the criteria outlined in this section.

Organization of Text

Collecting, Analyzing, and Reporting Qualitative Data is a resource for music education researchers, music education graduate students, and P–16 music teachers. The volume begins with a chapter examining ethics and qualitative research from the perspective of scholars within the University of Michigan's Heath Sciences and Behavioral Sciences Institutional Review Board. The middle five chapters describe data collection and analysis techniques as well as provide examples of studies in music education that have utilized these techniques, including: observation; individual interviews; focus group interviews; journals, multimodal and multimedia data; and music-making as data. A chapter on technology provides insight into the analysis process through technological support. The final two chapters address criteria for judging quality in qualitative data collection and analysis and ethics in relation to publication of qualitative work.

It was challenging for authors in this volume to situate music teaching and learning at the center of the conversation as the techniques used for qualitative research in general education and music education more specifically are closely aligned. Authors in this text did not attempt to provide a comprehensive collection of all music education qualitative researchers who used these techniques in their studies, but, rather, have selected exemplars for readers to consider.

Consideration of Issues Not Represented

The challenge for any book Editor is often to define the scope of the volume. Authors for this text were instructed to focus their chapters on qualitative research in American music education. The decision to be exclusive to studies conducted in North America (Canada and the US) was made to help focus and contain the volume. Many authors struggled with this restriction, as there is a rich traditional of qualitative research within international contexts. Another delimitation aimed at focusing the scope of this book was that authors include only qualitative studies that appear in published journals or as dissertations; not conference presentations or unpublished manuscripts.

Collecting, Analyzing, and Reporting Qualitative Data is quite comprehensive with regards to ways in which music education researchers have collected and analyzed their data. The one technique that some might consider missing from a text devoted to data collection and analysis is that of discourse analysis (Gee 2005). I am aware of several music education researchers who have used this technique (Dobbs 2005, 2008; Talbot 2010) but did not feel at the time of publication that there was enough work in music education in this area to create a chapter.

References

Dobbs, Teryl. 2005. "Discourse in the Band Room: How Talk Shapes Teaching, Learning, and Community in a Middle School Instrumental Music Classroom." Unpublished doctoral dissertation, Northwestern University, 3177710.

Dobbs, Teryl. 2008. "Discourse in the Band Room: The Role of Talk in an Instrumental Music Classroom." In *Diverse Methodologies in the Study of Music Teaching and Learning*, edited by Linda K Thompson and Mark R. Campbell, 137–160. Charlotte, NC: IAP-Information Age.

Gee, James Paul. 2005. *An Introduction to Discourse Analysis: Theory and Method*. New York: Routledge.

Lincoln, Yvonna S., and Egon G. Guba. 1985. *Naturalistic Inquiry*. Beverly Hills, CA: Sage Publications.

Schwartz, Henreitta. 1996. "The Changing Nature of Teacher Education." In *Handbook of Research on Teacher Education*, 2nd ed., edited by J. Sikula, T. J. Buttery, and E. Guyton, 2–13. New York: Macmillan.

Talbot, Brent. 2010. "Critical Discourse Analysis for Transformative Music Teaching and Learning: Method, Critique and Globalization." *Bulletin of the Council for Research in Music Education* 186: 81–93.

Contributors

Judith M. Birk, Director, Medical School Institutional Review Board, University of Michigan

Colleen M. Conway, Professor of Music Education, University of Michigan

John Eros, Associate Professor of Music, California State University, East Bay

Kristen Pellegrino, Associate Professor of Music Education, University of Texas at San Antonio

Mitchell Robinson, Associate Professor of Music Education, Michigan State University

Kathryn Roulston, Professor, Department of Lifelong Education, Administration, and Policy, University of Georgia

Margaret Schmidt, Associate Professor of Music Education, Arizona State University

Cynthia S. Shindledecker, Director, Health Sciences and Behavioral Sciences Institutional Review Board, University of Michigan

Evan S. Tobias, Associate Professor of Music Education, Arizona State University

Peter R. Webster, Scholar-in-Residence, Thornton School of Music, University of Southern California

COLLECTING, ANALYZING, AND REPORTING DATA

CHAPTER 1

ETHICS AND QUALITATIVE RESEARCH IN MUSIC EDUCATION

JUDITH M. BIRK AND CYNTHIA S. SHINDLEDECKER

1.1. INTRODUCTION

THE conduct of qualitative human participant research represents a complex intersection of terminology, techniques, and settings. Bresler and Stake (1992) provided a dizzying list of terminology: case study, field study, ethnographic, naturalistic, phenomenological, interpretive, and descriptive. Mills (2003) added action research to the list to describe the technique of systematic inquiries into self-practice in educational settings. Contributing to the mix are research environments varying from large cityscapes where an observational researcher is unlikely to be noticed, to intimate classroom settings where the researcher may also be the teacher. Music educators conducting human participant research are familiar with these concepts and the challenges they may present.

Music students and their teachers frequently gather in traditional classrooms or small group settings such as community ensembles. While these settings offer a convenient atmosphere to conduct research, the small environment may make it difficult for the researcher to maintain an anonymous presence or for the students or teachers in the classroom to feel that they retain autonomy relative to participation in research. This sense of autonomy may be further diminished when the teacher is the researcher and his or her own students are the object of the research investigation (Pritchard 2002).

Research conducted in the context of music education settings provides an interesting opportunity to consider ethical and regulatory oversight of human research participants within the boundaries of qualitative research design. The breadth of this topic is extensive. This piece provides a perspective on qualitative human participant research under the purview of United States federal regulations. It offers a guide to researchers to more easily navigate the Institutional Review Board (IRB) review process when approval is necessary for their research activities. Vignettes focusing on music education are provided to showcase research models and the corresponding IRB response. Suggestions are also offered to assist IRBs with maximizing regulatory flexibility to ease the regulatory burden on researchers while continuing to provide all necessary and appropriate protections for human participants.

1.2. Institutional Review Boards

Most individuals conducting academic research are familiar with the origins of current human participant research regulations. Atrocities committed during the prior century under the guise of biomedical research, especially those committed during World War II, led to the eventual development of regulations for oversight of human participant research in many countries of the world.

In the United States, the startling discovery of the unethical research protocols of the Tuskegee Syphilis Study conducted with African American men between 1930 and 1972 led to the creation of the National Commission for the Protection of Human Subjects of Biomedical and Behavioral Research. The work of this Commission, published in 1979 as the Belmont Report, formed the basis for US federal regulations for human participant research and the framework for IRBs. The report provided three core principles for the ethical conduct of human participant research:

1) Respect for persons—individuals should be treated as autonomous agents, and persons with diminished autonomy are entitled to protection;
2) Beneficence—do not harm; maximize possible benefits and minimize possible harms;
3) Justice—injustice occurs when some benefit to which a person is entitled is denied without good reason or when some burden is imposed unduly.

IRBs are primarily associated with institutions conducting human participant research funded or supported by US federal agencies but may also exist independently and not receive federal sponsorship. For entities receiving federal sponsorship, a Federalwide Assurance (FWA) indicating intent to comply with federal regulations (45 CFR 46) is required. In addition, each institution is required to choose a statement of ethical principles upon which it will discharge its responsibilities for protecting the rights and welfare of human participants in research conducted at or by the institution regardless of the source of support. Most US institutions select the Belmont Report.

This code, 45 CFR 46, is made up of five subparts, four of which are devoted to human participant protections. Subpart A, also known as the Common Rule, provides the basic framework for the IRB's composition, criteria for the approval of research, informed consent requirements, and record-keeping obligations. Subparts B, C, and D provide additional protections for pregnant women, fetuses, and neonates; prisoners; and children.

Many academic institutions have established IRBs, as they are major recipients of federal support for human participant research. Larger academic institutions may provide resources to constitute both biomedical and social/behavioral science IRBs in order to provide the specialized expertise necessary to review these distinct categories of research.

Depending on the nature and risk level of the research, IRBs are able to conduct their work utilizing several review pathways. Reviews of research posing more than minimal risk to the participants must be reviewed by the full, convened IRB; research meeting regulatory qualifications for expedited review is reviewed by a single, experienced member of the IRB; and research qualifying as exempt may be reviewed by a member of the IRB or other qualified individual.

Not all activities utilizing human participants are considered to be research regulated by an IRB. When IRB oversight is not required, professional codes of ethics or codes of conduct frequently provide an additional framework for protecting the rights of human participants in research. While the professional codes of conduct may provide less specificity than federal regulations, they outline the same ethical tenets to members of the profession. For example, the American Psychological Association Ethical Principles of Psychologists and Code of Conduct (2010 Amendments) and the Code of Ethics of the American Educational Research Association (approved February 2011) both provide discipline-specific requirements for conducting research with human participants.

1.3. Qualitative Research and Regulatory Ethical Review

Designing, conducting, and then overseeing qualitative research within the same regulatory framework as biomedical research poses challenges for researchers and IRBs. While all IRBs apply the same federal Common Rule requirements to research under their purview, a particular IRB's experience with reviewing qualitative research may affect regulatory outcomes for individual researchers. For example, the same definition of research applies to biomedical and qualitative research:

> Research means a systematic investigation, including research development, testing and evaluation, designed to develop or contribute to generalizable knowledge. (45 CFR 46.102(l))

Some, but not all, qualitative researchers point out that their work is often not systematic and may not be generalizable. Regulations are frequently interpreted and implemented via guidance documents. These documents are helpful to IRBs in providing clarification or additional direction on proceeding under the regulations. However, where the guidance is not prescriptive, varying interpretations may lead to inconsistent practice within an IRB or between IRBs at different institutions. This was likely the situation encountered by one researcher when she attempted to initiate a minimal risk music education survey at 26 academic institutions and was thwarted by varying IRB requirements (Thornton 2008).

Qualitative research may be especially susceptible to inconsistent review outcomes from IRBs. Open-ended or observational research designs do not have solid parameters upon which IRBs are able to make consistent determinations. For example, a researcher wishing to study the effect of music lessons in a home-schooling environment may need to convince the IRB that such an environment is considered to be a "... commonly accepted educational setting involving normal educational practices ..." under federal exemption #1. In the absence of specific guidance as to what constitutes a "commonly accepted educational setting" IRBs will arrive at different outcomes (45 CFR 46.104(b)(1)).

Not all qualitative research is without risks to participants. The American Anthropological Association Statement on Ethnography and Institutional Review Boards (2004, 2) states that "Ethnographic research may involve significant risks of harm—for example, discrimination, disruption of personal and family relationships, loss of rights, or claims, civil or criminal prosecution—usually as the result of disclosure of private, identifiable information such as data gathered in interviews filmed on video, or recorded on tape or field notes." Common Rule exemptions allow research to be free from IRB oversight if it involves the use of educational tests, surveys, interviews, or observation of public behavior but not if subjects can be identified directly or indirectly and "... any disclosure of the subjects' responses outside the research could reasonably place the subjects at risk of criminal or civil liability or be damaging to the subjects' financial standing, employability, or reputation" (45 CFR 46.104(d)(2)).

Risks to participants in biomedical research are usually evident. The research is stringently regulated to address the potentially significant, quantifiable risks associated with exposing participants to new or existing drugs, devices, therapies, or medical procedures. Standard protocols across one or more study sites assure consistent, reproducible data collection. Researchers can use lab values and other tools to monitor for significant changes in important body functions as an outcome of the research.

By contrast, qualitative research frequently proceeds without the exacting requirements required in biomedical research. The research design may be open-ended to allow for unconstrained exploration of the research topic and reproducibility may be limited by circumstance. Risks to participants are not easy to quantify. It may be difficult for a researcher to assess whether a participant who cries only a "little" during the interview is able to proceed without some lingering effects. If a video recording labeled with the name and school affiliation of a student teacher in a music classroom is stolen, does it mean that the teacher or students would not be at risk since it was "only" a music education classroom? What about the potential for misuse of the tape?

IRBs and researchers regularly struggle to reach consensus on risk to participants. IRBs are seen as over-managing risk to avoid institutional liability (Tierney and Corwin 2007; Gunsalas et al. 2007). However, IRBs are aware of the risks as they receive reports of research mishaps and must manage situations, including risks to participants when sensitive research data are lost or stolen. Even ethnographers acknowledge that publication of the work carries a very real possibility of exposing a participant and could result in a loss of confidentiality (Librett and Perrone 2010). Additionally, researchers, especially those new to the field, do not always plan appropriately for participant reactions. While qualitative research differs significantly in its data collection methodologies from the empirical data collection of quantitative research, it still requires careful consideration of the rights and welfare of the individuals under study as the risks are harder to quantify.

1.4. Designing Research Projects for Educational Settings

An understandable tension exists between the researcher preparing an application for review and the IRB. Like taxpayers completing their annual tax form, researchers hope to find one or more loopholes to avoid the extra work associated with IRB interactions. However, careful attention to research design and clear explanations provided to the IRB can improve the process for researchers and offer better protections for participants. Transparency at this juncture is important for IRBs to make exemption and other regulatory determinations.

When an activity meets the definition of research and involves human participants, the activity is considered to be regulated by an IRB unless the activity qualifies for a regulatory exemption. Frequently, research in the area of music education in the classroom qualifies for such an exemption. Whether the research qualifies for exemption or not, educational settings require special consideration of the study population, research location, data, and involvement of the teachers as researchers or as participants themselves.

1.4.1. Students as a Vulnerable Population

Students studied in a classroom setting, as the object of research, may be considered a vulnerable population. Researchers must assure that students are able to make fully informed, un-coerced decisions about their participation. Even observational research in the classroom may be perceived by students as limiting their autonomy to behave normally. When research is considered exempt from federal regulations, researchers continue to have an ethical obligation to obtain appropriate permissions from the students, and possibly their parents, if the students are minors.

Qualitative researchers should be careful to set boundaries between the research aspect of the relationship and the academic component. Where relationships might prove too confusing (as in teachers studying their own classroom practices), the researcher might consider assigning some of the research tasks to a third party to avoid any impression of limiting a student's autonomy or biasing grades or academic outcomes.

In cases where interactions with the students may involve sensitive data collection about illegal behaviors or child abuse inflicted upon the student, the researcher should work closely with an IRB to design appropriate protections for the data and to understand any reporting obligations necessary to protect the child. There may be additional issues related to obtaining parental permission in these circumstances and the IRB may ask the researcher to seek additional assurances to protect identifiable data such as a Certificate of Confidentiality.

1.4.2. Site Permissions

Education researchers wishing to work within school or classroom settings should plan to obtain explicit permission from school officials before engaging in the activity. Many school sites have their own operating procedures or are subject to local laws and may not be able or willing to cooperate with the researcher. So important are these permissions that many IRBs require documentation of site approval before completing their review. As school districts place more emphasis on curriculum requirements and the safety of their students, researchers may face additional challenges in attempting to access students or teachers to engage them in research activities.

1.4.3. Data and Its Management

Data in education research are collected and maintained in a variety of formats. Surveys, interviews, focus groups, field notes, and audio/video recording are common collection methods. Data may be maintained in hard copy, on local computer systems, or in a remote "cloud" storage facility. Some data are retained for future research use by the original researcher or intended for sharing with others in an archive or library format. If the research is not exempt, IRBs are required under the Common Rule to consider whether there are adequate provisions to protect the privacy of the participants and to maintain the confidentiality of the data. Researchers conducting exempt research are usually governed by professional codes of ethics that provide discipline-specific requirements.

All research studies should include a data management plan that describes how the researcher will protect, store, and use the data. Participants should be told of these plans during the informed consent process. Risks to participants are increased when research involves sensitive data collection. Care should be taken to protect participant confidentiality by de-identification of data when possible. Some data, especially video recordings or extensive field notes, may be difficult to de-identify due to their voluminous and qualitative nature. If the data are sensitive or may pose risks to participants, extra precautions should be taken. Data should be converted to storage mediums that allow for additional protections. For example, field notes and video recordings might be digitized and password protected. Data collected without participant identifiers, whenever possible, offers the best method of protecting the privacy of the participant and confidentiality of the data.

Occasionally a participant may decide to withdraw from research already underway and request that his or her data be destroyed. Researchers should contemplate such events in their study design and informed consent materials should provide information to participants about their options regarding return or destruction of their data. For example, data already de-identified and aggregated cannot be returned to the participant. However, identifiable interview or audio/visual materials may be able to be removed from the data set and destroyed or returned to the participant.

1.4.4. Teachers as Researchers

Teachers wishing to study instructional methods and practice have readily available participants from among the students in their own classroom. When a teacher studies his or her own practice, the intent may not be to produce "generalizable knowledge" but rather to inform and improve his or her own teaching. If so, this activity is not considered to be human participant research according to the Common Rule definition of regulated research. When the activities of a teacher meet the regulatory definition of research, regardless of whether the research qualifies as exempt, careful consideration must be given to the students who are now also participants.

If teachers conduct research in their own classrooms, they must seek to avoid bias in order to protect the non-research relationship with their students. For example, when both the researcher and the participant (who in this case are the teacher and the student) believe the research is being conducted for the good of the student participant, rather than the benefit of the research or researcher, participants may be misled. Pritchard (2002, 6) calls this the "educational misconception." So significant is the risk to students for coercion that some IRBs will not approve this research or will require additional protections before approval. Teacher-researchers might unintentionally single out one or more students in a manner that could draw unwarranted attention to them and constitute an invasion of their privacy. Teacher-researchers may subconsciously let knowledge of a student's participation in their research (or not) affect their grading of the student. Therefore, research should be designed to protect the identity of participating students from being disclosed to the teacher-researcher. Instead, it may be more appropriate for a third party to handle collection of completed survey instruments or to conduct interviews with students in order to shield the teacher from the direct knowledge of a student's participation. If participation in research is offered as extra credit, teacher-researchers must offer alternative, equivalent opportunities for individuals to receive extra credit if they decline to participate in the research.

All research, whether qualitative or quantitative, requires researchers to prioritize the interests of the participant ahead of their own. Music education research in its qualitative form is no exception. Even benign data, when mishandled, can raise issues of privacy and confidentiality for participants.

1.4.5. Teachers as Participants

A teacher may occasionally be the object of a research study. In the same way that students in a classroom might have their performance outcomes assessed by education researchers, teachers may be evaluated for the effectiveness of their teaching style or their delivery of a new curriculum. As with students being studied in the classroom, teachers should be provided with appropriate opportunities to provide informed consent and receive assurances of how their data will used and stored and how their confidentiality will be protected. Even when the research intervention is directed toward the teacher, students may indirectly enter the data collection, as is the case when teachers are video recorded as part of the research. Researchers should examine school policies to determine how to manage these situations. In the case of video recording, some schools require that students without permission to be photographed be moved out of camera range.

1.5. Activities Outside the Scope of IRB Oversight

Not all activities connected with music education research are under the oversight of an IRB. IRBs regulate only those activities that are non-exempt and meet the definition of research conducted with human participants as defined by the Common Rule. To determine which activities qualify as research regulated by an IRB, IRBs systematically evaluate the basis for the activities and the nature of the interaction with human participants. Vignettes are useful as a method of illustrating IRB decision-making and may help music educators assess whether their efforts require IRB review and approval, are considered exempt from regulatory oversight, or do not represent research with human participants as defined by the regulations. The following vignettes describe common situations and discrete components of IRB decision-making to illustrate when activities do not meet the test for IRB oversight.

> Vignette 1: Research on Organizational Systems (research not involving human participants)
> For his master's thesis, a music education student is interested in assessing the current level of state support for music education in the Midwest and its effect on individual districts. The researcher will collect data by reviewing public records of state agencies, including budget information and transcripts of public meetings. In

addition, he will conduct a telephone survey of school district administrators to seek information regarding current funding levels and the ability of the district to support music education. Since the student will be conducting surveys and using transcripts that identify participants from public meetings, his faculty advisor recommended that he submit an application to the IRB.

IRB Considerations

An IRB's first decision point for a project is to determine whether it is an activity that meets the regulatory definition of research with human participants requiring IRB oversight. The Common Rule defines research as:

> A systematic investigation, including research development, testing and evaluation, designed to develop or contribute to generalizable knowledge (45 CFR 46.102(l)).

The proposed study meets the regulatory definition of research as it is a systematic data collection and the student intends to use the data for his thesis.

Next, the IRB considers whether human participants are involved in the research. The Common Rule defines a human participant as:

> A living individual about whom an investigator (whether professional or student) conducting research: (i) Obtains information or biospecimens through intervention or interaction with the individual, and uses, studies, or analyzes the information or biospecimens; or (ii) Obtains, uses, studies, analyzes identifiable private information or identifiable biospecimens (45 CFR 46.102(e)(1)).

Before determining whether the research includes human participants, the IRB must consider additional elements of the research design to characterize the source and nature of the data.

1. Defining "About whom"
   Conducting a telephone survey involves an interaction with a person. The key question is whether the survey collects information about that individual. If the survey questions directed at the institutional spokesperson are limited to collecting facts about district budgets and curriculum offerings, the activity does not involve a human participant. The information collected is about the organization, not the individual responding. However, if the survey elicits identifiable private information, such as personal opinions, the district official would be a human participant. District administrators did not provide identifiable, private information about themselves in this vignette.
2. Identifiable private information
   The student will review transcripts of public meetings. The student is not conducting an intervention or interaction with these individuals nor is the information collected considered private as the meetings were public and the transcripts are publicly available. Thus, the individuals involved in the public meeting are not considered human participants.

IRB Determination

After considering the student's IRB application, the IRB determined that while the activity was research, it did not involve human participants. Therefore, it did not require IRB oversight.

Vignette 2: Student Teacher in a Classroom (regulatory definition of research not met)

A middle school student with a disability is enrolled in choir for the academic year. A graduate student working with the choir tries various methods to engage the student with the music and with her fellow singers. At the end of a successful year, the graduate student presents her experiences in working with this student as part of a class assignment for her master's program. Her advisor suggests that she present her work to other music educators at a national meeting. The graduate student contacts the IRB to see if her project requires IRB review.

IRB Considerations

As with the first vignette, the IRB must assess whether this activity meets the definition of research with human participants. The graduate student did not start the academic year intending to systematically engage in planned interactions, interventions, and data collection with the middle school student. Only after hearing the graduate student's presentation at the end of the year did her advisor realize that the experience offered value and should be shared with other educators. In this situation, the project does not meet the regulatory definition of *research*—a systematic investigation designed to contribute to generalizable knowledge. This situation is similar to that of a physician who reports on an interesting or unusual clinical case. Reporting of one or two interesting cases where research was not originally contemplated does not require IRB review and approval. Consistent with her own professional ethics, the graduate student should be careful to protect the confidentiality of the student or else obtain assent from the student and permission from the student's parents to share the student's identity.

IRB Determination

IRB review and approval of this activity is not necessary, as the activity does not meet the definition of research. However, going forward, if the student decided to design and implement specific educational interventions and methodology using this experience as a basis, and her intent is scholarly publication, IRB consultation and/or review should be sought before beginning the project, as the project may constitute research with human participants.

1.6. Exempt Research

The Common Rule identifies eight categories of human participant research that are considered to be exempt from the requirements of the regulations and from IRB oversight (45 CFR 46.104). It is important to note that activities considered exempt from the federal regulations are still considered research with human participants. While federal regulations are silent on who may make a determination of exemption, the federal Office of Human Research Protections (OHRP) recommends that the researcher not make the determination due to an inherent conflict of interest. Most academic institutions vest within the IRB the authority to determine whether an activity meets the criteria for exemption, but may designate other institutional components, such as research administration offices or the researcher's academic unit, with responsibility to issue exemptions. However,

OHRP will allow institutions, by local policy, to use methods such as validated checklists or web-based decision tools to permit researchers to make an exemption determination.

Receiving an exempt determination does not negate the need for the researcher to conduct the research in an ethical manner. The same ethical principles requiring minimizing risks to participants, maximizing research benefits, and protecting participant privacy and confidentiality must be met by the researcher. Additionally, if any modification to the study design exceeds the exemption category, then review by an IRB is required to determine if the activity now requires regulatory oversight by an IRB. The following vignettes describe common applications of exemption criteria to music education research.

Vignette 3: Academic Collaborations in Classroom Research (exempt research #1)
A faculty member from the music department of a university collaborates with a local fifth-grade teacher to add an African drumming module to her music classes. The faculty member plans to instruct the teacher on how to administer brief assessments to students before and after the module to evaluate the module's impact. They also plan to videotape the classroom during the drumming activities for further evaluation at a later date. The module, as designed, meets required elements of the music curriculum for the school district. Results will be reported to the district as part of an effort to innovate music education. Additionally, the faculty member plans to publish the methodology and findings in a peer-reviewed journal. The faculty member consults with the IRB to determine if review necessary.

IRB Considerations
Because this project is taking place in a school setting, the IRB considers whether the project meets the criteria for exempt category #1:

Research, conducted in established or commonly accepted educational settings, that specifically involves normal educational practices that are not likely to adversely impact students' opportunity to learn required educational contant or the assessment of educators that provide instruction. This includes most research on regular and special education instructional strategies, and research on the effectiveness of or the comparison among instructional techniques, curricula, or classroom management methods (45 CFR 46.104(d)(1)).

The introduction of an African drumming module is consistent with normal educational practices already in place in the district. Use of the innovative module and assessment of its impact do not pose risks to students. The IRB recommends that the faculty member submit an application for exemption. According to institutional policy, the IRB is responsible for issuing exempt determinations.

IRB Determination
The IRB issues an exempt #1 determination for the project. The activity is considered research and involves human participants, but is exempt from IRB oversight, including any consent procedures for students and parents. The IRB reminds the researchers of their ethical obligation to notify parents about the research project according to school district guidelines and to design a process by which parents might opt out of having their child's data used for research purposes.

Vignette 4: Qualitative Interviews with Adults in a Community Choir (exempt research #2)

As part of her dissertation research, a university graduate student is interested in studying the interactions among the members of a local symphonic choir as well as exploring their motivations for participation. The student plans to conduct one-on-one interviews with choir members who agree to participate. The student will publish the results of her research and share it with the choir. The student's advisor recommends that she discuss her project with the IRB office to determine the correct type of review for her project.

IRB Considerations

First, the IRB office inquires as to whether the community choir involves any high school or college students who might be under age 18. The student notes that group does not typically include student members and thinks it unlikely that any potential interview participants will be minors. Second, the IRB office asks whether the interview questions will elicit responses that might be embarrassing or pose a reputational risk to participants. The student does not believe that her questions are sensitive. Based upon these responses, the IRB office assesses that the project may qualify as exempt under category #2:

Research that only includes interactions involving educational tests (cognitive, diagnostic, aptitude, achievement), survey procedures, interview procedures or observation of public behavior (including visual or auditory recording) if at least one of the following criteria is met: (i) The information obtained is recorded in such a manner that the identity of human subjects cannot be readily ascertained, directly or through identifiers linked to the subjects; (ii) Any disclosure of the human subjects' responses outside the research would not reasonably place the subjects at risk of criminal or civil liability or be damaging to the subjects' financial standing, employability, educational advancement, or reputation; or (iii) The information obtained is recorded by the investigator in such a manner that the identity of the human subjects can be readily ascertained, directly or through identifiers linked to the subjects, and an IRB conducts a limited IRB review to make the determinations required by 45 CFR 46.111(a)(7) (45 CFR 46.104(d)(2)).

The IRB office recommends that the student submit an application for exemption. Per institutional policy at the student's university, only the IRB has the authority to make exemption determinations. The IRB reviews the proposed interview questions to determine if they meet the exemption criteria. The IRB notes that some questions about relationships among members might pose a reputational risk to individuals and suggests that the student eliminate data elements that could potentially identify a participant. Alternatively, the IRB suggests that the student could retain identifying elements, but revise the questions to eliminate the potential sensitivity. The student decides to collect the data without identifying information.

IRB Determination

The IRB issues an exempt #2 determination for the project. Because use of the exemption for interviews is limited to interactions with adults, the IRB cautions the student to include a screening question to ensure she does not interview anyone under 18. The IRB reminds the student that it is ethically appropriate to include an informed consent process for her participants even though the IRB does not review or approve consent materials for exempt projects. The project is considered to be research with human participants, but is exempt from IRB oversight after this initial determination.

1.7. Research Regulated by an IRB

When activities are non-exempt and meet the definitions for research conducted with human participants, the research is regulated by an IRB. The nature of IRB review varies depending on the risk level of the study and whether the research involves any vulnerable populations as defined under the regulations. No more than minimal risk research that meets one of nine federal expedited review categories may undergo review by a single, qualified member of the IRB. Research that does not meet one of these categories and all research posing more than minimal risk to participants must be reviewed by the full, convened IRB.

The following vignettes describe two types of IRB review.

Vignette 5: Academic Research in the Classroom (expedited review)
   A university researcher wishes to study the persistence of students from a minority population participating in the concert band program at a suburban high school. The researcher is not affiliated with the school and asks the band director to help recruit the students. The band director as well as other teachers and students from the target population will be interviewed. The interviews will elicit private (though not necessarily sensitive) information about the individuals. The researcher will also observe band practice and videotape only the minority students during practice. Written informed consent will be obtained from the teachers. Parents of the minority students will provide written permission and the researcher will obtain assent from the participating students. Recognizing the activity involves research with human participants, the investigator submits an application for IRB review.

IRB Considerations
IRB review identified several issues with the researcher's study design as described in the application. Changes were required to assure the protection of research participants.
   1. Voluntary Participation
      Human research regulations offer special protections for children who are considered to be vulnerable to undue influence (45 CFR 46 Subpart D). Since the research is designed to use the band director to recruit minority students in the band, the IRB expressed concern that the students (and their parents) might feel compelled to participate. To avoid the possibility of this undue influence, the IRB indicated the band director may only forward information about the research to the families and provide the contact information for the researcher.

Given that the band director will ultimately know whether any given student decides to participate, the students' participation is not confidential. However, minimizing the band director's involvement in the recruitment process limits his influence on the decision-making of the students and retains their autonomy.

2. Privacy and Confidentiality

The researcher indicated that only a very small percentage of the school's concert band are members of the minority study population. Interviews with the students will occur after school to ensure their privacy. However, the videotaping of the students during practice will focus only on the minority students. The IRB pointed out that it would be obvious to everyone in the class that these students were being singled out for some purpose. The IRB required that the researcher either revise the informed consent information to more fully disclose the taping process, devise a procedure that did not single out individual students, or utilize field notes to capture the observations of interest, rather than videotaping.

3. Informed Consent

The IRB noted that the consent materials were generally well-prepared but the researcher should prepare translations of relevant materials if English comprehension for students or parents might be limited. In addition, since the band director and other teachers were to be asked questions about individual minority students, the IRB noted this process should be completely disclosed to the students and parents and they should be told that the students' participation would not be completely confidential.

4. Assessment of Risk

The IRB noted that the questions pertaining to the minority students would not elicit sensitive information and did not pose a risk to the students. Given the small sample size, this was particularly important in that knowledgeable individuals might be able to identify some of the students in published results.

IRB Determination

After revision of the study to respond to the IRB's concerns, the research posed no more than minimal risk to the participants and met the criteria for expedited review by a single member of the IRB.

Vignette 6: Classroom Research Combining Qualitative and Quantitative Components (full IRB review)

A doctoral music education student is interested in studying the impact of high school music teachers on at-risk students facing serious personal challenges such as substance abuse and homelessness. The research is a two-year study focusing on one teacher, in one classroom, at a small school for at-risk students. The school provided documentation of its support for the project. The doctoral student is not affiliated with the school. The research includes classroom observation, interviews with the teacher, focus groups, and a survey with the students. The survey will ask sensitive questions about the students' use of drugs and alcohol and their participation in illegal behaviors. The researcher plans to obtain informed consent from the teacher, as well as signed parental permission and student assent. The doctoral student submits an IRB application and requests exemption #1 based upon the fact that she is conducting the research in a high school, an established educational setting.

IRB Considerations
IRB review determined that the proposed research did not meet the criteria for exemption #1 as it did not focus on curriculum-based activities considered to be normal, educational practices under the Common Rule, but rather on the relationships between the teacher and individual students. Since the study design requires identity-linked data collection points from individual students and the students are likely to reveal participation in activities that are considered illegal, the IRB determined that the research poses more than minimal risk to the students. Consequently, the IRB undertook a full regulatory review of the proposed research at a convened board meeting. The IRB identified a number of issues associated with the project that required reconciliation before granting approval.

1. Confidentiality Issues

    Surveys of the students include questions about specific illegal behaviors to be tracked over the study period. The data are individually identifiable and identities are maintained during the data collection period. Unauthorized access to the data through loss or intentional sharing could pose a risk to the students. Additionally, the sensitive nature of topics to be explored in open-ended interviews with the teacher and in student focus groups raised concern for the IRB that information might be revealed about the students or others. Unauthorized use of this information could prove damaging.

2. Informed consent issues

    The researcher proposes to use written consent materials and obtain signatures on parental permissions and student assents. The IRB acknowledged that there may be a challenge in obtaining signed parental permissions for students in this population, but given the sensitive nature of the questions, the IRB determined the research did not qualify for a waiver of signed parental permission. The IRB noted some students may be considered legally emancipated or qualify as adults under state law. No parental permission is required for these individuals and students may provide their own consent, rather than assent.

IRB Determination
Given that the federal regulatory framework for review and approval of research with children requires the IRB to make specific determinations of risk as weighed against direct or indirect benefit, the IRB determined that the researcher must devise strategies to minimize the risks to the student participants to ensure that the research poses no more than minimal risk to them. As this project involves both qualitative and quantitative research methods, the IRB offered suggestions to minimize the risk of breach of confidentiality in the focus groups by having students refrain from naming individuals in the discussion and suggested that the researcher use coded identifiers rather than participants' names when collecting sensitive survey information.

1.8. WORKING WITH AN IRB

Brydon-Miller and Greenwood (2006, 122) describe what happens when researchers and IRBs do not work well together: ". . . simply knowing the hurdles we will face in attempting to gain IRB approval may dissuade many researchers of all kinds from even attempting to address the truly important issues facing us, settling instead for studies that skirt the issues or in some other way 'play it safe' as a strategy for streamlining the approval process and completing their research in a timely manner."

While each IRB office functions under the same federal regulatory authority, each IRB has a distinct personality. Those housed within academic institutions are subject to institutional oversight and any additional parameters set by the institution. Operational budgets may also be limited by levels of institutional funding. Non-academic IRBs able to operate on a fee-for-service basis have more freedom to determine their staffing levels and workflows.

The smoothest and, ideally, most efficient outcomes of an IRB review are usually the result of transparency in communication between the IRB and the researcher. IRBs are responsible for conducting reviews and regulatory assessments for numerous research disciplines. Within each discipline, the application of scientific methodologies to human participants may present unique circumstances for reviewers. Researchers who complete their IRB applications with only the details they *think* the IRB needs to know are likely to provide only a partial or inaccurate description of the research. Researchers who take the time to clearly and completely describe their research are usually rewarded with fewer questions and requests for clarification from the IRB. These suggestions are equally important for qualitative or quantitative researchers.

Bresler and Stake (1992, 84) describe the researcher in music education research as the "principal instrument" in determining whether the observations are providing sufficient data. Observations may be audio or video recorded, but these are only the storage media, as the data lie within the interpretation of the observations. When data are interpreted as insufficient, researchers desire the flexibility to return to the location of the participants to engage again in the same manner or perhaps to employ a new tactic. Qualitative researchers and IRBs should seek an open dialogue to develop the broadest parameters for the IRB-approved protocol. IRBs typically require specific details regarding when and how interactions with participants will occur. When a researcher takes care to fully outline the research protocol and its relevant factors, the IRB can review and approve a study design to offer greater flexibility for the researcher in the field and a reduced regulatory burden for both the researcher and the IRB. For example, rather than stating that the research interview will be completed in a single session, the researcher should indicate it might take up to three sessions to accomplish the desired data collection. This simple, broad statement eliminates the need for the investigator to seek an additional IRB review to add the extra interviews.

Simple strategies such as contacting the IRB office to seek a consult can improve the application process. Researchers should also make an effort to attend or complete any training offered by an IRB, as this offers an excellent opportunity to ask questions about expectations and workflows.

IRBs also have responsibilities to researchers. Gunsalas et al. (2007) describe the tendencies of IRBs to over-regulate research that is not biomedical as "mission creep."

The authors note that IRBs are misdirecting their energies in an effort to avoid lawsuits instead of focusing on difficult ethical issues. They describe limited use of exemptions and the incorrect application of IRB regulations to activities that are not research with human participants. While not every IRB functions in this manner, these concerns have some validity.

IRBs can address these issues with careful attention to workflow and the correct application of regulations to the research design. Thoughtful IRBs provide guidance to improve confidentiality protections and thereby reduce risk for the participants. IRBs can serve as a repository of best practices and offer recommendations to researchers based on their experience with well-designed and well-executed research. IRBs can partner with researchers to consider the most appropriate response in challenging research situations. For example, Dubois (2002) described IRB consideration of informed consent in educational settings. The best IRBs make an effort to listen to researchers and learn from their experiences and challenges.

Even well-designed research protocols rarely proceed according to the written plan and IRB-approved protocol. Researchers should expect the unexpected and develop responses to common interruptions to their research. IRBs should work with investigators to develop a breadth and depth to the IRB-approved research design in order to allow the investigator the necessary flexibility to make modifications to the research design without compromising participant safety.

1.9. Conclusion

Music education researchers face the classic qualitative science regulatory conundrum: how to develop a study protocol that meets ethical and regulatory obligations to participants as required by the IRB, while maintaining the flexibility to adapt the research to natural settings and circumstances. IRBs should be seen as partners with researchers in the development and conduct of human participant research. Many IRBs have broad and substantive experiences with a variety of qualitative research designs. A thoughtful dialogue between the IRB and the researcher can usually solve many of the review challenges associated with qualitative research designs.

To address the unique qualities of qualitative research design, IRBs and the institutions that house them should make every effort to review these studies with an eye toward maximizing flexibility within the approved research protocol. Music education research generally does not pose a direct risk to participants in the same manner as biomedical research or other quantitative research designs. Federal research regulations make specific allowances to exempt certain types of research from ongoing regulatory oversight, including research conducted within classrooms for educational purposes. When IRBs correctly apply these exemptions, researchers are able to fluidly adjust their research designs to accommodate the natural educational settings, without IRB review and approval for each change to the research design. When research is subject to ongoing IRB oversight, the IRB and researchers should work together to assure that the study is designed with sufficient flexibility.

The conduct of human participant research is based on a fluid trust model between the participant, the researcher, and the IRB. Each entity trusts the other to do the right thing—to assure that the research is conducted in an ethical and compliant manner and safeguards the rights and welfare of the participants. Participants in qualitative research often receive little or no direct benefit or compensation for contributing their time and their data. Paramount for the participants is their expectation that research is well-conducted and may produce some future benefit.

Whether a researcher's activities are exempted from the regulations or subject to federal regulatory oversight, they remain ethically obligated to protect their participants. When directly interacting with students in academic settings, it is imperative that qualitative researchers remain cognizant of their role, eliminate bias and coercion, and conduct their activities in an ethical manner to respect the rights and autonomy of their participants.

References

American Anthropological Association. 2004. "Statement on Ethnography and Institutional Review Boards." http://www.aaanet.org/stmts/irb.htm.
American Educational Research Association. 2011. "AERA Code of Ethics." *Educational Researcher* 40: 145–56.
American Psychological Association. 2010. "Ethical Principles of Psychologists and Code of Conduct." http://www.apa.org/ethics/code/index.aspx.
Bresler, L., and R. Stake. 1992. "Qualitative Research Methodology in Music Education." In *Handbook of Research on Music Teaching and Learning: A Project of the Music Educators National Conference*, edited by R. Cowell, 75–90. New York: Schirmer Books.
Brydon-Miller, M., and D. Greenwood. 2006. "A Re-Examination of the Relationship between Action Research and Human Subjects Review Processes." *Action Research* 4 (1): 117–28.
Code of Federal Regulations, Title 45. 2018. "Public Welfare." Department of Health and Human Services, Part 46: "Protection of Human Subjects."
DuBois, J. M. 2002. "When Is Informed Consent Appropriate in Educational Research? Regulatory and Ethical Issues." *The Hastings Center. IRB: Ethics and Human Research* 24 (1): 1–8.
Gunsalus, C. K., E. Bruner, N. C. Burbules, L. Dash, M. Finkin, J. Goldberg, W. T. Greenough, G. A. Miller, M. G. Pratt, M. Iriye, and D. Aronson. 2007. "The Illinois White Paper: Improving the System for Protecting Human Subjects: Counteracting IRB 'Mission Creep.'" *Qualitative Inquiry* 13 (5): 617–64.
Librett, M., and D. Perrone. 2010. "Apples and Oranges: Ethnography and the IRB." *Qualitative Research* 10 (6): 729–47.
Mills, G. 2003. *Action Research: A Guide for the Teacher Researcher*. 2nd ed. Upper Saddle River, NJ: Merrill/Prentice Hall.

National Commission for the Protection of Human Subjects of Biomedical and Behavioral Research. "The Belmont Report: Ethical Principles and Guidelines for the Protection of Human Subjects of Research." Washington, DC: US Government Printing Office (1978).

Pritchard, I. A. 2002. "Travelers and Trolls: Practitioner Research and Institutional Review Boards." *American Educational Research Association* 31 (3): 3–13.

Thornton, L. C. 2008. "The Role of IRBs in Music Education Research." In *Diverse Methodologies in the Study of Music Teaching and Learning*, edited by Linda K Thompson, 201–14. Charlotte, NC: Information Age.

Tierney, W. G., and Z. Corwin. 2007. "The Tensions between Academic Freedom and Institutional Review Boards." *Qualitative Inquiry* 13 (3): 388–98.

CHAPTER 2

GENERATING AND ANALYZING OBSERVATION OF MUSIC TEACHING AND LEARNING DATA

MARGARET SCHMIDT

Humans are born observers—observation is a primary tool that permits us to learn about and make sense of the world around us. However, if we noticed every detail in our environment, we would quickly become overwhelmed. Instead, our brains simplify routine visual information and direct our attention to more important or meaningful features. With practice, we can become discriminating observers. For example, a collector of Dresden china will observe details in a flea market display that others pass by. A music teacher will notice details about the behavior and musical performance of students in his classroom that a parent volunteer might not see. A cardiologist will see more than squiggles in an EKG report. These people have developed what Eisner (1991) calls "connoisseurship" of a particular facet of human activity: well-honed perceptual skills that allow them to observe more detail in and attribute greater meaning to what they observe than one who has a mere acquaintance with that activity.

John Dewey (1934) distinguishes between two modes of observing: *recognition*, or "bare identification," and *perception*, where we "begin to study and to 'take in'" what we observe (52–53). Such perception is the goal of qualitative observation. Adler and Adler (1994) suggest,

> What differentiates the observations of social scientists from those of everyday-life actors is the former's systematic and purposive nature. Social science researchers study their surroundings regularly and repeatedly, with a curiosity spurred by theoretical questions about the nature of human action, interaction, and society. (377)

Generating and analyzing observation data relies on the researcher's connoisseurship of the research setting, the willingness to observe "regularly and repeatedly," and the ability to perceive details, "taking them in" in order to make meaning from them through analysis. In this chapter, I discuss nine aspects of observational research: preparing for observations, determining the researcher's role, planning to enter and leave a site, processes of observation, generating data, maintaining a data record, analyzing data, writing the research report, and ethical considerations in working with observation data.

2.1. Preparing for Observations

Qualitative studies that rely solely on observation data are rare; however, nearly all researchers generate data through observation. Even a study that draws almost completely on interview data involves some observation of interviewees' body language, verbal pauses, and tone of voice. Observation data are often used to corroborate or triangulate data from multiple other sources. For example, by comparing participants' observed actions with their perspectives as revealed through interviews, written documents, or informal conversations, a researcher can learn a great deal about unnoticed, implied, or unvoiced rules or relationships within the setting under study. For example, Norgaard (2008) observed seven professional jazz musicians as they improvised a blues form. By comparing his observations of their performances with the comments they made as they listened to a recording of their own improvisations, Norgaard was able to identify common strategies they used to improvise.

A study's research questions help determine whether observation offers a useful source of data and, if so, what might be observed to address those questions. Qualitative research methods texts offer a variety of perspectives on site and participant selection or "sampling" (Glesne 1999; Stake 1995), including, for example, purposeful, intensity, criterion, critical case, convenience, or maximum variation sampling (Creswell 2007, 127). "The researcher should have a connoisseur's appetite for the best persons, places, and occasions. 'Best' usually means those that can best help us understand" the study's questions (Stake 1995, 56). A pilot study in the prospective or a similar setting may provide opportunities to identify potential benefits and challenges, as well as to practice and refine observation techniques. Selecting sites and participants often requires balancing different trade-offs, including practical issues such as time and funding required and accessibility and availability of participants. Tobias (2010, 89–98) provides extensive detail about his selection of research site and participants in a study of a high school songwriting class, describing the range of options he identified and his reasons for his final selection.

Gaining access to a desired research setting requires approval of procedures by the appropriate Institutional Review Board (IRB). In some cases, researchers make preliminary contact with a proposed site to determine feasibility of the study in that site before submitting a proposal to the IRB. In other cases, IRB approval precedes contacts with possible sites. Gaining access may be a relatively simple or an extremely complex process. For example, to generate observation data in a public school classroom, a researcher may need approval from both a university and a school district IRB. Sometimes the process begins with contacting official gatekeepers, such as a school principal, the administrator of a club, or the director of a community ensemble. Other times, a friend or acquaintance with access can introduce the researcher to the official gatekeepers. When a study involves only adults in everyday settings, an IRB may declare it "exempt," allowing researchers to contact participants directly. For example, although Pellegrino's (2010) study included classroom observation, because she focused her observations only on the teachers, the IRB did not require her to obtain permission from the school or the students' parents.

Obtaining access usually involves generating informed consent forms signed by participants or their guardians, and assent forms signed by minors under age 18 or other vulnerable individuals. The researcher prepares an overview of the study's purposes and methods in language participants can understand. Particular concerns that must be addressed include whether photos, student work, interviews, audio, or video recordings will be collected. Researchers must provide specific information about how data will be used, with appropriate guarantees of anonymity and other privacy protections for all participants. In some cases, the formal language required by IRBs in consent/assent forms may be off-putting to participants, and researchers may plan a verbal "translation," speaking with participants in more familiar terms when they present the forms. The appendices and method chapters of many dissertations include examples of consent/assent forms and other IRB-approved documents.

Issues of access may require changes in research focus or design as the researcher proceeds with observations. Glesne (1999) writes,

> Access is a process. It refers to your acquisition of consent to go where you want, observe what you want, talk to whomever you want, obtain and read whatever documents you require, and do all of this for whatever period of time you need to satisfy your research purposes. If you receive full and unqualified consent, then you have obtained total access. If your access is qualified somehow, then you must explore the meaning of the qualifications for meeting research expectations: Should you redefine your research? Should you select another site? (39)

For example, although Soto, Lum, and Campbell (2009) had planned to collect data from two school sites, they discovered more limited access than anticipated at one of the schools, and had to reassign that school to "an occasional rather than the central feature of the project" (339). They also had to revise their intentions to interview all the participants, as some "could not commit the time to sit-down interviews with one or more members of the research team" (340–41). Similarly, a researcher may intend to study interactions among students in a classroom, but several parents may not provide consent for their children to participate. In such cases, the researcher may need to reposition recording equipment to exclude those participants, eliminate some collected data from analysis, or revise the research questions.

2.2. Determining the Researcher's Role

In each observation study, researchers create their role from an array of possibilities. These choices commonly involve identifying one's place on the participant-observer continuum, using oneself as the primary research instrument, and establishing relationships with participants.

2.2.1. The Participant-Observer Continuum

As data generators, researchers function as both participants and observers in any research study. Spradley (1980) distinguishes five possible levels of participation as an observer. *Non-participation* is the rare case where the researcher simply observes, with participants sometimes unaware of being observed. For example, Duke and Simmons (2006) analyzed 25 hours of video-recorded studio lessons taught by three artist-teachers, and described the teaching strategies they observed.

Passive participation involves minimal interaction with the participants, as when the researcher sits in a corner of a classroom taking notes. Studies of young children's musical activities often rely primarily on observation of the children's music-making on the playground or other settings, with minimal interaction between children and researchers (e.g., Jackson-Gough 2003; Lum and Campbell 2007; Stauffer 2002).

An example of *moderate participation* is studying interactions in a third-grade music class, where the researcher determines ahead of time to chat with children and answer their questions before and after class, but also remains on the sidelines unless approached while the class is formally in session. Seddon and Biasutti (2010) video recorded three college students using a text in an asynchronous e-learning environment to create 12-bar blues; only when participants requested assistance did the researchers provide support.

Spradley's fourth level of involvement, *active participation*, is when the researcher "seeks to *do* what other people are doing, not merely to gain acceptance, but to more fully learn the cultural rules for behavior" (60). Manes (2009) took shamisen lessons himself, observed other students' lessons, and interviewed the teacher to study traditional Japanese teaching strategies and playing techniques.

Complete participation involves the researcher in a setting in which he or she is a full participant, as in an action research study of one's own classroom, or an examination of the implicit workings of an ensemble of which one is a member. Gackle (Gackle and Fung 2009) studied her choir's experience learning traditional Chinese songs in a community youth choir organization of which she was founder, artistic director, and conductor of the choir. She and co-author Fung together analyzed videos of her rehearsals. Most often, researchers function as moderate or active participants, becoming directly involved in some degree, as determined by both the research questions and the nature of what is being observed.

2.2.2. Researcher as Research Instrument

In qualitative research, researchers themselves are the primary research instruments; they cannot "completely disappear [as] a distinct person" (Angrosino 2005). Peshkin (1988) defines this researcher subjectivity as "an amalgam of the persuasions that stem from the circumstances of one's class, statuses, and values interacting with the particulars of one's object of investigation" (17). The researcher's own positionality, of having particular experiences of gender, class, ethnicity, profession, and place, may provide valuable insight into the situation under study. However, it may just as easily create blinders or encourage "*selective inattention*, tuning out, not seeing, and not hearing" (Spradley 1980, 55). Researchers are obligated to account for both the benefits and limitations of their subjectivity. For example, Tsugawa's (2009) 25 years of band and orchestra teaching experience allowed him to quickly understand the rehearsal processes of a senior adult band and orchestra. However, in reviewing his observation notes, Tsugawa noticed he was critiquing the participants' performance skills as if he were the teacher. He realized that, to better understand the participants' experiences, he needed to move beyond his prior experience and "change role by removing [his] teacher-adjudicator glasses and putting on [his] participant-observer glasses" (56–57).

Members of a research team can challenge each other's selective vision (e.g., Soto, Lum, and Campbell 2009), while individual researchers can invite peer review of their work to help them eliminate blind spots in generating and analyzing data. Creswell's (2007) Chapter 10 provides one overview of multiple "validation strategies" for qualitative research. He outlines eight procedures that are commonly accepted as standards to establish credibility and account for researcher subjectivity. These include prolonged engagement and observation in the study site, triangulation of multiple data sources, peer review, negative case analysis, clarification of researcher bias, member checks, "rich, thick description," and external audits (207–09). Creswell recommends that researchers plan to employ at least two of these strategies.

2.2.3. Relationships with Participants

Atkinson and Hammersley (1994) argue that "we cannot study the social world without being part of it"; therefore they suggest "that participant observation is not a particular research technique but a mode of being-in-the-world characteristic of researchers" (249). Deciding on this "mode of being-in-the-world" for a study is less straightforward than it may seem. In the ways researchers design a study and generate, analyze, and report observation data, they convey their understandings of their relationship with participants (e.g., Angrosino and Rosenberg 2011; Atkinson and Hammersley 1994; Flinders and Richardson 2002; Spradley 1980). Relationships can range from an authoritative researcher positioning participants as others to a view of "observer and observed as inhabitants of a shared social and cultural field, their respective cultures different but equal, and capable of mutual recognition by virtue of a shared humanity" (Atkinson and Hammersley 1994, 256).

Spradley (1980) suggests that much useful information arises as researchers position themselves as learners, allowing participants to serve as teachers and experts: "Fieldwork, then, involves the disciplined study of what the world is like to people who have learned to see, hear, speak, think, and act in ways that are different. Rather than *studying people*, [participant observation] means *learning from people*" (3). The music education researchers cited in this chapter describe ways they assured participants that they wanted to learn their perspectives. For example, Abramo (2009) studied his own high school students rehearsing in rock bands. Concluding that "the social dynamic of 'outnumbering the adult' would yield more honest answers than the asymmetrical power relationship of teacher/student" (120), he sought to empower the students by conducting the study in spaces where they normally "hung out," providing food, using their language, and allowing their friends to be in the room during individual interviews.

2.3. Generating Observation Data: Entering and Leaving a Site

Stake (1995) points out, "Almost always, data gathering is done on somebody's 'home grounds.' . . . [The] burden on the host should be acknowledged. The researcher may be delightful company, but hosting delightful company is a burden" (57–58). In beginning an observational study, researchers will want to plan carefully how they will enter those "home grounds" in a respectful way. Will the researcher suddenly appear, or will a collaborator already familiar to the participants prepare them for the researcher's coming? Will the researcher begin formal observations immediately or start with a period of "informal hanging out" (Jansen and Peshkin 1992, 709)? How will the study be explained to the participants? What will they want to know about the researcher's personal background and interests?

Answers to these and similar questions will depend on variables such as the study's purposes, the researcher's familiarity with the site or participants, the researcher's anticipated role on the participant-observer spectrum, and the type of relationship the researcher intends to establish with the participants. No matter the approach chosen, the goal is to bring the researcher into the setting in ways that promote his or her ability to eventually become a part of the setting, so that participants act much as they normally would were the researcher not present.

To blend in, researchers aim to establish trust with participants. Rapport may be created in a variety of ways, as fits the purpose of the study. Sometimes, the researcher is already familiar with the research site and participants. In her dissertation, Lum (2007, 18–27) provides a detailed explanation of selecting and entering an elementary school in her native Singapore, where she had taught for five years and had already earned a high level of trust. When researchers have no prior relationship with the site or participants, they will need to plan ways to build trust. Tobias (2010, 115–19) describes his theoretical goals and internal debates as he negotiated his relationships with high school students and their teacher. Koops (2010) wanted to study the learning processes of children in The Gambia. In the year prior to the study, she learned the Wolof language. While in The Gambia, she lived closely with the children and their families, and found that her limited knowledge of Wolof was helpful in establishing rapport, allowing her "to greet people, bargain at the market, interact with children, and explain [her] research" (23).

The credibility of both the researcher and the study may be enhanced when relationships with participants are consciously negotiated. In his study of a middle-school technology classroom, Ruthmann (2006, 73–77) describes his progression from being a stranger in the classroom to becoming a "collaborative participant" as students began to seek his advice on their compositions, and the teacher asked his ideas about curricular, technological, and pedagogical issues that arose in her work. Alert researchers use their intuition as a guide to identify and resolve challenges that arise in establishing and maintaining rapport, as Blair (2009) did in studying her colleague Sue's classroom:

> Though my role as researcher was transparent to me, Sue regarded me as a fellow teacher, as that was how our relationship had begun and, as I entered her classroom, I once again assumed this role. Though always carefully observing while in the classroom, my researcher role was largely conducted outside of her classroom as I constructed field notes and journals and studied the literature, much of which was not a part of Sue's world as an educator. The conversations in which we engaged were "teacher talk," . . . a sharing of the professional landscape now held in common. (21)

Blending in, however, can become a potential concern in leaving a site at the conclusion of the study. The researcher often comes to feel a part of the group, and may be reluctant to sever ties. If a close relationship has developed, or if the researcher has been providing assistance to them, participants may feel abandoned once the researcher ceases to be part of the setting. It may be helpful to keep open the option to return, in case additional observation is needed to clarify questions that arise during later analysis. If appropriate, researchers can gradually withdraw by coming less frequently until visits cease (Bogdan and Biklen 2003). Stake (1995) recommends that researchers use good judgment, common sense, and good manners to respectfully enter and leave a research site, having "made no one less able to carry out their responsibilities" during or at the conclusion of the study (60).

2.4. Generating Observation Data: How to Observe

Initially, novice researchers may experience unsettling feelings of not knowing how or what to observe. With practice, they can develop the skills to notice key features relevant to a study's purpose. Stake (1995) suggests that effective observation requires both sensitivity and skepticism: the sensitivity to remain alert for potentially useful information, and the skepticism to constantly question whether other important things are being overlooked. The skilled observer seeks both to "make the obvious obvious" (Wolcott 1992, 24) and to "make the familiar strange" (Spindler 1982, 313). The most effective researchers constantly search for alternative perspectives and explanations, being slow to conclude that they have observed the whole picture.

Skilled researchers learn to determine clear foci for each observation; a large quantity of unfocused observation notes might actually needlessly complicate data analysis, by obscuring the information most pertinent to the study's research questions. Spradley (1980) describes three levels of observation. In a *descriptive observation,* researchers try to address the question, "What is going on here?" (73). At this level, Angrosino (2005) suggests observing as many details as possible, setting aside preconceptions and taking nothing for granted. This wide lens, he suggests, will yield a great deal of data. Although some of these data may later prove to be irrelevant, the discipline of detailed looking assures that important information is not too easily dismissed.

A second level is *focused observation.* Spradley (1980) suggests using five or six broad categories derived from the research questions to guide increasingly more focused observations. Key information begins to surface over repeated visits, as the researcher becomes more familiar with the setting and more aware of "what's going on."

Selective observation is a third level, where the researcher plans to observe for specific details. These foci change and evolve throughout the study, often based on questions that arise in reviewing data from previous observations. "Most researchers find they do their best work by being thoroughly prepared to concentrate on a few things, yet ready for unanticipated happenings that reveal the nature of the case" (Stake 1995, 55). Spradley's (1980) book, *Participant Observation,* offers detailed guidance in maintaining the "balanced tension" (102) between big-picture and in-depth observation.

Rarely will a researcher begin with descriptive observation, proceed in order through the next two levels, and conclude data generation. It is also unusual for an observation study to close with the original research questions unchanged. With each return visit to the site, the researcher tacks back and forth among all three levels, as newly observed data raise questions that provoke a shift in observation focus or suggest refinement or revision of research questions. The method chapter of dissertations often provides details about the evolution of a study. For example, Lewis (2004, 22–23) describes the gradual revision of her research questions. She intended to study whether kindergarten teachers made connections between music and other subject areas. As data collection proceeded, reading and literacy emerged as the key focus.

2.5. Generating Observation Data: What to Collect

Observers typically collect multiple types of data. Field notes and audio or video recordings are common. Pertinent documents and artifacts, such as songbooks, photographs, music program brochures, or examples of students' work, may be appropriate. In addition, the researcher maintains a journal throughout the study (Creswell 2007). The more different kinds of data sources, the more credible the findings will be. Miles and Huberman (1994) suggest,

> Triangulation is a state of mind. If you *self-consciously* set out to collect and double-check findings, using multiple sources and modes of evidence, the verification process will largely be built into the data-gathering process. (235)

In this section, I discuss field notes, artifacts, preliminary data analysis, and the researcher journal.

2.5.1. Field Notes

Researchers make field notes in a variety of ways, depending on the circumstances of a particular study. Glesne (1999), Stake (1995, 2010), Spradley (1980), and Bogdan and Biklen (2003) are among the many texts that provide detailed examples of processes for making field notes. If the researcher's role is primarily as observer, notes may be made by hand in a notebook or on a computer while observing. Sometimes, however, this may create a disturbance or discomfort for the participants, or researchers may be participating fully during an observation. For example, Tobias's (2010) data gathering procedures in a high school songwriting class required considerable multitasking, keeping him too busy to make notes on-site beyond "in-process analytic writing such as asides, commentaries, and in-process memos." After leaving the site each day, he reviewed the videos to make detailed descriptive notes (105, examples on 106–07).

Spradley (1980) notes a particular challenge related to field notes: "the moment you begin writing down what you see and hear, you automatically encode things in language . . . [and while] this may seem a rather straightforward matter, the language used in field notes has numerous long-range consequences for your research" (64). Especially important are the use of participants' own language and concrete, descriptive terms. The most useful field notes record terms and phrases participants themselves use to label, describe, or discuss what the observer sees. Additionally, precise descriptions of a participant's behaviors and actions will yield more useful data than simply noting that a child is "angry." Evaluative descriptors, such as "wonderful," "boring," or "enthusiastic," may record more about the researcher's perspective than the views of the participants.

To separate their own feelings and interpretations from description of what is observed, researchers may find it helpful to record field notes on a divided page, using one side to describe events and the other side to record the researcher's own thoughts or questions. Another option is writing researcher memos, entered directly in the field notes using a different font or other special notation, as Schmidt did (1994, 471–75). Berg's (1997) Appendices H and I offer complete transcripts of her observations of two high school chamber ensembles' rehearsals; Jackson-Gough's (2003) Appendices D and E provide both raw observation notes and descriptive summaries of her video recordings.

2.5.2. Artifacts

For some studies, site diagrams, participant e-mails, concert programs, and other artifacts may provide invaluable information, while in others, they may be irrelevant. To record the contexts in which four urban music teachers worked, Fitzpatrick (2008) "drove around the school neighborhood, taking photographs of local housing, area businesses, and otherwise trying to document aspects of the local culture" (110). Soto, Lum, and Campbell (2009), studying a school-university partnership, collected "class handouts, songs and song sheets, teaching schedules, and lesson plans," as well as "the school's annual calendar, local news coverage on the program, and articles published in the university magazines and faculty/staff weekly" (351), to triangulate observation and interview data. To supplement her classroom observations, Blair (2009) took photos of student group work completed on the classroom white board, reviewed student work saved to classroom computers, and archived e-mail conversations with the classroom teacher.

Occasionally, participants may not mention key documents and artifacts simply because they assume they are not important. A researcher's ability to follow hunches and ask good questions can be useful in revealing or locating important artifacts. Stake (1995) suggests using logic, intuition, and careful observation, recommending that "one needs to have one's mind organized, yet be open for unexpected clues" (68).

2.5.3. Researcher Journal

Because the researcher is the key research instrument, another important data source is the record of the observer's own experience of conducting the study (Bogdan and

Biklen 2003; Creswell 2007; Stake 2010). The research journal "contain[s] a record of experiences, ideas, fears, mistakes, confusions, breakthroughs, and problems that arise during fieldwork. A journal represents the personal side of fieldwork; it includes reactions to informants and the feelings you sense from others" (Spradley 1980, 71).

Peshkin (1988) believes an awareness of feelings can alert researchers to important data. He writes,

> I looked for the warm and the cool spots, the emergence of positive and negative feelings, the experiences I wanted more of or wanted to avoid, and when I felt moved to act in roles beyond those necessary to fulfill my research needs.... I had to monitor myself to sense how I was feeling. (18)

Schmidt (1994) was surprised by the strong emotional reactions the student teachers in her study revealed as casual conversations after class evolved into discussions of major issues. She later made notes about these exchanges, and also recorded the tensions this created for her, finding that "keeping records of 'friendly' conversations reflected an attitude [she] did not want to convey: that the student teachers were 'subjects' for research" (42).

The journal also documents the evolution of research questions or data generation methods. Spradley (1980) explains that "rereading your journal at a later time will reveal how quickly you forget what occurred during the first days and weeks of fieldwork" (71). The journal becomes part of the data record, and can be used in creating the final report to inform readers about the researcher's process, permitting readers to better interpret the study's findings.

2.5.4. Preliminary Data Analysis

Novice researchers often fail to plan adequate time for review of data as it is generated. Although it is tempting to assume that recordings will preserve data adequately for analysis several months later, timely review of field notes and recordings are essential components of data generation and analysis. As Stake (1995) points out, "There is always too little time.... We need some deep thinking, perhaps a data-gathering plan, a plan that protects time for the less attractive work, such as writing up observations" (51).

Following each observation, researchers return to field notes to "thicken" them, reviewing recordings or mentally recreating the visit and filling in additional details to describe the people, setting, and events as thoroughly as possible. Memories are most vivid within the first 24 hours following an observation. Observation data will be most complete if researchers review field notes within that time frame, recalling their own sensations during the observation and adding information about participants' actions or body language. As researchers note possible interpretations, questions, or foci for subsequent observations, this review process informs preliminary data analysis.

Ongoing preliminary analysis is also important in determining when enough data have been generated. Sometimes a study is limited by the amount of time granted for access, for example, when a music program's schedule dictates the end. The ideal end of data generation occurs when data become "saturated" (Adler and Adler 1994; Glesne 1999), i.e., when repeated visits yield redundant information or "diminishing returns" (Bogdan and Biklen 2003, 62). To help in deciding when data are saturated, Spradley (1980) recommends that occasionally "you need to climb a very tall tree and gain a broad perspective on how far you have come, what tasks lie ahead, and which direction you should take" to keep "from losing sight of the forest because of the trees" (35).

2.6. Maintaining a Data Record

Observational studies can generate a large volume of data, requiring the researcher to develop systematic and accessible methods for organizing it. Technology has made it possible to collect hundreds of photographs or hours of recordings. These data permit repeated examination and allow researchers to review an observation in more detail. However, the benefits of digital records should be weighed against the time, energy, and intrusiveness required to collect and transcribe the data. Wolcott (2001) warns,

> Audiotapes, videotapes, and now computer capabilities... have gargantuan appetites *and* stomachs. Because we can accommodate ever-increasing quantities of data—mountains of it—we have to be careful not to get buried by avalanches of our own making. (44)

Very early in the study, researchers need to develop systems for handling data, clearly labeling files with dates, participants' names, locations, and other pertinent information. Some researchers like to work with an electronic archive of field notes; others prefer to maintain hard copy of field notes in binders. Recordings may be kept on a computer or transferred to other digital formats. Photographs and other documents may be digitally scanned or stored in paper files. Frequent backup of digital files can avoid catastrophe. (Tobias's chapter 5 in this volume offers practical suggestions for data management.)

Markers within field notes that easily identify the location of data are particularly helpful during analysis and writing the final report. For example, labeling field notes with "4/12.O3A.6.23" could identify the date the notes were made (April 12), the observation (the third observation of classroom A), and the page (6) and line number (23) (e.g., Schmidt 1994, 471–75). Most word processing systems will configure documents with this type of marker for easy reference. Similarly, a system for classifying and labeling recordings can simplify review and analysis. It is important to be aware that transcription can take five to eight hours per hour of recorded data; sometimes a paid transcriptionist can expedite the process, getting the basics on paper for the researcher to thicken in reviewing recordings. An indexed timeline entered in the corresponding transcript for each recording, marking major points or predetermined time intervals, will facilitate later analysis. For example, Hornbach's (2005) Appendix E shows field notes using a timeline to note shifts in children's musical activities.

2.7. Analyzing Observation Data

Preliminary analysis, described in section 2.5.4, continues from the first observation to the last. While preliminary analysis reveals some important information, once data generation is complete, formal analysis involves a more systematic search. Most approaches to analysis share a common understanding of the researcher as the primary research instrument, whose job is to describe and interpret what was observed. Through analysis, researchers seek to document the "complex meaning systems [people use] to organize their behavior, to understand themselves and others, and to make sense out of the world in which they live" (Spradley 1980, 5).

For novice researchers, analysis may seem mysterious or unsettling, with few easy-to-follow guidelines. Stake (1995) defends a view of data analysis as a largely intuitive, subjective process, learned through practice.

> I defend it because I know no better way to make sense of the complexities of my case. I recognize that the way I do it is not "the right way." ... Each researcher needs, through experience and reflection, to find the forms of analysis that work for him or her.... The nature of the study, the focus of the research questions, the curiosities of the researcher pretty well determine what analytic strategies should be followed. (77)

In the following subsections, I discuss the analytical processes of developing and refining data codes.

2.7.1. Developing Data Codes

Formal analysis requires "perform[ing] some kinds of dissection, to see the parts separately and how they relate to each other" (Stake 1995, 72). Generally, researchers begin by reviewing all the generated data, rereading field notes and documents, listening to or watching recordings, and making notes about larger patterns, themes, or categories that emerge. In this initial review, it is important to keep an open mind, looking not only to confirm ideas that have arisen during preliminary analysis, but also searching for things that may have been overlooked or that challenge those initial thoughts.

Researchers often use this first review of data to develop an initial coding scheme. Qualitative research methods texts provide a variety of approaches to and detailed examples of coding (e.g., Bogdan and Biklen 2003; Creswell 2007; Glesne 1999; Miles and Huberman 1994; Stake 2010). They generally describe a process of identifying key categories, or codes, with subcategories of related data. The data itself may suggest codes; for example, Brewer (2009) found that his data documenting preservice music teachers' conceptions of good teaching could initially be grouped into three large categories: personal skills and knowledge, teaching skills and knowledge, and musical skills and knowledge. Over time, these data categories suggested a model of role-identity in music teaching, which he continued to refine over the course of his study (72–82). Alternatively, codes may be initially determined from prior research. Abramo (2011, 121) set out to specifically study the ways that high school students performed gender roles as they worked in small rock groups. He began initial data analysis by coding the data for issues of power, gender, and musical gesture that informed the study's theoretical framework, developed through his review of literature.

Using these preliminary codes, researchers review the entire data set again, coding individual bits of data, either by hand or using a software program. Others may prefer tactile manipulation of data; Wolcott (2001, 41–43) writes data on cards and manually sorts them into coded piles. Hornbach's (2005) Appendices E and H show her field notes with codes written beside each data segment. Some researchers prefer to work with lists of codes; for others, charts, tables, or diagrams may help clarify codes, subcodes, and the relationships among them. Berg (1997, 301–16) provides a detailed table of her final set of codes, with a definition and example given for each.

In some cases, numerical analysis of codes may be helpful, such as Norgaard's (2008, 202–05) Code Table, which counts the number of references to each code made by each participant, or Jackson-Gough's (2003, 51–52) Tables 12 and 13, which count the frequencies with which kindergartners engaged in specific musical events and the types of musical events observed at each of her eight research sites. A comprehensive quantitative analysis of rehearsal communication and thought patterns appears in Berg's Chapter 4 (1997, 110–39). She also includes diagrams to explain relationships in her coding scheme.

2.7.2. Refining Codes

In the process of assigning codes to specific data, initial codes are often revised by combining, dividing, adding, or deleting categories, until the researcher is satisfied that categories account as well as possible for the generated data. Although coding is time-consuming and can seem tedious, it is important to spend adequate time in this stage of analysis, recognizing that "as you choose what to attend to and how to interpret it, mental doors slam shut on the alternatives" (Agar, cited in Jansen and Peshkin 1992, 706). Stake (1995) suggests being deliberate, "looking [data] over again and again, reflecting, triangulating, being skeptical about first impressions and simple meanings" (78). Not all data, no matter how interesting, will be relevant to the purpose of a study; therefore, those data are not coded. Alternatively, data that do not fit a code may signal the need to revise or divide codes. They may also point to inconsistencies or contradictions in participants' beliefs and behaviors that the researcher should consider.

Matsunobu's (2011) study of North American shakuhachi practitioners offers details about the evolution of his analysis. He began his coding process using five dimensions of spirituality identified by other researchers. From those initial categories, four contrasting pairs of concepts emerged, which in turn suggested questions that guided further analysis. In the process, Matsunobu was forced to question his original understandings of music as culturally specific, and identified a key theme which he had not considered earlier in his research. As Wolcott (2001) suggests, "Good qualitative research ought to confound issues, revealing them in their complexity rather than reducing them to simple explanation" (36); it ought to "trouble certainty" (Barrett and Stauffer 2009). While this may sometimes lead to researcher frustration and somewhat messy research findings, it can also lead to a more holistic understanding of the complexity of the observation setting and participants.

2.8. Writing about Observation Data

The previous section described the process of data analysis, which involves searching for patterns and themes within the data themselves. As the researcher reviews the data set multiple times and refines codes, larger patterns or themes begin to emerge. These themes and broad categories, now supported by specific coded data, help determine the organization of the report of the study's findings, and writing of findings can begin. Wolcott (2001) suggests first writing a *description* of what was observed. A separate process, *interpretation* of the findings, involves researchers in "sensemaking" (Wolcott 2001, 33), explicating their own understandings of the meaning of what was observed. In published research, *descriptions* are often titled "findings" or "results," and *interpretations* "discussion" or "implications." In the following subsections, I first consider writing descriptions, then writing interpretations, followed by a discussion of the author's voice in research writing.

2.8.1 Writing Descriptions of Observation Data

The first phase of writing is to describe what was observed, creating rich and vivid descriptions of the context and providing key details that "develop *vicarious experiences* for the reader, to give them a sense of 'being there'" (Stake 1995, 63). A major premise of qualitative research is that no one "correct" view of reality exists; "reality is socially constructed, complex, and ever changing" (Glesne 1999, 5). The most carefully crafted descriptions still position some things to be noticed while others are ignored. Therefore, the researcher faces "the possibility of arriving at different descriptions of the same data. This is sometimes regarded as a problem, but I would argue it could also be regarded as an opportunity of seeing new dimensions in a phenomenon" (Larsson 1986, 38). In this sense, writing descriptions of observed data is both an analytical and a creative process, as the researcher makes decisions about what to include and omit, as well as choices of writing style and language. The goal is to craft a story that conveys the most important details from one's vast collection of data, those details that best illustrate the large patterns or themes determined through the analysis process. Reflecting on a previous study, Peshkin (1982) described his goal in writing:

> Any number of observers could have joined me in Mansfield and shared my "scientific observation." To be sure, they might have seen something else, something I overlooked or valued less and therefore ignored in my reconstruction. Indeed, they could have overlooked what I was seeing, by fastening upon some dimension of the phenomena before us that was central to them. But I believe that if I pointed to what I was seeing, the overlookers would then be able to say, "Yes, I see what you see." (62–63)

2.8.2. Writing Interpretations of Observation Data

Description of findings is the section of the written report that brings the researcher's observations to life for readers. In contrast, "interpretation involves explaining and framing your ideas in relation to theory, other scholarship, and action, as well as showing why your findings are important and making them understandable" (Bogdan and Biklen 2003, 147). The interpretation section presents researchers' own understandings of key relationships and connections among the people, actions, and beliefs they observed, and discusses these in relation to the crucial questions, "So what?" and "What difference does this study make?" (Flinders and Richardson 2002, 1169).

Writing interpretation is similar to constructing a convincing argument. Carter (1993) states, "We are, in the very act of story making, deciding what to tell and what to leave out and imposing structure and meaning on events" (9). Carefully crafted descriptions will include details that foreshadow points made in the interpretation. Skilled writers make many revisions of both description and interpretation sections, until the vivid portrayals of observed data hang together in a convincing way with the ideas raised in the interpretation. Bogdan and Biklen's Chapter 5 (2003, 185–207) presents a thorough discussion of choices writers face; Wolcott's chapter, "Tightening Up" (2001, 109–34), offers invaluable practical advice for editing one's own writing.

Because a goal of qualitative research is to present multiple perspectives on the observed setting, writers are obligated to consider and report participants' differing perceptions and to account for plausible alternative or discarded explanations. Equally critical in writing interpretations is connecting a study's findings to other research, articulating where the current findings support prior work and where they may challenge others' findings or suggest questions for further research. In addition, interpretations include implications of the findings for practitioners in the field.

Music education researchers use a variety of formats for reporting a study's findings and interpretations. Koops (2010) presents her data in a "Results" section, followed by "Interpretations" revealing the three main themes she found, and "Discussion" suggesting implications of those themes for music educators' practice and for further research. Rather than writing a separate "Findings" section, Silverman (2011) describes the choral ensemble she studied in the "Method" section, then presents specific descriptions to support her interpretation of the four themes that emerged from her data.

Dissertations offer additional examples for organizing description and interpretation. Paise's (2010) Chapters 4 and 5 present her data, first as individual case studies of participants, then as cross-case analysis of similarities and differences in their teacher role identities; in Chapter 6 she discusses interpretations and implications. Eros (2009), Berg (1997), and Schmidt (1994) each wrote individual chapters to describe findings related to one of their three research questions; subsequent chapters offer further interpretation of themes and discussions of implications of the three description chapters.

2.8.3. Establishing the Writer's Voice

Language "is not merely a conveyor of [experience]. Language shapes, focuses, directs our attention; it transforms our experience in the process of making it public" (Eisner 1991, 28). By the language they use, researchers craft a writer's voice, assuming a position that implies varied degrees of omniscience and authority over, under, or alongside participants and readers. Most often, researchers are the primary writers, although they may invite participants to read and comment on some or all of the final report (e.g., Eros 2009, 71–72; Gray 2011, 99–100; Pellegrino 2010, 88–89). Schmidt and Canser (2006) demonstrate one example of researcher and participant sharing in analyzing and writing a study's findings. Researchers will want to consider whether their language reflects the kind of relationship with participants and readers they intend.

The voice a researcher assumes is thus an ethical decision, because "all types of educational research, both quantitative and qualitative, employ rhetorical forms and thus privilege those who know how to use the rules of the discourse to their advantage" (Flinders and Richardson 2002, 1167). Voice and vocabulary concern not only whose perspective is presented, but whether the language of the report permits participants to read, debate, or own it (Carter 1993; Eisenhart and Howe 1992; Stake 1995). The tone may range from detached or scholarly to warm and poetic. No matter the choices made, writers are obligated to articulate their decisions for readers. In writing about a study, Peshkin (1985) was surprised to catch himself "red-handed, with [his] values at the very end of [his] pen," but then decided that is "right where they belong" (277). Such disclosures allow readers to evaluate the credibility and applicability of the findings for their own work.

Recognizing that multiple possible interpretations of events exist suggests that readers will add their own voices to the researcher's discussion. It is important for researchers to "inform readers where self and subject have been joined"; otherwise, the researcher's experiences remain "beyond control in the research process" (Jansen and Peshkin 1992, 710). Although the word "generalization" is problematic in qualitative research (see Bogdan and Biklen 2003, 31–32; Stake 2010, 197–98), Wolcott (1990) makes a useful point in distinguishing "propositional generalizations" (stated directly by the researcher) from "naturalistic generalizations" (made as readers compare their own experiences with those the researcher reports):

> We have choices to make in terms of how much we should organize our analyses and interpretations to produce the researcher's propositional generalizations (which I have been calling assertions) or to provide input into the reader's naturalistic generalizations. We will ordinarily do both, but how much of either is an important strategic choice. (86)

Words suggesting that readers "should," "must," or "need to" do something based on the study's findings position the writer as more of an authority. In contrast, words suggesting that readers "may," "consider," or "might" do something invite more input from readers' perspectives in determining the usefulness of the findings for their own situations. Flinders and Richardson (2002) provide a good discussion of issues of authorship, suggesting that qualitative researchers "write in a voice that frees the reader to find the meaning of the qualitative research report" for themselves (1169).

2.9. Ethical Issues in Observational Studies

Deyhle, Hess, and LeCompte (1992) offer a history and extensive discussion of ethical issues that may arise in qualitative research. For example, a researcher may be observing a group where several participants have not provided consent forms. No matter how interesting the data these participants provide, their words and work cannot be used in the study, unless the researcher devises a mechanism for collecting such data that meets IRB approval.

Other issues, while within the ethical guidelines of IRBs, are less clear-cut. When the video or audio recording captures the interactions of the whole group, including those participating without permission, can researchers use the video for data analysis, if they use only data pertinent to participants with appropriate permission? Conversations not intended for the researcher's ears may be overheard, or confidential information may be offered off the record or in informal exchanges. Is this data appropriate to include for analysis? Skilled researchers also remain aware of participants who find recording or photography uncomfortable, disruptive, or even disrespectful. For example, Blair (2009) turned off her video recorder because two girls in the class she studied were very sensitive to being photographed. Similarly, in studying his own teaching of private percussion lessons, Smith made only audio recordings and notes, deciding that video would be too intrusive for his students in that intimate setting (Smith and Durant 2006).

Other ethical concerns may arise as researchers seek to establish positive relationships with participants, for example, offering something to participants in exchange for the privilege of observing. To establish rapport and thank participants, Berg (1997, 94) regularly brought snacks for students in the high school chamber music programs she studied, offered to help the coordinators and provide them with information about their programs and, at the conclusion of the study, bought a meal or small gift for the teachers and coaches.

Stake (1995) recommends caution in making promises or offers of help, particularly in the early stages of a study. For example, researchers may promise participants the opportunity to review the final research report, and then discover that findings raise issues that participants are not able to or may prefer not to acknowledge. Descriptions that participants find unflattering or that could reveal sensitive information may be important findings. Are these findings essential to reporting the study? Should they be shared with participants?

Angrosino (2005) offers guidelines for such slippery questions under a principle he calls "proportionate reason."

> First, *the means used will not cause more harm than necessary to achieve the value*. . . . If we take "the value" to refer to the production of some form of ethnography, we must be careful to ensure that the means used (e.g., inserting oneself into a social network, using photographs or other personal records) do not cause disproportionate harm. . . . The second criterion is that *no less harmful way to protect the value currently exists*. (737, italics in the original)

Angrosino proposes that proportionate reason may be judged through intuition, trial and error, and commonsense guidelines such as respecting community norms. Acknowledging that researchers cannot always predict the consequences of their choices, he also offers, "The moral advantage of the proportionate reasoning strategy is that it encourages researchers to admit to errors once they have occurred, to correct the errors so far as possible, and to move on" (737).

2.10. Parting Thoughts

Observational studies have made important contributions to our understanding, illuminating processes of music teaching and learning, and articulating a wealth of individually and socially constructed meanings among music-makers, listeners, teachers, learners, and music itself. More studies of formal and informal music teaching and learning in outside-of-school settings could deepen our understanding of individuals' motivations to make music and the meanings of music-making in their lives. Observational studies of small groups who gather to make music for themselves or to share with others, such as garage bands, woodwind quintets, drumming groups, country-western bands, vocal quartets, laptop orchestras, or fiddle bands, are lacking. Also unexplored are the behaviors of those who, as their primary way of interacting with music, choose to listen to live or recorded music, as audience members, fans, or avid and knowledgeable collectors. Such studies could offer insights into teaching and learning processes and suggest ways for music educators to more effectively prepare individuals with skills for lifelong involvement with music.

Technological advances continue to provide expanded options for data generation (see chapters 5 and 7 in this volume). Researchers are gaining the technical capabilities to conduct observations remotely, rather than on-site. What are the possibilities for combining on- and off-site observations in a study? What is gained or lost, for example, observing music-making in a remote area by Web camera, rather than in person? In addition, Angrosino (2005) warns that it is easy to forget that photographs, recordings, and other digital data are partial and decontextualized. He urges researchers to remember that, far from being a neutral record, technology "has the perceived power to objectify and turn into 'data' everything it encounters" (743). He therefore recommends that, rather than focusing on digital records themselves, researchers concentrate on understanding participants' and their own lived experience.

In my experience as a researcher, I have been privileged to be allowed to observe and share in participants' worlds and lives. In the process, I have gradually learned to become a more skilled observer. I have learned to plan more carefully and to deal with unanticipated occurrences that disrupt my careful plans. There is no shortcut for developing observation skills—we learn to observe by *doing* observation. Through continued practice, we discover that

> All researchers have great privilege and obligation: the privilege to pay attention to what they consider worthy of attention and the obligation to make conclusions drawn from those choices meaningful [to others]. . . . Added to the experience of ordinary looking and thinking, the experience of the qualitative researcher is one of knowing what leads to significant understanding, recognizing good sources of data, and consciously and unconsciously testing out the veracity of their eyes and the robustness of their interpretations. (Stake 1995, 49–50)

Studying music teaching and learning through observation offers an adventure with few specific rules or recipes. General principles, such as those outlined in this chapter, can help us develop useful questions and determine appropriate methods of data gathering and analysis, offering vivid descriptions and considered interpretations to participants, readers, and our field.

References

Abramo, Joseph Michael. 2009. "Popular Music and Gender in the Classroom." PhD diss., Teachers College, Columbia University.

Abramo, Joseph Michael. 2011. "Gender Differences of Popular Music Production in Secondary Schools." *Journal of Research in Music Education* 59 (1): 21–43.

Adler, Patricia A., and Peter Adler. 1994. "Observational Techniques." In *Handbook of Qualitative Research*, edited by N. K. Denzin and Y. S. Lincoln, 377–92. Thousand Oaks, CA: Sage Publications.

Angrosino, Michael V. 2005. "Recontextualizing Observation: Ethnography, Pedagogy, and the Prospects for a Progressive Political Agenda." In *The SAGE Handbook of Qualitative Research*, edited by N. K. Denzin and Y. S. Lincoln, 729–45. Thousand Oaks, CA: Sage Publications.

Angrosino, Michael V., and Judith Rosenberg. 2011. "Observations on Observations: Continuities and Challenges." In *The SAGE Handbook of Qualitative Research*, edited by N. K. Denzin and Y. S. Lincoln, 467–78. Thousand Oaks, CA: Sage Publications.

Atkinson, Paul, and Martyn Hammersley. 1994. "Ethnography and Participant Observation." In *Handbook of Qualitative Research*, edited by N. K. Denzin and Y. S. Lincoln, 248–61. Thousand Oaks, CA: Sage Publications.

Barrett, Margaret S., and Sandra Lee Stauffer. 2009. *Narrative Inquiry in Music Education: Troubling Certainty*. Dordrecht, London: Springer.

Berg, Margaret H. 1997. "Social Construction of Musical Experience in Two High School Chamber Music Ensembles." PhD diss., Music Education, Northwestern University.

Blair, Deborah V. 2009. "Nurturing Music Learners in Mrs. Miller's 'Family Room': A Secondary Classroom for Students with Special Needs." *Research Studies in Music Education* 31 (1): 20–36.

Bogdan, Robert C., and Sari Knopp Biklen. 2003. *Qualitative Research For Education: An Introduction to Theories and Methods*. 4th ed. Boston, MA: Allyn and Bacon.

Brewer, Wesley. 2009. "Conceptions of Effective Teaching and Role-Identity Development among Preservice Music Educators." PhD diss., Arizona State University.

Carter, Kathy. 1993. "The Place of Story in the Study of Teaching and Teacher Education." *Educational Researcher* 22 (1): 5–12, 18.

Creswell, John W. 2007. *Qualitative Inquiry and Research Design: Choosing among Five Approaches*. 2nd ed. Thousand Oaks, CA: Sage Publications.

Dewey, John. 1934. *Art as Experience*. New York: Perigee Books.

Deyhle, Donna L., G. Alfred Hess Jr., and Margaret D. LeCompte. 1992. "Approaching Ethical Issues for Qualitative Researchers in Education." In *The Handbook of Qualitative Research in Education*, edited by M. D. LeCompte, W. L. Millroy, and J. Preissle, 597–641. San Diego, CA: Academic Press.

Duke, Robert A., and Amy L. Simmons. 2006. "The Nature of Expertise: Narrative Descriptions of 19 Common Elements Observed in the Lessons of Three Renowned Artist-Teachers." *Bulletin of the Council for Research in Music Education* 170: 7–19.

Eisenhart, Margaret A., and Kenneth R. Howe. 1992. "Validity in Educational Research." In *The Handbook of Qualitative Research in Education*, edited by M. D. LeCompte, W. L. Millroy, and J. Preissle, 643–80. San Diego, CA: Academic Press.

Eisner, Elliot W. 1991. *The Enlightened Eye: Qualitative Inquiry and the Enhancement of Educational Practice*. New York: Macmillan.

Eros, John D. 2009. "A Case Study of Three Urban Music Teachers in the Second Stage of Their Teaching Careers." PhD diss., The University of Michigan.

Fitzpatrick, Kate R. 2008. "A Mixed Methods Portrait of Urban Instrumental Music Teaching." PhD diss., Northwestern University.

Flinders, David J., and Carol P. Richardson. 2002. "Contemporary Issues in Qualitative Research and Music Education." In *The New Handbook of Research on Music Teaching and Learning*, edited by R. J. Colwell and C. Richardson, 1159–71. New York: Oxford University Press.

Gackle, Lynne, and Victor Fung. 2009. "Bringing the East to the West: A Case Study in Teaching Choral Music to a Youth Choir in the United States." *Bulletin of the Council for Research in Music Education* 182: 65–77.

Glesne, Corrine. 1999. *Becoming Qualitative Researchers: An Introduction*. 2nd ed. New York: Longman.

Gray, Lori F. 2011. "The Impact of Changing Teaching Jobs on Music Teacher Identity, Role, and Perceptions of Role Support." PhD diss., Arizona State University.

Hornbach, Christina M. 2005. "Ah-eee-ah-eee-yah-eee, Bum and Pop, Pop, Pop: Teacher Initiatives, Teacher Silence, and Children's Vocal Responses in Early Childhood Music Classes." PhD diss., Michigan State University.

Jackson-Gough, Julie J. 2003. "Music Events among Four-Year-Old Children in Naturalistic Contexts, within Selected New Zealand Kindergartens." PhD diss., Florida State University.

Jansen, Golie, and Alan Peshkin. 1992. "Subjectivity in Qualitative Research." In *The Handbook of Qualitative Research in Education*, edited by M. D. LeCompte, W. L. Millroy, and J. Preissle, 681–725. San Diego, CA: Academic Press.

Koops, Lisa Huisman. 2010. "'Deñuy Jàngal Seen Bopp' (They Teach Themselves): Children's Music Learning in The Gambia." *Journal of Research in Music Education* 58 (1): 20–36.

Larsson, S. 1986. "Learning from Experience: Teachers' Conceptions of Changes in Their Professional Practice." *Journal of Curriculum Studies* 19 (1): 35–43.

Lewis, Carolyn E. 2004. "Music's Role in the Kindergarten Classroom: A Qualitative Study." Master's Thesis, University of Louisville.

Lum, Chee-Hoo. 2007. "Musical Networks of Children: An Ethnography of Elementary School Children in Singapore." PhD diss., University of Washington.

Lum, Chee-Hoo, and Patricia Shehan Campbell. 2007. "The Sonic Surrounds of an Elementary School." *Journal of Research in Music Education* 55 (1): 31–47.

Manes, Sean Ichiro. 2009. "The Pedagogical Process of a Japanese-American Shamisen Teacher." *Bulletin of the Council for Research in Music Education* 281: 41–50.

Matsunobu, Koji. 2011. "Spirituality as a Universal Experience of Music: A Case Study of North Americans' Approaches to Japanese Music." *Journal of Research in Music Education* 59 (3): 273–89.

Miles, Matthew B., and A. Michael Huberman. 1994. *Qualitative Data Analysis: An Expanded Sourcebook*. Thousand Oaks, CA: Sage Publications.

Norgaard, Martin. 2008. "Descriptions of Improvisational Thinking by Artist-Level Jazz Musicians." PhD diss., University of Texas.

Paise, Michele. 2010. "Six Beginning Music Teachers' Music Teacher Role Identities." PhD diss., Arizona State University.

Pellegrino, Kristen 2010. "The Meanings and Values of Music-Making in the Lives of String Teachers: Exploring the Intersections of Music-Making and Teaching." PhD diss., The University of Michigan.

Peshkin, Alan. 1982. "The Researcher and Subjectivity: Reflections on an Ethnography of School and Community." In *Doing the Ethnography of Schooling*, edited by G. Spindler, 48–67. New York: Holt, Rinehart and Winston.

Peshkin, Alan. 1985. "Virtuous Subjectivity: In the Participant-Observer's I's." In *Exploring Clinical Methods for Social Research*, edited by D. N. Berg, and Kenwyn K. Smith, 267–82. Beverly Hills, CA: Sage Publications.

Peshkin, Alan. 1988. "In Search of Subjectivity—One's Own." *Educational Researcher* 17 (7): 17–21.

Ruthmann, Stephen Alexander. 2006. "Negotiating Learning and Teaching in a Music Technology Lab: Curricular, Pedagogical, and Ecological Issues." PhD diss., Oakland University.

Schmidt, Margaret. 1994. "Learning from Experience: Influences on Music Student Teachers' Perceptions and Practices." PhD diss., The University of Michigan.

Schmidt, Margaret, and Jelani Canser. 2006. "Clearing the Fog: Constructing Shared Stories of a Novice Teacher's Success." *Research Studies in Music Education* 27: 52–66.

Seddon, Frederick, and Michele Biasutti. 2010. "Strategies Students Adopted When Learning to Play an Improvised Blues in an E-Learning Environment." *Journal of Research in Music Education* 58 (2): 147–67.

Silverman, Marissa. 2011. "Music and Homeschooled Youth: A Case Study." *Research Studies in Music Education* 33 (2): 179–95.

Smith, Gareth Dylan, and Colin Durrant. 2006. "Mind Styles™ and Paradiddles—Beyond the Bell-Curve: Towards an Understanding of Learning Preferences, and Implications for Instrumental Teachers." *Research Studies in Music Education* 26 (1): 51–62.

Soto, Amanda Christina, Chee-Hoo Lum, and Patricia Shehan Campbell. 2009. "A University-School Music Partnership for Music Education Majors in a Culturally Distinctive Community." *Journal of Research in Music Education* 56 (4): 338–56.

Spindler, Gary, ed. 1982. *Doing the Ethnography of Schooling*. New York: Holt, Rinehart and Winston.

Spradley, James P. 1980. *Participant Observation*. New York: Holt, Rinehart and Winston.

Stake, Robert E. 1995. *The Art of Case Study Research*. Thousand Oaks, CA: Sage Publications.

Stake, Robert E. 2010. *Qualitative Research: Studying How Things Work*. New York: The Guilford Press.

Stauffer, Sandra. 2002. "Connections between the Musical and Life Experiences of Young Composers and Their Compositions." *Journal of Research in Music Education* 50 (4): 301–22.

Tobias, Evan. 2010. "Crossfading and Plugging in: Secondary Students' Engagement and Learning in a Songwriting and Technology Class." PhD diss., Northwestern University.

Tsugawa, Samuel. 2009. "Senior Adult Music Learning, Motivation, and Meaning Construction in Two New Horizons Ensembles." PhD diss., Arizona State University.

Wolcott, Harry F. 1990. *Writing up Qualitative Research*. 1st ed. Vol. 20. SAGE Qualitative Research Methods Series. Newbury Park, CA: Sage Publications.

Wolcott, Harry F. 1992. "Posturing in Qualitative Inquiry." In *The Handbook of Qualitative Research in Education*, edited by M. D. LeCompte, W. L. Millroy, and J. Preissle, 3–52. San Diego, CA: Academic Press.

Wolcott, Harry F. 2001. *Writing Up Qualitative Research*. 2nd ed. Thousand Oaks, CA: Sage Publications.

CHAPTER 3

GENERATING AND ANALYZING INDIVIDUAL INTERVIEWS

KATHRYN ROULSTON

DAILY life in the twenty-first century is saturated with information generated in interviews and disseminated via a spectrum of print and digital media. Citizens globally know the "interview" as both spectators and participants and have participated in some form of interview in educational settings, clinical encounters, or job interviews. Given the ubiquity of interviews in social life, it is easy to overlook the complexity of the interview as a specialized interaction characterized by question and answer sequences. This chapter discusses a particular form of individual interview—namely, the "research interview." Research interviews are used as a method to generate data to explore research problems and topics. Although some research interviews involve groups, the most common of which is focus groups, these are not discussed here (see chapter 4 in this volume for further information). This chapter focuses on the use of individual research interviews to examine topics in music education in North America.

First, different structures and types of interview used by researchers are reviewed. Second, the process of research design using interviews is reviewed. Third analytic and representational approaches to interview data are discussed. Ethical issues are threaded throughout the chapter, as are relevant exemplars of research studies in music education. The chapter concludes by considering the future of interviewing in music education research, including the impact of new technologies; how methodological and theoretical developments in the social sciences might impact music education research; and implications of these developments for the assessment of quality in research.

The research interview is an interaction in which an interviewer asks a research participant questions to generate information about a research topic. What distinguishes research interviews from mundane conversations in which people ask and answer one another's questions is that information generated ("data") is used to examine research questions about the social world. Interviews are commonly audio and/or video recorded, transcribed, and systematically analyzed to generate knowledge about people's experiences of engaging with music, music learning and teaching, and the meanings that they attribute to their experiences.

3.1. Types of Interviews

Interviews range in structure from *standardized* in which highly structured protocols are used, through *semi-structured*, to *unstructured* or conversational interviews. In all these interview types, questions are posed to research participants with the expectation that they elicit factual descriptions of experiences, beliefs, or events. Yet, the kinds of descriptions generated by standardized question guides are likely to be quite different from those provided in unstructured conversations. In unstructured formats, talk is more likely to be symmetrical, with interviewers and interviewees free to initiate topics of discussion and ask questions. In contrast, standardized interviews rely on the interviewer asking the same questions in the same sequence, with minimal deviation from pre-formulated scripts. Midway between structured and unstructured formats are semi-structured interviews in which researchers use topical guides to generate talk. Semi-structured interviews provide freedom for interviewers to pursue further detail concerning topics that arise in discussions with individual participants. Semi-structured interviews are frequently used in music education research.

While many researchers describe their use of interviews via the structures mentioned earlier, methodological literature describes other interview formats. These include phenomenological interviews, ethnographic interviews, life history and oral history interviews, feminist interviews, dialogic interviews, and new materialist conceptualizations of interviews. Researchers also make use of visual methods such as graphic elicitation and photos, and material objects in interviews to elicit descriptions.

Recent innovations in technology also afford opportunities to conduct interviews via telephone, as well as using synchronous and asynchronous online tools. Broadly speaking, most qualitative inquiries are "phenomenological" in that the intent is to develop knowledge about human experience through examining people's descriptions of their lived experiences and life worlds. In *phenomenological interviews* interviewers ask questions of participants in order to generate in-depth descriptions of participants' experiences. Some researchers situate their use of phenomenological interviews within one of the many strands of philosophical phenomenology, including transcendental (Moustakas 1994), hermeneutic (van Manen 1990, 2014), or post-intentional (Vagle 2014) phenomenology, among others. Others use phenomenological interviews to generate rich descriptions of human experience that are analyzed via other approaches to human science research (e.g., constant comparative or narrative methods).

In a phenomenological interview, the interviewer's responsibility is to listen carefully to the participant and ask thoughtful and relevant follow-up questions to elicit further details about the phenomenon of interest. Interviewers usually refrain from contributing their own ideas and experiences during conversations, and aim to provide supportive, non-therapeutic environments in which participants are comfortable to talk about their life worlds. A typical opening question posed is:

- Think of a time when you experienced..., and describe that in detail.

Follow-up questions or probes may incorporate the participants' utterances in order to facilitate storytelling in participants' own words. For example:

- You mentioned..., tell me more about that.
- You talked about..., what was that like for you?

Elizabeth Parker (2017) used phenomenological interviews to explore the experiences of long-term singing among participants in a Southeastern African American church choir. Drawing on Maurice Merleau-Ponty's embodiment phenomenology, Parker generated six themes that outlined the "texture" of participants' experiences (growing as young people, building and sustaining the choir family, inspiring directors with vision, becoming part of my music, contributing and ministering to others, and loving God and gospel music), before outlining the essence of the phenomenon examined as the "development of the spiritual self" (Parker 2017, 68).

A second example of the use of phenomenological interviews is described by Bridget Sweet (2015) in her study of adolescent female changing voice. Although phenomenological interviews are typically conducted face-to-face, Sweet innovated on this process. Her young interviewees, who ranged from 6th- to 12th-graders, were asked to complete written responses to initial questions prior to participating in a series of three interviews. Data generated were subject to phenomenological reduction and findings are discussed under the broader themes of phonation and emotional experiences, and contexts of singing. The "essence" of the phenomenon derived from data is explained as the "vulnerability and fear of embarrassment determined all use of the females' singing voices, resulting in risk assessment for each singing situation and setting" (Sweet 2015, 70). Another example of phenomenological research is Ryan Hourigan's (2009) study of preservice teachers' fieldwork experiences in special needs classrooms and Adam Kruse's exploration of hip-hop musicians of hip-hop musical learning. Phenomenological interviews are typically used as the primary source of data (e.g., Sweet 2015), although multiple sources of data are frequently used also (Kruse 2018; Parker 2017; see also chapter 7 in Volume 1 of this *Handbook* for more detail on phenomenological research in music education).

3.1.1. Ethnographic Interviews

Ethnographic interviews (Roulston, 2019) are used to elicit information in face-to-face contexts about social practices, culture, and meaning-making. With roots in anthropological and sociological field studies, ethnography uses participant observation as a primary source of data, with informal and formal interviews as a complementary data source. Ethnographers typically spend considerable amounts of time observing participants in naturalistic settings before asking questions in informal settings or arranging formal interviews. More recently, researchers have conducted online and digital ethnographies.

The range of questions asked in any ethnographic study varies considerably with respect to the topic(s) of study, and may include questions about the researcher's observations concerning space, objects, activities, events, time, people, goals, and feelings (Spradley 1979; Spradley 1980). Question types described in relation to ethnographic work have become commonplace in other kinds of research, and include "the grand tour question" (e.g., "Describe the rehearsal room for me" or "Describe the final rehearsal for me from the moment you arrived until you left") and "mini-tour questions" (e.g., "Describe how you plan for a lesson").

Informal interviews are conversations that researchers might initiate in response to actions and activities that they observe. In ethnographic work, researchers might not audio-record interviews, but rather jot down details and information at a later time. In both informal and formal interviews, the ethnographic interviewer must express genuine interest in learning about others and their actions and contexts. Researchers must also develop a high level of rapport and engage in ethical ways with participants. While all research involving human subjects requires respect for and ethical treatment of participants, ethnography calls upon researchers to be keenly aware of how data are collected over prolonged periods of time, and to let participants know about their rights as participants. Because researchers may develop friendly relationships with participants, it is the ethical responsibility of researchers to let participants know the boundaries within which data-gathering occurs. This avoids misunderstandings when information gained from informal conversations is later used as "data," when a participant may have thought they were reporting confidential information to a "friend." Multiple ethnographic interviews are likely to occur over time, with analysis occurring simultaneously with data generation. Thus, findings and questions from earlier interviews are used to structure different sorts of questions in later interviews (for example, Spradley 1979 discusses the use of descriptive, structural, and contrast questions at different points during an ethnographic study).

Sarah Bartolome's (2013) study of perceived values and benefits of the Seattle Girls' Choir experience combined semi-structured interviews with prolonged observations and examination of documentary data in an ethnographic study over the period of a year. Bartolome includes the semi-structured interview guides she used with choristers, their parents, and faculty, and reports that interviews with younger choristers were conducted in small groups of three or four. Findings are represented in relation to discussion of social, musical, personal, and external and community benefits.

Adam Kruse (2016) explored a hip-hop musician's experiences and perspectives of school from an ethnographic perspective. Use of a combination of autoethnography and ethnographic methods that involved participant observation and informal conversations allowed Kruse to compare his own experiences as a music teacher to those of his participant, Terrence, over the period of two and a half years. Kruse represents his findings in the form of themes, with text boxes entitled "addressing assumptions," in which he examines his responses to what he learned from Terrence.

Additional examples of the use of ethnographic interviewing may be found in Andrew Goodrich's (2007) ethnographic study of peer mentoring in a high school jazz ensemble, Stephen Paparo's (2013) study of a collegiate a cappella ensemble, and Mary Kennedy's (2004) study of the American Boychoir School (ABS) (also see chapter 6 in Volume 1 for more information on ethnographic research in music education).

Oral and life history interviews have long been used by oral historians and folklorists such as Studs Terkel (1912–2008) and Alan Lomax (1915–2002) to document peoples' life stories. Countless oral histories of musicians and folk performers have been collected and archived in the Smithsonian Museum. One such collection is the *Smithsonian Jazz Oral History Program*, established in 1992 by the Smithsonian's National Museum of American History to record interviews with senior jazz musicians. Various institutions (e.g., Yale University, and University of California, Los Angeles) have extensive oral history collections related to musicians. As one example, Roy Legette's collection of video- and audio-recorded oral histories of music teachers in Georgia, *Music Teachers' Stories Collection*, has been made available through the Special Collections at the University of Georgia.

Music education researchers have also used narrative interviews to represent the life stories of those who have been formerly excluded within the literature. For example, Jeananne Nichols (Cape and Nichols 2012, Nichols 2015, 2016) has contributed an understanding of the role of women in military bands in the United States Air Force through a combination of archival research and life history interviews, and Nichols (2013) and Sarah Bartolome (2016) have developed life histories of transgender persons. Both Nichols and Bartolome gained extensive feedback from their participants prior to representing their stories. These studies attend to Gordon Cox's (2002) call for music education researchers to make more use of life history research to document the lives and experiences of those involved in music education.

Music education researchers have yet to utilize other forms of interviewing such as feminist, dialogic, and new materialist approaches to interviewing that are found in qualitative research methods literature. I have yet to locate work on feminist interview methods (DeVault 1990; DeVault and Gross 2007; Linabary and Hamel 2017) that has been applied in music education research, even though researchers make use of feminist research approaches (e.g., Hess 2014, 2018). Typical principles and practices on the part of feminist interviewers include striving to listen to and respond sincerely to participants, promoting non-hierarchical and/or dialogic relationships with women, and representing women in ways that avoid objectification. It may be that feminist scholars in music education conduct interviews using feminist principles, but are focused on the emancipatory emphasis of feminist work in their reports, rather than methodological issues.

Writing on *dialogic interviews* explores approaches that demonstrate a greater degree of back-and-forth conversation between interviewers and interviewees. Rather than taking a "neutral" or "objective" role in interviews, interviewers are more likely to express opinions, discuss their experiences, and even challenge participants' accounts. Writing on this form of interview (Brinkmann 2007; Tanggaard 2007; Tanggaard 2008; Way, Zwier, and Tracy 2015) has yet to have an impact in music education research, although these articles provide insight into how these approaches might be applied.

The most recent innovation in writing on interviewing to emerge in methodological literature is that of new materialist theorizations of interviews (Kuntz 2015; Kuntz and Presnall 2012). From this perspective, interviews are seen as sites in which the human and non-human are entangled in an "assemblage." From this view, any research project includes people, ideas, social collectivities, and institutions (Fox and Alldred 2015). Data, from this perspective, is no longer viewed as information that can be determined, but rather a "becoming" involving the interviewer, interviewee, and the non-human elements co-present—that are constituted in an assemblage of "multiple historical, present and future encounters" (Kuntz and Presnall 2012, 736). Given that one can find writing that draws on scholars who use new materialist approaches in music education literature (e.g., Allsup 2017), these approaches may well emerge in forthcoming work.

Finally, visual methods and stimulus materials have also been incorporated into interviews, as researchers ask participants to take photos, respond to photos (Clark-Ibáñez 2004), draw images or diagrams (Crilly, Blackwell and Clarkson 2006), or respond to stimulus materials (Stacey and Vincent 2011) and objects (De Leon and Cohen 2005) such as a guitar. Music education research is ripe with possibility here, since questions might be asked about instruments people play, the music they listen to, and musical scores and tools used in learning.

3.2. Modes of Interacting with Interviewees

Researchers make use of telephones and computer-mediated communication to conduct interviews. Social research has made extensive use of telephones (Genovese 2004) and cell phones (Carley-Baxter, Peytchev, and Black 2010; Steeh, Buskirk, and Callegaro 2007) to ask participants questions, although this work predominantly relies on standardized surveys administered to participants who have been randomly selected. Yet these methods are increasingly used by qualitative researchers (Lechuga 2012). Similarly to Raymond Opdenakker (2006), Judith Sturges and Kathleen Hanrahan (2004) argue for the advantages of using telephones to conduct interviews, noting that they are effective for examining sensitive topics, enable researchers to involve participants who may be difficult to access, involve cost-savings, and ensure researcher safety. For researchers intending to use telephone interviews, Genovese (2004,

216) points out that these differ from face-to-face interviews because the interviewer does not have access to visual cues supplied by facial expressions and body language. A good telephone interviewer, according to Genovese (2004, 225), creates a comfort zone, engages the listener, visits a little with the person interviewed, exhibits patience, takes time, maintains a persona, is consistent, and communicates clearly. As one example, Catherine Bell-Robertson (2014) used telephone interviews to talk to geographically dispersed novice instrumental teachers who participated in an online community.

New modes of computer-mediated communication (CMC) provide opportunities to recruit participants previously unavailable because of geographical distance, as well as fresh topics for examination. *Online interviewing* may be conducted asynchronously (e.g., via e-mail), or synchronously (e.g., via Internet chat rooms, instant messaging, or Voice over Internet Protocols [VoIPs] such as Skype or in multi-user domains [MUDs]) (Deakin and Wakefield 2014). While online methods of communication provide ways to recruit participants from groups who otherwise may not be able to participate in interviews face-to-face, a range of issues must be considered. First, in online interviews, researchers must consider whether persons interviewed are who they say they are. This can be an issue in both synchronous and asynchronous settings when researchers cannot see parties to the interaction. Second, researchers cannot necessarily ensure the confidentiality of electronic communications. Third, researchers need to consider participants' level of skill in the use of technologies in addition to the robustness of Internet connections. For participants lacking skill in the use of technologies, participating in an online interview may be onerous and difficulties may also be encountered if connections fail during interactions. With advances in online technologies, reliance on CMCs for social research is likely to increase, as researchers incorporate new technologies to conduct interviews online, in addition to examining online settings as contexts for music learning and teaching. For example, Adam Kruse (2018) used a combination of interviews that encompassed in-person meetings and use of telephone and online video conference software for his phenomenological study of hip-hop musicians' experiences of learning to create and perform.

3.3. Designing Studies Using Interviews

The process of designing a study using interviews encompasses developing a research topic and research questions, decision-making concerning the overall design and methods for the study, and formulating interview questions for a study. Questions used for a study are called "interview guides" or "interview protocols." Once a proposal for a study has been developed, the researcher must gain approval for the study from relevant institutional review boards (IRBs)[1] (these may include both university and ethical review boards in school districts), and outline plans for sample selection and recruitment of participants. Proposals for studies involving human subjects usually include the following elements:

- Background to the study and outline of the research problem (including reference to relevant literature);
- Research design and methods statement explaining:
  - A description of the study's design (e.g., interview study, case study, ethnography etc.);
  - The population from which participants for the study will be selected, and criteria for selection;
  - Plans for recruitment and relevant recruitment materials;
  - Research settings and contexts;
  - Projections concerning what data will be collected over what time period;
  - Plans for data analysis;
  - Interview guides;
- Risks and benefits for participants;
- Benefits for humankind.

Researchers bound the scope of qualitative studies by specifying research contexts, methods of data collection, time periods, and sampling strategies for participant selection. Qualitative researchers typically use purposeful sampling strategies rather than the random sampling commonly used in standardized interviewing. Depending on the research purpose of a study, researchers outline inclusion criteria for a study. For example, participants might be sought because they represent a "typical case," an "information-rich case," an "extreme case," or because they fit specific criteria (e.g., they are recommended by others as "exemplary" teachers). Patton (2002) identifies "convenience sampling," in which participants are selected and recruited because they are easily accessible and willing to volunteer, as the least defensible and weakest form of sampling. To ensure that a research study meets standards for quality used by music education researchers to judge the merit of research, considerable thought must be given to decision-making concerning research contexts, sample selection, and recruitment in order to allow maximum opportunities for the generation of rich information to respond to the research questions.

Since qualitative interviewing involves the researcher in the generation of data, researchers need to consider the implications of the subject positions that they occupy in relation to the research topic and participants. Alan Peshkin referred to this sort of investigation as searching for one's own "subjectivity." Peshkin (1988, 17) defined subjectivities as the "amalgam of the persuasions that stem from the circumstances of one's class, statuses, and values interacting with the particulars of one's object of investigation." In any project, different "researcher subjectivities" are mobilized in relation to topics and participants that have varied implications for the data generated. As a starting place, these might include gender, race, ethnicity, age, educational attainment, sexual orientation, and socioeconomic status. For example, Mary Kennedy (2004) reported that her identity as a woman studying boys' experiences of the changing voice likely impacted the data generated in interviews. The search for one's subjectivity will unfold differently for each and every research project, given that contexts and human beings change, and participants orient to different aspects of a researcher's self-presentation. One example of how a music education researcher has discussed his subject positions is provided by Adam Kruse (2016).

The identification of one's subjectivities has become a standard practice among qualitative researchers, although it has been critiqued by some scholars (Harding 2007; Pillow 2003). Yet, identifying one's subject positions is frequently identified with the idea of demonstrating reflexivity as a researcher. Kim Etherington (2004, 31–32) defines researcher reflexivity as "the capacity to acknowledge how their own experiences and contexts (which may be fluid and changing) inform the process and outcomes of inquiry." Linda Finlay (2002) has reviewed the multiple ways in which "reflexivity" is conceptualized by qualitative researchers. Although there is no one "right" path to demonstrating researcher reflexivity, this is an important consideration in planning for and conducting research.

3.4. Asking Questions

The type of interview question that is formulated for a research project is integrally connected with the theoretical and conceptual framework for a study, the research purpose, the research questions posed, research design and methods used, and the analytic methods that are projected. For example, if the object of a research project is to gain rich descriptions of a participant's experiences and lifelong involvement as a music educator, then a life history interview would be appropriate. Open interview questions would need to be formulated to elicit stories. For example, a beginning question might be formulated as:

- Think back to your first memories of being involved in music, and tell me about that.

In contrast, if the research purpose is to generate comparable factual data across a range of participants about their perspectives of a topic, then a non-qualitative interview (i.e., standardized survey questions with fixed-response choices) might be more appropriate. Clearly, the selection of the type of interview and how questions are formulated are linked to methods of data analysis and representation.

Patton (2002, 348–51) describes six types of interview questions, including questions concerning (1) experiences and behaviors; (2) opinions and values; (3) feelings; (4) knowledge; (5) sensory observations; and (6) background and demographics. Table 3.1 includes examples of each question type.

Numerous methods texts provide advice on how questions should be posed during interviews. One frequent recommendation is that researchers using qualitative interviews should pose "open" rather than "closed" questions. As I have written

Table 3.1 Examples of Question Types

Experiences and behaviors	Tell me how you came to be involved in learning music/taking music lessons.
	Describe a typical music lesson.
Opinions and values	
	Tell me what you see as the role of your teacher.
	What else do you think would be helpful?
Feelings	Tell me about the feelings you experience when you perform.
Knowledge	Tell me about how the Community Band is organized.
Sensory observations	Describe what you hear and see when you are performing in the ensemble.
Background and demographics	Age
	Ethnicity/race
	No. of years of teaching experience

elsewhere (Roulston 2010), open questions call upon participants to respond to question topics using their preferred terms rather than those of the interviewer. Closed questions, in contrast, provide parameters in which participants may answer. These sometimes generate yes/no responses or short answers. For example, with respect to the topic of learning an instrument as an adult, the following questions illustrate these open and closed formulations:

Open:

- Tell me about your childhood experiences in taking music lessons.

Closed:

- Have you been able to meet that goal?

Open questions are more likely to generate rich, in-depth descriptions, and may be used to elicit detailed stories, or initiate new topics within the interview as whole. While many texts recommend that researchers avoid the use of closed questions, I have found these to be useful when clarifying details of earlier talk, or making requests for specific, factual information (e.g., "And how many people were in your group to begin with?"). Nevertheless, closed questions should be used judiciously.

Another guideline for asking questions is to pose short, simple, and clear questions, one at a time. This helps participants by asking them to address one topic at a time. Novice interviewers frequently find themselves asking multiple questions, particularly if interviewees do not immediately respond. To avoid this, interviewers need to provide sufficient wait time for participants to think about the question posed before replying. For interviewers who find it difficult to wait before asking more questions or commenting, a useful guideline is to count to five, *slowly*, before saying more.

An effective strategy for posing follow-up questions with participants includes incorporating the participant's prior talk in the formulation of the question. For example, these are follow-up questions I posed in an interview:

- And so you said that this is something you'd always wanted to do. And what was that like for you?
- Can you say more about what you enjoy about it?

By using participants' utterances in the formulation of follow-up questions, interviewers can avoid posing questions that are "leading." (See Excerpt 1 for examples of leading questions).

If interviewers are not vigilant in how they ask questions, it is possible to generate precisely the kind of information that is being sought. Participants may also disagree with assumptions embedded in interviewers' questions. If researchers are aiming to learn about participants' lives and their interpretations of their experiences, formulating questions that facilitate spaces for interviewees to use their own words is crucial. Formulating open follow-up questions that orient to interviewees' talk requires intensive listening, careful thought, and a good deal of practice. By learning how to ask these kinds of questions, interviewers can facilitate spaces for participants to respond to questions in ways that provide rich descriptions in their own terms.

Excerpt 1 (Roulston 2000)

1.	IR	so do you find because of this (.) um (.) I guess compression of more classes into
2.		the same period of time that you're just doing less and less?
3.		(1.0)
4.	P	oh yes it's it's not half as good it's about a quarter as good you know=
5.	IR	=yeah=
6.	P	=yes you're doing less and less as far as what what you [accomplish in literacy=
7.	IR	[yes
8.		yeah (.) so less in terms of quantity song material=
9.	P	=oh less [less in terms of quantity yep
10.	IR	[but also less
11.		in terms of u:m (1.0) u:h (.) I guess (.) conceptual knowledge=
12.	P	=yes (.) less in term yeah less in both ways and of course it's a vicious circle

IR: Interviewer
P: Participant

3.5. Preparing Interview Data for Analysis

To prepare interview data for analysis and representation of findings, researchers must first transcribe the words spoken by both interviewers and interviewees. It is a good idea to include the following information on a transcript:
  Project name

- Date, place, and time of interview;
- Interviewer's name;
- Interviewee's pseudonym (unless permission has given to reprint the interviewee's name);
- Duration of interview.

There is enormous variation in what kind of detail might be included in an interview transcript. A basic transcript will include the words spoken, together with identification of speakers. Utterances are usually punctuated and edited for clarity—that is, overlapping talk, pauses, and continuers such as "um," "yeah," and "uh" are typically omitted. Since speakers make use of all kinds of conversational resources to communicate, transcriptions may include annotations indicating laughter, sighs, coughs, pauses, crying, or moments when participants punctuate descriptions by singing melodies. If interviews have been conducted in another language, researchers must note in methods descriptions at what point data are translated. Data analysis may take place in the original language or in the translated language. If findings are represented in a language other than the original talk, researchers must choose whether to include the original language in representations of findings. Decisions about what level of detail to include in a transcript are related to the method of analysis selected and the audience(s) to whom the researcher wishes to communicate. If the topic of talk is the primary focus of analysis, then other features of talk (such as pauses, or laughter) are usually omitted. In contrast, if researchers want to account for how talk is co-constructed in interviews, then further detail is included (for an example of transcription conventions from conversation analysis with naturally occurring data, see Forrester 2010).

Researchers conducting unfunded research usually transcribe their own interviews, whereas in funded research, funds are routinely allocated for transcription. Applications such as oTranscribe (http://otranscribe.com/) or Express Scribe (http://www.nch.com.au/scribe/index.html) may be used to transcribe digital audio-files. Rapid progress had been made with the development of voice-to-text software, so it is possible that in the near future transcriptions will be generated automatically. At the time of this writing, considerable editing is still needed. As a general rule, it takes four hours to transcribe one hour of audio-recorded talk. Depending on the amount of detail required and the speed of delivery of talk, this may take considerably longer. In cases in which a professional transcriber has been employed, it is good practice to check the transcripts for accuracy by listening to the audio-recordings, adding further details in the transcript where necessary. As a preliminary step in analysis, re-listening to audio-recordings of interviews is productive, and researchers can use this phase to note down emerging ideas and insights for analysis, as well as methodological reflections concerning the conduct of the interview.

3.6. Analyzing Qualitative Interview Data

Of the numerous ways to analyze interview data, coding and categorization approaches are most commonly used (Saldaña 2013). Inductive approaches to coding data were first codified in Barney Glaser and Anselm Strauss's seminal book, *The Discovery of Grounded Theory* (Glaser and Strauss 1967). Since that time, grounded theory as an approach to research has developed into a diversity of approaches (Charmaz 2014; Corbin and Strauss 2015; Morse et al. 2009). The basis of coding and categorization of data is that data in the form of interview transcripts, field notes of observations, or documents are condensed by labeling sections of data with "codes" that reflect some combination of topical content, structural features, and/or concepts derived from literature in the field (Miles, Huberman, and Saldaña 2014). Researchers frequently develop "code books" or "code dictionaries" that include definitions for each code and the parameters by which codes might be applied, as well as examples of data that illustrate the code (Bernard and Ryan 2010). Systematic coding involves an iterative and recursive process in which the analyst reads and re-reads data, and develops concepts and ideas represented by the codes through memo-writing. Once a set of codes has been systematically developed and applied across a data set, researchers then sort the codes into larger categories, comparing data with data, events with events, codes with codes, and categories with categories in a process identified by grounded theorists as the "constant comparative method."

Over the last two decades, a variety of Qualitative Data Analysis (QDA) software programs have been developed. With each new version, these programs display ever-increasing capacities to assist in coding, searching, retrieving, and theorizing of qualitative data. QDA software do *not* analyze the data—instead, the analyst is fully responsible for using these as a tool to code, analyze, and interpret data, and thoughtful decision-making and careful reflection are required throughout the analytic process. For an introduction to QDA and specific packages, see Silver and Lewins (2014) and Woolf and Silver (2018a, 2018b, 2018c). QDA programs are regularly updated by software developers, so researchers should check product websites for the latest versions and training opportunities.

Grounded theorists vary considerably in relation to how and what constitutes a "theory." In much qualitative research, the coding processes first described in grounded theory literature are used not so much to develop "theory," but to generate "themes" that are supported by excerpts from the data set (Braun and Clarke 2006). The processes of coding and categorizing that fragment data and then reassemble data into "themes" is described by Donald Polkinghorne (1995) as a "paradigmatic" approach to the analysis of narrative data.

Another approach to analysis of qualitative interview data is that of the generation of narratives, or what Polkinghorne (1995) describes as "configuration of narratives." Rather than comparing and contrasting data to examine commonalities and differences, some narrative researchers aim to preserve the unique features of individual stories through the development of narratives. This approach is illustrated in autobiographies, biographies, and autoethnographies (Jones, Adams, and Ellis 2013). In narrative inquiry, researchers work to configure a variety of data—which may include interviews, documents, visual data, and field notes—into a story with a plot that answers the question of how and why events occur as they do (Clandinin 2007; Riessman 2008). In music education, Margaret Barrett and Sandra Stauffer (2009) have forwarded the application of narrative approaches to the analysis and representation of data. In their edited collection, Barrett and Stauffer review the origins of narrative inquiry, provide seven examples of narrative inquiry by music education researchers, and include invited commentaries from other researchers on the narrative examples and the potential for the use of narrative inquiry in music education (see also chapter 8 in volume 1).

More recently, qualitative inquiry has been profoundly influenced by new initiatives in the arts and humanities as "art-based inquiry" and "arts-based educational research" (Cahnmann-Taylor and Siegesmund 2018), although application of these approaches is seldom seen in music education research. A wide-ranging assortment of influences—including fiction, nonfiction, theater, dance, performance texts, poetry, visual arts, and music—has influenced the ways in which interview data are represented. One example of the use of poetic representation is found in an article by Monica Prendergast, Peter Gouzouasis, Carl Leggo, and Rita Irwin (Prendergast et al. 2009). All of the authors identify with the "a/r/t/ography" movement and are accomplished as artists, teachers, and researchers. This paper represents findings from a study of secondary school students' musical engagement in the form of a haiku suite. Gouzouasis had worked with the students and their teacher in a rhythm and blues class over a three-year period in a high school in Vancouver, Canada, and interviews were conducted with students about their involvement. The purpose of the haiku suite is described as a "collective portrait of these students' thoughts, attitudes, reflections, and philosophical statements" in response to interview questions (307). This representation of findings breaks with long-standing traditions in how music education research might be presented and is notable because it is published in a music education journal.

3.7. THE FUTURE OF INTERVIEWING IN MUSIC EDUCATION RESEARCH

Here, I comment on emerging trends and future possibilities. I focus on three issues: emerging avenues for research made possible by new technologies; how methodological and theoretical writing in the social sciences might inform the use of interviews in music education research; and implications of these developments for the assessment of quality in research.

First, new technologies are providing new contexts for conducting research as well as innovative ways to conduct interviews. Given that musicians have long embraced new technologies and integrated these in music education contexts, the possibilities for embracing these for the purpose of doing interview research are great. Music education researchers are using interviews to explore the ways in which people engage with digital technologies, online tools, and online communities to learn and teach music. For example, Nathan Kruse, Steven Harlos, Russell Callahan, and Michelle Herring (2013) and Nathan Kruse and Kari Veblen (2012) have explored online music teaching and learning involving Skype and YouTube videos. Researchers are also using new technologies such as VoIPs to conduct interviews with participants who, in prior times, may have not participated due to distance. Future research will likely make greater use of asynchronous and synchronous CMCs to conduct and record interviews that contribute to an understanding of significant topics in music education.

Second, theoretical and methodological writing on interviewing in the social sciences continues apace. There is heightened awareness that research interviews are sites in which interviewers and interviewees collaboratively co-construct data (Roulston 2018), in addition to continued questioning of the search for objective truth (St. Pierre 2011). Music education researchers have begun, and will continue to "trouble certainty" (Barrett and Stauffer 2009) by using diverse theoretical perspectives to examine research topics of interest and innovative approaches to represent findings. These approaches might draw on feminist, transformative, or new materialist conceptualizations of interviews, or make use of participatory and collaborative ways to involve participants in the generation of interview data. Music education researchers are likely to continue to de-emphasize representations of objectives truths in favor of varied and partial representations of humans' meaning-making.

Third, and finally, the interview as a technology for generating research data continues to be questioned. This questioning involves epistemological issues concerning the status of self-reported data (Lubet 2018), and methodological issues involving the analysis and representation of interview data (Potter and Hepburn 2012; Schaeffer and Alvesson, 2017; Silverman 2017). In music education research there has been an emphasis in qualitative inquiry on verifying the truth value of participants' accounts through the use of multiple forms of data over lengthy periods of time. This aligns with a neo-positivist (Roulston 2010) conceptualization of interviewing. Although contested, there are other ways of conceptualizing interviews (e.g., as a socially situated and active meaning-making sites in which interviewers and interviewees co-construct data, or as an assemblage). There are many other possibilities for music education researchers to consider. One thing is clear. The future is bright with promise for using interviews to conduct innovative research on significant topics that will continue to inform the field of music education.

Note

1. In 2018, the Office for Human Research Protections in the US published "The Final Rule," which revised expectations for what was required of researchers conducting research with human subjects. The effective date for general compliance was January 20, 2019. What this means is that researchers need to consult local institutions for any changes required in consent procedures with human subjects.

References

Allsup, Randall E. 2017. "Ifs, Ands, *and* Buts: A Polyphonic Vision of Qualitative Research in Music Education." *Bulletin of the Council for Research in Music Education* 214: 7–18. http://www.jstor.org/stable/10.5406/bulcouresmusedu.214.0007.

Barrett, Margaret S., and Sandra Lee Stauffer. 2009. *Narrative Inquiry in Music Education Troubling Certainty*. Dordrecht, London: Springer.

Bartolome, Sarah J. 2013. " 'It's Like a Whole Bunch of Me!': The Perceived Values and Benefits of the Seattle Girls' Choir Experience." *Journal of Research in Music Education* 60 (4): 395–418. doi:10.1177/0022429412464054.

Bartolome, Sarah J. 2016. "Melanie's Story: A Narrative Account of a Transgender Music Educator's Journey." *Bulletin of the Council for Research in Music Education* 207–08: 25–47. doi:10.5406/bulcouresmusedu.207-208.0025

Bell-Robertson, Catherine G. 2014. " 'Staying On Our Feet': Novice Music Teachers' Sharing of Emotions and Experiences within an Online Community." *Journal of Research in Music Education* 61 (4): 431–451. doi:10.1177/0022429413508410.

Bernard, H. Russell, and Gery. W. Ryan. 2010. *Analyzing Qualitative Data: Systematic Approaches*. Thousand Oaks, CA: Sage Publications.

Braun, Virginia, and Victoria Clarke. 2006. "Using Thematic Analysis in Psychology." *Qualitative Research in Psychology* 3 (2): 77–101. doi: 10.1191/1478088706qp063oa.

Brinkmann, Svend. 2007. "Could Interviews be Epistemic? An Alternative to Qualitative Opinion Polling." *Qualitative Inquiry* 13 (8): 1116–38. doi.org/10.1177/1077800407308222.

Cahnmann, Melisa, and Richard Siegesmund. 2018. *Arts-Based Research in Education: Foundations for Practice*. 2nd ed. New York; London: Routledge.

Cape, Janet, and Jeananne Nichols. 2012. "Engaging Stories: Co-constructing Narratives of Women's Military Bands." In *Narrative Soundings: An Anthology of Narrative Inquiry in Music Education*, edited by Margaret Barrett and Sandra Stauffer, 23–36. Dordrecht, London: Springer.

Carley-Baxter, Lisa, Andy Peytchev, and Michele Black. 2010. "Comparison of Cell Phone and Landline Surveys: A Design Perspective." *Field Methods* 22 (1): 3–15. doi.org/10.1177/1525822X09360310.

Charmaz, Kathy. 2014. *Constructing Grounded Theory*. 2nd ed. Thousand Oaks, CA: Sage Publications.

Clandinin, D. Jean, ed. 2007. *Handbook of Narrative Inquiry*. Thousand Oaks, CA: Sage Publications.

Clark-Ibáñez, Marisol. 2004. "Framing the Social World with Photo-Elicitation Interviews." *American Behavioral Scientist* 47 (12): 1507–27. doi.org/10.1177/0002764204266236.

Corbin, Juliet, and Anselm Strauss. 2015. *Basics of Qualitative Research: Techniques and Procedures for Developing Grounded Theory*. 4th ed. Los Angeles: Sage Publications.

Cox, Gordon. 2002. "Transforming Research in Music Education History." In *The New Handbook of Research on Music Teaching and Learning*, edited by Richard Colwell and Carol Richardson, 695–706. New York: Oxford University Press.

Crilly, Nathan, Blackwell, Alan F., and P. John Clarkson. 2006. "Graphic Elicitation: Using Research Diagrams as Interview Stimuli. *Qualitative Research*, 6 (3): 341–66. doi:10.1177/1468794106065007.

Deakin, Hannah, and Kelly Wakefield. 2014. "Skype Interviewing: Reflections of Two PhD Researchers." *Qualitative Research* 14 (5): 603–16. doi.org/10.1177/1468794113488126.

De Leon, Jason P. and Jeffrey Cohen. 2005. "Object and Walking Probes in Ethnographic Interviewing." *Field Methods* 17 (2): 200–04. doi.org/10.1177/1525822X05274733.

DeVault, Marjorie L. 1990. "Talking and Listening from Women's Standpoint: Feminist Strategies for Interviewing and Analysis." *Social Problems* 37 (1): 96–116.

DeVault, Marjorie L., and Glenda Gross. 2007. "Feminist Interviewing: Experience, Talk, and Knowledge." In *Handbook of Feminist Research: Theory and Praxis*, edited by Sharlene Nagy Hesse-Biber, 173–98. Thousand Oaks, CA: Sage Publications.

Etherington, Kim. 2004. *Becoming a Reflexive Researcher: Using Our Selves in Research*. London; Philadelphia: Jessica Kingsley.

Finlay, Linda. 2002. "Negotiating the Swamp: The Opportunity and Challenge of Reflexivity in Research Practice." *Qualitative Research* 2 (2): 209–30. doi.org/10.1177/146879410200200205.

Forrester, Michael A. 2010. "Emerging Musicality during the Pre-School Years: A Case Study of One Child." *Psychology of Music* 38 (2): 131–58. doi: 10.1177/0305735609339452.

Fox, Nick J., and Pam Alldred. 2015. "Inside the Research-Assemblage: New Materialism and the Micropolitics of Social Inquiry." *Sociological Research Online* 20 (2): 1–19. doi:10.5153/sro.3578.

Genovese, Barbara J. 2004. "Thinking inside the Box: The Art of Telephone Interviewing." *Field Methods* 16 (2): 215–26. doi: 10.1177/1525822x04263329.

Glaser, Barney G., and Anselm L. Strauss. 1967. *The Discovery of Grounded Theory: Strategies for Qualitative Research*. New York: Aldine de Gruyter.

Goodrich, Andrew. 2007. "Peer Mentoring in a High School Jazz Ensemble." *Journal of Research in Music Education* 55 (2): 94–114. doi.org/10.1177/002242940705500202.

Harding, Sandra. 2007. "Feminist Standpoints." In *Handbook of Feminist Research: Theory and Praxis*, edited by Sharlene N. Hesse-Biber, 45–70. Thousand Oaks, CA: Sage Publications.

Hess, Juliet. 2014. "Radical Musicking: Towards a Pedagogy of Social Change." *Music Education Research* 16 (3): 229–50. doi:10.1080/14613808.2014.909397.

Hess, Juliet. 2018. "Interrupting the Symphony: Unpacking the Importance Placed on Classical Concert Experiences." *Music Education Research* 20 (1): 11–21. doi:10.1080/14613808.2016.1202224.

Hourigan, Ryan M. 2009. "Preservice Music Teachers' Perceptions of Fieldwork Experiences in a Special Needs Classroom." *Journal of Research in Music Education* 57 (2): 152–168. doi.org/10.1177/0022429409335880.

Jones, Stacy Holman, Tony E. Adams, and Carolyn Ellis. 2013. *Handbook of Authoethnography*. Walnut Creek, CA: Left Coast Press.

Kennedy, Mary Copland. 2004. "'It's a Metamorphosis': Guiding the Voice Change at the American Boychoir School." *Journal of Research in Music Education* 52 (3): 264–280. doi: 10.2307/3345859.

Kruse, Adam. J. 2016. "'They Wasn't Makin' My Kinda Music': A Hip-Hop Musician's Perspective on School, Schooling, and School Music." *Music Education Research* 18 (3): 240–53. doi:10.1080/14613808.2015.1060954.

Kruse, Adam J. 2018. "'Hip-Hop Wasn't Something a Teacher Ever Gave Me': Exploring Hip-Hop Musical Learning." *Music Education Research* 20 (3): 317–29. doi:10.1080/14613808.2018.1445210.

Kruse, Nathan B., Steven C. Harlos, Russell M. Callahan, and Michelle L. Herring. 2013. "Skype Music Lessons in the Academy: Intersections of Music Education, Applied Music and Technology." *Journal of Music, Technology and Education* 6 (1): 43–60. doi:10.1386/jmte.6.1.43_1.

Kruse, Nathan B., and Kari K. Veblen. 2012. "Music Teaching and Learning Online: Considering YouTube Instructional Videos." *Journal of Music, Technology and Education* 5 (1): 77–87. doi:10.1386/jmte.5.1.77_1.

Kuntz, Aaron M. 2015. *The Responsible Methodologist: Inquiry, Truth-Telling, and Social Justice*. London; New York: Routledge.

Kuntz, Aaron M., and Marni M. Presnall. 2012. "Wandering the Tactical: From Interview to Intraview." *Qualitative Inquiry* 18 (9): 732–44. doi:10.1177/1077800412453016.

Lechuga, Vicente M. 2012. "Exploring Culture from a Distance: The Utility of Telephone Interviews in Qualitative Research." *International Journal of Qualitative Studies in Education* 25 (3): 251–68. doi.org/10.1080/09518398.2010.529853.

Linabary, Jasmine R., and Stephanie A. Hamel. (2017). "Feminist Online Interviewing: Engaging Issues of Power, Distance and Reflexivity in Practice." *Feminist Review* 115 (1): 97–113.

Lubet, Steven. 2018. *Interrogating Ethnography: Why Evidence Matters*. New York: Oxford University Press.

Miles, Matthew B., A. Michael Huberman, and Johnny Saldaña. 2014. *Qualitative Data Analysis: A Methods Sourcebook*. 3rd ed. Los Angeles: Sage Publications.

Morse, Janice M., Phyllis Noerager Stern, Juliet Corbin, Barbara Bowers, Kathy Charmaz, and Adele E. Clarke. 2009. *Developing Grounded Theory: The Second Generation*. Walnut Creek, CA: Left Coast Press.

Moustakas, Clark. 1994. *Phenomenological Research Methods*. Thousand Oaks, CA: Sage Publications.

Nichols, Jeananne. 2013. "Rie's Story, Ryan's Journey: Music in the Life of a Transgender Student." *Journal of Research in Music Education* 61 (3): 262–79. doi:10.1177/0022429413498259.

Nichols, Jeananne. 2015. "Living History: Pioneering Bandswomen of the United States Air Force." *Music Educators Journal* 101 (3): 55–62. doi:10.1177/0027432114563719.

Nichols, Jeananne. 2016. "Into the Wild Blue Yonder: A History of the United States 'Women in the Air Force' (WAF) Band 1949–1961." In *Women's Bands in America: Performing Music and Gender*, edited by J. M. Sullivan. Lanham, MD: Rowman and Littlefield.

Paparo, Stephen A. 2013. "The Accafellows: Exploring the Music Making and Culture of a Collegiate A Cappella Ensemble." *Music Education Research* 15 (1): 19–38. doi:10.1080/14613808.2012.712508.

Opdenakker, Raymond. 2006. "Advantages and Disadvantages of Four Interview Techniques in Qualitative Research." *Forum: Qualitative Social Research* 7 (4), Art. 11. http://www.qualitative-research.net/index.php/fqs/article/view/175/392.

Parker, Elizabeth C. 2017. "A Phenomenology of One Southeastern African American Church Choir." *Bulletin of the Council for Research in Music Education* 212: 57–74. doi: 10.5406/bulcouresmusedu.212.0057.

Patton, Michael Quinn. 2002. *Qualitative Research and Evaluation methods*. 3rd ed. Thousand Oaks, CA: Sage Publications.

Peshkin, Alan. 1988. "In Search of Subjectivity: One's Own." *Educational Researcher* 17 (7): 17–22.

Pillow, Wanda S. 2003. "Confession, Catharsis, or Cure? Rethinking the Uses of Reflexivity as Methodological Power in Qualitative Research." *International Journal of Qualitative Studies in Education* 16 (2): 175–96. doi.org/10.1080/0951839032000060635.

Polkinghorne, D. E. 1995. "Narrative Configuration in Qualitative Analysis." *International Journal of Qualitative Studies in Education* 8 (1): 5–23. doi.org/10.1080/0951839950080103.

Potter, Jonathan, and Alexa Hepburn. 2012. "Eight Challenges for Interview Researchers." In *The SAGE Handbook of Interview Research: The Complexity of the Craft*, edited by Jaber F. Gubrium, James A. Holstein, Amir Marvasti, and Karen McKinney, 555–70. Los Angeles: Sage Publications.

Prendergast, Monica, Peter Gouzouasis, Carl Leggo, and Rita L. Irwin. 2009. "A Haiku Suite: The Importance of Music Making in the Lives of Secondary School Students." *Music Education Research* 11 (3): 303–17. doi: 10.1080/14613800903144262.

Riessman, C. K. 2008. *Narrative Methods for the Human Sciences*. Thousand Oaks, CA: Sage Publications.

Roulston, Kathryn. 2010. *Reflective Interviewing: A Guide to Theory and Practice*. London; Thousand Oaks, CA: Sage Publications.

Roulston, Kathryn. 2018. "Qualitative Interviewing and Epistemics." *Qualitative Research* 18 (3): 322–41. https://doi.org/10.1177/1468794117721738.

Roulston, Kathryn. 2019. "Ethnographic Interviewing." In *The SAGE Research Methods Foundations*, edited by Paul Atkinson, Sara Delamont, Melissa Hardy, and Malcolm Williams. London: Sage Publications. http://dx.doi.org/10.4135/9781526421036.

Saldaña, Johnny. 2013. *The Coding Manual for Qualitative Researchers*. 2nd ed. Los Angeles: Sage Publications.

Schaefer, Stephan M., and Mats Alvesson. 2017. "Epistemic Attitudes and Source Critique in Qualitative Research." *Journal of Management Inquiry*, 1–13. Online first. doi.org/10.1177/1056492617739155.

Silver, Christina, and Ann Lewins. 2014. *Using Software in Qualitative Research: A Step-by-Step Guide*. 2nd ed. Los Angeles, CA: Sage Publications.

Silverman, David. 2017. "'How Was It for You?': The Interview Society and the Irresistible Rise of the (Poorly Analyzed) Interview." *Qualitative Research* 17 (2): 144–58. doi.org/10.1177/1468794116668231.

Spradley, James. 1979. *The Ethnographic Interview*. Belmont, CA: Wadsworth.

Spradley, James. 1980. *Participant Observation*. New York: Holt, Rinehart and Winston.

Stacey, Kaye, and Jill Vincent. 2011. "Evaluation of an Electronic Interview with Multimedia Stimulus Materials for Gaining In-Depth Responses from Professionals." *Qualitative Research* 11 (5): 605–24. doi.org/10.1177/1468794111413237

Steeh, Charlotte, Trent D. Buskirk, and Mario Callegaro. 2007. "Using Text Messages in U.S. Mobile Phone Surveys." *Field Methods* 19 (1): 59–75. doi.org/10.1177/1525822X06292852.

St. Pierre, Elizabeth. 2011. "Post Qualitative Research: The Critique and the Coming After." In *The SAGE Handbook of Qualitative Research*, 4th ed., edited by Norman K. Denzin and Yvonna S. Lincoln, 611–25. Los Angeles: Sage Publications.

Sturges, Judith, E., and Kathleen Hanrahan, J. 2004. "Comparing Telephone and Face-to-Face Qualitative Interviewing: A Research Note." *Qualitative Research* 4 (1): 107–118. doi.org/10.1177/1468794104041110.

Sweet, Bridget. 2015. "The Adolescent Female Changing Voice: A Phenomenological Investigation." *Journal of Research in Music Education* 63 (1): 70–88. doi:10.1177/0022429415570755.

Tanggaard, L. 2007. "The Research Interview as Discourses Crossing Swords." *Qualitative Inquiry* 13 (1): 160–76. doi.org/10.1177/1077800406294948.

Tanggaard, Lene. 2008. "Objections in Research Interviewing." *International Journal of Qualitative Methods* 7 (3): 15–29. doi.org/10.1177/160940690800700302.

Vagle, Mark D. 2014. *Crafting Phenomenological Research*. Walnut Creek, CA: Left Coast Press.

van Manen, Max. 1990. *Research Lived Experience: Human Science for an Action Sensitive Pedagogy*. London, Ontario, Canada: The Althouse Press.

van Manen, Max 2014. *Phenomenology of Practice: Meaning-Giving Methods in Phenomenological Research and Writing*. New York; London: Routledge.

Way, Amy K., Robin Kanak Zwier, and Sarah J. Tracy. 2015. "Dialogic Interviewing and Flickers of Transformation: An Examination and Delineation of Interactional Strategies That Promote Participant Self-Reflexivity." *Qualitative Inquiry* 21 (8): 720–31. doi:10.1177/1077800414566686.

Woolf, Nicholas H., and Christina Silver. 2018a. *Qualitative Analysis using ATLAS.ti: The Five Level QDA® Method*. New York; London: Routledge.

Woolf, Nicholas H., and Christina Silver. 2018b. *Qualitative Analysis using MAXQDA: The Five Level QDA® Method*. New York; London: Routledge.

Woolf, Nicholas H., and Christina Silver. 2018c. *Qualitative Analysis using NVivo: The Five Level QDA® Method*. New York; London: Routledge.

CHAPTER 4

CONDUCTING AND ANALYZING FOCUS GROUP DATA

JOHN EROS

THE interview has long been an element of qualitative research in music education. In chapter 3 of this volume, Roulston examines the use of interviewing in qualitative music education research. Researchers might take a number of approaches to conducting interviews (Seidman 2006) and might use them as a data collection device in a variety of qualitative paradigms, such as case study, ethnography, and phenomenology. Although interviews are usually conducted between one interviewer and one participant at a time, this chapter discusses a specific type of interview that involves several participants simultaneously: the focus group interview.

The primary objective of this chapter is to discuss strategies for the collection and analysis of data through the use of focus group interviews within the context of music education research. I will begin with a brief history of the focus group, followed by a definition of key terms. I then examine ways in which focus groups have been employed in recent research in music education. I next discuss the logistical issues that researchers must address, followed by a discussion of conducting focus groups. I conclude with a discussion of analytic strategies. There will be overlap between this particular topic and the more general topic of qualitative interviewing, so this chapter assumes that the reader has at least some familiarity with qualitative interviewing.

4.1. HISTORY OF FOCUS GROUP INTERVIEWS

Although the focus group interview has been used as a data collection device since the 1950s, particularly in areas such as market research and politics, it is in recent decades that it has developed a presence in the qualitative research tradition. The earliest published use of the focus group was by Merton and his collaborators, who used focus groups to study the effectiveness of wartime propaganda (Merton and Kendall 1946; Merton et al. 1956; Merton 1987). The term "focus group interview" became more widespread in the 1960s (Lee 2010), and the focus group interview gained more of a foothold in the qualitative research tradition during the 1980s (Morgan 1988). Focus groups began to appear within qualitative methodologies in music education in the 1990s and have been used frequently in the 2000s (Beegle 2010; Conway 2000, 2003; Conway, Eros, Hourigan, and Stanley 2007; Conway, Eros, Pellegrino, and West 2010a, 2010b; Eros 2009; Mantie and Tucker 2008; Morgan, 1993, 2001; Morgan, Fellows, and Guevara 2008; Robinson 2005; Roulston et al. 2005; Yourn, 2000).

4.2. Defining Characteristics

Morgan (1988) suggests that focus group interviews are not equivalent to traditional interviews "in the sense of an alternation between the researcher's questions and the participants' responses" (9). Rather, Patton defines a focus group interview as "an interview with a small group of people on a specific topic" (2002, 385). The principal defining trait of focus group interviews as a specific type of interview, therefore, is the element of group interaction.

Brenner (2006) discusses the difference in interaction between individual and group interviews: "group interviews such as the focus group (Morgan 1988) offer a way to move beyond the personal interaction of an interviewer and informant" and Morgan states that the primary characteristic of a focus group is "the explicit use of the group interaction to produce data and insights that would be less accessible without the interaction found in a group" (1988, 12). While there will obviously be interaction between the interviewer and the participant in the setting of an individual interview, the element of interaction between numerous persons not including the interviewer is particular to focus group interviews. Morgan (1988) states that focus group interviews actually combine the element of participant observation (a foundational data collection method in qualitative research) with the already present element of interviewing, creating the potential for data that would otherwise not be obtainable.

Another crucial characteristic of focus group interviews is that they are *focused* on a specific topic. It is not the same as gathering a number of people together for a general discussion related to the research questions, or even a serendipitous meeting of several participants. The interview itself must be prepared for and structured such that it, and the resulting data, will be focused on the study's purpose.

Finally, it is important to remember that a focus group interview is still only one interview. It is not several individual interviews conducted simultaneously. To take such an approach would compromise the foundational component of interaction.

4.3. RATIONALE: WHY INCLUDE FOCUS GROUP INTERVIEWS?

Focus group interviews have the potential to generate particularly rich data. Kamberelis and Dimitriadis (2005, 904) suggest that focus groups "allow for the proliferation of multiple meanings and perspectives as well as for interactions between and among them." An example of a good candidate for the use of focus group interviews would be a study involving the perspectives of several teachers who share a common trait, such as middle school band directors, recent graduates, or rural music teachers. Another example would be a study in which the researcher is interested in the interaction among the members of a small performance ensemble (such as a jazz combo, garage band, or string quartet).

Additionally, focus group interviews may serve not only as a data collection device, but also as a component of the validity (trustworthiness) of the research study. Kamberelis and Dimitriadis (2005 904) suggest that focus group dialogue and its resulting shift of power away from the researcher may prevent the researcher from drawing hasty conclusions: "[T]he dialogic possibilities afforded by focus groups help researchers to work against premature consolidation of their understandings and explanations."

Finally, there may be an element of convenience, due to the fact that one meeting with several people will take less time to conduct than several meetings with individuals. Focus group interviews may be easier to schedule, particularly if they are to take place during an already regularly scheduled meeting, such as a seminar, rehearsal, or class meeting. However, as with any research design, convenience should not be the sole determining factor for the use of a data collection device if it is to be included in a rigorous research design.

4.4. FOCUS GROUP INTERVIEWS IN MUSIC EDUCATION

Focus group interviews have been used in music education research with an increasing frequency in recent years both in the United States (Conway 2000, 2003; Conway, Eros, Hourigan, and Stanley 2007; Conway, Eros, Pelligrino, and West 2010a, 2010b; Eros 2009; Mantie and Tucker 2008; Roulston et al. 2005; Yourn 2000) and abroad (Byrne and MacDonald 2002; Gouzouasis, Henrey, and Belliveau 2008; Marshall and Hargreaves 2007; Papageorgi et al. 2010a, 2010b). Common topics include research on the perspectives of beginning teachers, students' transitions between grade levels, teachers' common experiences with specific events, and interaction among ensemble members or students in a class. It is also common for research in music education to use the terms "focus group," "focus group discussion," or even "focus group meeting" in place of "focus group interview." Whichever term is selected, it should be described clearly in the research design.

Yourn (2000) used focus group interviews, along with individual interviews and observations, to study the perspectives of nine beginning music teachers, as well as their mentors and supervisors. While one finding was that the new teachers had a number of concerns on an individual level, such as classroom management, an "unexpected finding" was the degree to which the beginning teachers valued the relationships that they developed with their peers: "The beginning music teachers enjoyed discussing their concerns and found comfort in having their peer group identify and listen to how they felt. We consoled each other and laughed together" (189). Had the methodology not included focus group interviews, this important finding might not have become known.

As part of a study on perceptions of music teacher education by beginning teachers, their mentors, and administrators that was held over the course of a school year, Conway (2003) conducted four focus group interviews, including one each at the beginning and ending of the school year. The study began with a focus group interview, at which the participants discussed "issues pertinent to the study" (25). Moreover, Conway states that this first focus group interview "served as the starting point for data collection," which went on to include individual interviews, observations, questionnaires, and a researcher log.

In a similar example of the importance of the placement of focus group interviews within the overall design, in a study on beginning teachers' perceptions regarding instrumental techniques classes, Conway, Eros, Hourigan, and Stanley (2007) conducted a focus group with the four participants in their study after each participant had been individually interviewed. The focus group interview served as both analysis and data collection, as the researchers had begun preliminary analysis before the focus group and were therefore able to use the focus group to follow up on early findings. The focus group also generated additional data, as the participants were able to listen and respond to one another's perceptions.

At times, researchers have identified the use of focus groups as a data collection device, but have not necessarily identified them as focus group interviews. In a study of experienced music teachers participating as scorers in a two-week new teacher assessment institute, Robinson (2005) used as a data source the "informal, impromptu focus-group meetings" that took place between the teachers during the institute itself. Although arguably not a focus group interview due to the absence of a moderator to ensure that the discussion remain focused on the topic, the value of these informal discussions by the participants, focused on the research topic, should not be discounted. Considering the research setting of a two-week institute at which the participants spend a great deal of time with one another, spontaneous group conversations on research-focused topics certainly present fertile ground for rich (and sustained) data collection. The researcher must be careful, however, to qualify how the focus group was used in the design, and hence if it is a researcher-led interview or a self-directed group discussion.

Typically, research that uses focus group interviews is conducted with adult participants. The focus group is much less common in studies involving K–12 students. However, Beegle (2010) described using focus groups as part of an investigation into fifth-grade students' improvisation, interaction, and musical self-evaluation during class. Within a larger study of two classrooms, four sets of four students were placed into focus groups for extended study of their music-making, including group interviews. Prompts at these interviews included such questions as "What was it like working together?" and "What did you like/dislike about each of your performances?" While this configuration differs somewhat from the more conventional focus group interview procedures as described elsewhere in this chapter, it provides an interesting glimpse into how the overall focus group interview concept might be expanded beyond a purely discussion-based paradigm.

4.5. Before the Focus Group Interview

4.5.1. Confidentiality and Informed Consent

Confidentiality requires particular consideration in the focus group interview context. As several persons are present during the data collection session, and they will all ostensibly hear what each other says, confidentiality will be more difficult to maintain. It is possible that a university's Institutional Review Board (IRB) will have specific regulations regarding the use of focus group interviews. Chapter 1 in this volume discusses the ethics of qualitative research, including the IRB. An IRB may require a specific mention in the informed consent form that will be given to the participants, such as in the following example, required by the IRB at California State University, East Bay:

> California State University East Bay
> Focus Group Consent
> (Directions: focus groups require an additional layer of privacy protection, because the researcher cannot guarantee that the participants of the group will not reveal each other's contributions to the group discussion once it has ended.
>
> In addition to the usual warning about "loss of privacy is a potential risk," the "risks" section of the protocol and the informed consent should contain the "*focus group consent*" wording below, adapted to the individual research project.)
>
> Also, because the focus groups include discussion of personal opinions, extra measures will be taken to protect each participant's privacy. The researcher will begin the focus group by asking the participants to agree to the importance of keeping information discussed in the focus group confidential. She will then ask each participant to verbally agree to keep everything discussed in the room confidential, and will remind them at the end of the group not to discuss the material outside.
>
> Only the researcher will have access to the data collected. Any tapes and transcripts of the focus group will be destroyed after one year or at the end of the study.

In proposing focus group interview research, then, researchers should examine their particular IRB's rules regarding specific regulations for focus group interviews.

4.5.2. Selection of the Participants: Implications for the Group Dynamic

Although the selection of participants is critical to any qualitative design, it is worth noting the specific reasons why this might be considered in focus groups. The number of participants in a focus group is one of the first steps. A common figure among research texts is six to ten (Merriam 2009; Patton 2002), although fewer might also be used. Conway and Hodgman (2008) used two focus groups of eight. Larger numbers have been used, as in a study of a music technology class, in which Ruthmann (2008) conducted two focus group interviews with all 16 members of a class. With a group of that size, however, it might be difficult for one moderator to maintain an awareness of all participants, such that all voices are heard.

It is recommended that the researcher know a bit about each of the participants. Conway (2000) had observed all of her participants during their student teaching. In another study, as the focus group was the final data collection device, Conway, Eros, Hourigan, and Stanley (2007) were familiar with all of their participants based on earlier interactions during the research. In a study of her own fifth-grade students using focus groups, Beegle (2010) placed students into four four-person focus groups based on input from a variety of sources: "Groups were selected using suggestions from the participants, classroom teachers, [and] based on harmonious and productive group dynamics during previous grouping experiences in their regular classrooms" (221). Research settings in which researchers are studying students in their own classes might allow for more carefully planned groupings. Researchers might also consider characteristics such as age, gender, or ethnic background. Yourn's (2000) focus group was composed of eight female and one male participant. The male student, who is in the minority, might be less inclined to speak.

Familiarity will help the researcher to consider the dynamic that will be created among the participants and, hence, to consider the nature of the interaction. Who is gregarious? Who is reserved? How well do the participants know one another? If the participants are complete strangers, it might take longer for them to develop a level of comfort among themselves. Patton notes that participants commonly have "similar backgrounds" (2002, 385) although, conversely, Merriam (2009) suggests that the participants should be quite unfamiliar with one another.

Another factor to be considered is the nature of the rapport between the interviewer and subjects. Conway stated:

> As director of the music student-teaching program, I had previously established relationships with all of the teacher participants in this study because I had observed

all of them at least once during their student teaching semester. This previously established relationship made it easier for me to maintain the necessary rapport for in-depth observation and interviewing. (2000, 24)

Conway (2000, 27) also discussed rapport as a factor in strengthening the validity of the study, considering rapport to be a factor in attention to researcher expertise: "I had enough background in the content area and association with the participants to be empathetic in my interview approach and to establish the necessary rapport."

While a positive rapport is generally viewed as advantageous, an overly comfortable rapport might impact the data collected. Seidman (2006, 97) states that "the rapport an interviewer must build in an interviewing relationship needs to be controlled. Too much or too little rapport can lead to distortion of what the participant reconstructs during the interview (Hyman et al. 1954)."

4.5.3. Logistics

The researcher must determine an appropriate site for the focus group interview. The location should be one in which a good quality audio recording can be made, as the primary form of data is typically the audio recording (Morgan 1988). A "neutral" location such as a university conference room, a school classroom, or a similar meeting place often works well. Other possibilities might be the researcher's office or home. The location should be a reasonable distance for the participants to travel, as well as easy to find. In a study that I conducted with three participants, two lived in the same metropolitan area and one lived in another city approximately 90 miles away. We were able to find a location nearly equidistant from both areas. Although the participants' considerations must take precedence, the researcher should also not commit to a time or location that is not practical. In another study in which I participated, two researchers and four participants met at my home.

4.6. Preparing for the Focus Group Interview

4.6.1. The Interview Protocol

In the interest of keeping the discussion focused, an interview protocol is necessary (Patton 2002). However, the focus group interview protocol will typically be shorter than that of an individual interview, as the interaction within the focus group interview will theoretically generate its own questions and prompts. Knodel (1994, 36) advocates the use of guidelines in outlining the format for focus group interviews:

The first step in designing a focus group study should be to define and clarify the concepts that are to be investigated. . . . The general concepts to be explored need to be formulated as a set of discussion guidelines that can be used by the moderator during the focus group sessions.

He also states that "guidelines tend to be general in nature, be open-ended, and seek to find what is going on without specifically asking directly about the situation of the individual participants" (37). He gives the following examples, taken from a study of support and exchange systems involving the elderly: "Do most elderly work in this community?" and "Do elderly work because they want to or because they have to?" (38). Similarly, Youn (2000, 184) began her study with a focus group meeting, at which the time "was spent discussing two questions in some depth: what concerns they had prior to going out to schools, and how they could manage their concerns."

4.6.2. Recording

Many individual interviews are audiotaped. However, focus group recordings will have numerous voices. The listener must be able to discern which participant is speaking. Also, with a larger number of people, there is a greater chance of participants talking simultaneously. The interviewer should establish a baseline for identifying everyone's voices. The interviewer might begin the focus group interview by having the participants introduce themselves, making sure to state their names clearly. Also, in the interest of keeping track of who is speaking, and considering the ready availability of portable video-recording equipment (i.e., smart phones and tablets) at present, focus group interviews might also be video recorded. That might make it easier to keep track of who is speaking, as well as to observe any nonverbal responses or cues among the group, although the quality of the sound itself might not be as good as with audio equipment. The researcher would, of course, need to include mention of video recording in the informed consent.

Finally, to return to the topic of confidentiality, it is quite possible that the participants will have their own personal electronic devices (smart phones and tablets) with them and, as such, will also have the capacity to record the focus group interview. The researcher should make it clear that, to maintain confidentiality, the researcher's is the only recording that is to be made.

4.7. DURING THE INTERVIEW

4.7.1. Interviewer vs. Moderator

The researcher's role in a focus group interview is not equivalent to that played in an individual interview. The role takes a different form: that of a moderator rather than an interviewer (Krueger 1994; Morgan 1988). Rather than posing specific questions to particular people, the researcher will more likely be establishing an initial topic and direction for the focus group interview and then moderating the interview as needed.

4.7.2. Opening

The focus group interview should begin when all participants are assembled. The interviewer should begin by introducing himself or herself, and briefly describing the topic for the focus group. Based on where the focus group is in the research design, the researcher might comment on previous focus group interviews or other data collection, in the interest of setting the stage. The focus group interview should then continue with brief introductions from the participants. Even if they already know one another, it will serve to focus the participants on the discussion format. With music educators, for example, the interviewer might begin by having the participants state their names and a bit about their current teaching situations (location, type of school, specific discipline, grade levels, etc.).

Although my participants (Eros 2009) were already somewhat familiar with each other, I began a focus group interview with the following prompt:

> [It] would be helpful to talk for a second about the schools where everybody teaches, because we have elementary general, high school band, and middle school band. Perhaps we can talk for a minute or so in order to know what each school is like.

This has the intended effect of getting the participants talking, establishing a reference for each voice, making the participants more comfortable with one another, and allowing the participants to begin the discussion "in familiar territory."

The interviewer should also take the time to establish a few ground rules for a productive discussion, such as respecting one another's contributions, speaking one at a time, not maintaining side conversations, encouraging everyone to speak freely, etc.

It is important for the participants to feel sufficiently comfortable with one another that all are willing to participate. Some members may be more naturally gregarious than others, and some more reserved, particularly among a group of strangers. Focus groups themselves might be held in "less formal" settings, such as a gathering or even a meal. However, the researcher must maintain an awareness of the intended focus, rather than letting the group drift more toward a social encounter with little or no relevance to the research topic.

4.7.3. Moderating the Interview

As mentioned previously, it is incumbent on the researcher to moderate the discussion. The researcher should remember that focus group interviews must remain *focused* on the research topic at hand. Therefore, the interviewer must be able to quickly determine if "tangents" are relevant to the research questions and objectives for the interview.

The interviewer should also take note of the degree to which all participants are responding. The interviewer might maintain a checklist of each person's name and make checkmarks each time the person speaks, so as to have a clear reference for how well each person is represented. Not only is it important to have all members of the focus group contribute, it provides for richer data and also serves to support the validity of the study. An hour can pass by quickly, and if there are eight people in the focus group, the researcher will need to ensure that two or three talkative people do not dominate the hour, while another two or three barely speak at all.

Nonverbal communication may also play a role. It is possible that the participants are showing responses to one another rather than verbally articulating them. In this case, the interviewer should think ahead to the act of transcription, if an audio recording is being made. Since recordings will not catch nonverbal communication, it is the interviewer's job to make sure that these details are captured. For example, several participants might be nodding their heads in agreement while one is shaking his head in disagreement. While this is significant in individual interviews, it takes on an added dimension in focus group interviews inasmuch as it is an element of interaction.

The interviewer might use comments such as, "Jim, I noticed that you were shaking your head. Do you disagree with Janice?" both to make the nonverbal communication evident for audio recordings and to potentially draw out participants who have been somewhat quieter. Moreover, the interviewer should take note of times when multiple gestures are being made, such as, "It looks like Evan and Nate both agree. Is that accurate?" or "Alan, I notice that you're nodding your head but Bill is shaking his. In what ways do you disagree?"

Finally, as the transcripts will be a crucial data set, the researcher must think ahead to what the transcriber will encounter. For example, the researcher should be aware of participants talking over one another. If there is an overlap in statements, the interviewer might say, "James, what was that you said again?" And "Peter, you were saying . . . ?" Statements should be made in a non-threatening manner, such that the participants are not made to feel as though they are being reprimanded for talking out of turn.

4.7.4. Posing Questions

Numerous texts exist with guidelines for asking interview questions (for example, Patton 2002). Most importantly in the focus group interview context, the researcher should recall that he or she is posing one question to a group of six rather than asking the same question six times. The researcher will pose questions, and guide activities based on the research questions, but the objective is to conduct one focus group interview of six people rather than six simultaneous individual interviews.

The potential for new topics to emerge in focus group interviews is greater than in individual interviews. In the following example, although the second participant's questions are of the yes/no variety, all three demonstrate the phenomenon of participants beginning to "interview each other," leading to additional related discussion (Eros 2009):

TOM: But I have no lesson plan structure to go back and look at. So that makes me really frustrated because I can't sit down and figure out what to do to improve.
JAMES: Do you have support? Like administrative support? Supervisory support?
TOM: Yes. I love my principal.
JAMES: Do you feel like those are people that can assist you with that?
TOM: No.
SAM: I definitely understand. Is it an issue where your administrators see that you have it together, that your kids are doing great things, that there are no problems....

At other times, the interviewer might pose an initial question that leads to answers from several participants that are in agreement, disagreement, or response to one another, such as in this excerpt (Conway, Eros, Pelligrino, and West 2010b):

INTERVIEWER: Did you feel like it established a bond with the graduate students?
PARTICIPANT #1: I thought so—I thought I talked to Lisa more after than I probably would have walking down the hallway or whatever, yeah.
PARTICIPANT #2: I feel the observations, like when you watched us teach was more interactive than the PhD buddy thing because we didn't really have a connection at that point. It was just like what I said, "Tell me what you're learning in class." But there, they are watching you and giving you direct feedback on your teaching or future career, so it seemed more personal.
PARTICIPANT #3: I agree. I found it extremely helpful to have PhD buddies or, you guys around because you are not teachers. I can talk freely with you. Especially, for instance, on the Detroit trip, I had a chance to just have a conversation with Chad. Whenever I have a conversation with a GSI in these classes, I get a lot of really good advice. It's not so much someone telling me, "No, you're wrong, it's actually like this," which isn't so helpful for me. It's just sort of like having a dialog with someone who has a lot more experience, which is more helpful than only having teachers you can't necessarily have a free conversation with.
PARTICIPANT #5: I think we got to know you guys more, too, when you were observing us this year. Like, after we would teach and you guys would talk about it with us. It wasn't like, "This is what you did, this is what you did, this is what you did. Well..." I don't think any of the GSIs did that. It was good to hear a perspective from you guys.

In this case, one question produced four answers, including affirmation of one answer, via another participant.

4.8. Analysis

Morgan (1988) states, "The fundamental data that focus groups produce are transcripts of the group discussions" (10). Many researchers, once the transcript is prepared, read and reread the transcripts, leading to the development of codes and categories. Another option is the use of qualitative analysis software such as NVIVO.

4.8.1. Transcription

There are different issues to address in the transcription of focus group interviews than in individual interviews. There will be more spoken text and there is also the potential for participants to talk simultaneously. It has been my experience that participants generally listen attentively when others are speaking, and are quite willing to "yield the floor" should someone interject.

The researcher will have to decide on the approach that will be taken to transcription. In some cases, the transcription might be absolutely verbatim, including any instances of repeated words and expressions such as "uh-huh." Other sounds might be included, such as laughter. There is a certain advantage to transcription that includes gestures of this sort, given the fact that focus group interviews have such a focus on interaction. At other times, the discussion might be transcribed at specific times only. Ruthmann (2008, 47) stated that data were "transcribed when salient."

In addition to transcribing participants' statements, a transcription makes it possible for the researcher to get a sense of reactions from those who are not speaking. It is common for transcribers to eliminate words such as "um," "yeah," "you know," and so forth, as well as to change affirmative words such as "uh-huh" and "mm-hm" into "yes" for purposes of clarity in the transcript. Similarly, similar instances of agreement, such as a combination of simultaneous "uh-huh," by several persons might be transcribed as such:

> JAMES: I have found that students have difficulty with dotted quarter–eighth patterns.
> ELLEN: Jordan, Kim: *verbal agreement*

Transcripts must clearly identify each speaker. The larger the group, the more important this becomes. If there is an overlap in statements, the interviewer might say, "James, what was that you said again?" And "Peter, you were saying . . . ?" At times, researchers may take notes during the course of the focus group, and those might serve as an additional data set, as well as a way to keep track of participation.

Moreover, it is often valuable for the researcher to do the transcription, as an additional element of both analysis and trustworthiness. However, transcription is time-consuming, particularly for focus group interviews. A one-hour focus group discussion with six participants, if transcribed verbatim, could easily equal 50 pages of raw data. If a study includes multiple focus group interviews, the amount of raw data can quickly become imposing. If the researcher is working with research assistants, or using technological aids, this might be less of an issue. Finally, while there are currently voice-recognition programs and devices available, capable of converting speech to text (dictation-style), these devices are usually designed to recognize and work with only one voice at a time, making them impractical for use in transcribing focus groups. As yet, technology capable of transcribing several voices simultaneously is not available.

Once the transcript is obtained, the procedure will unfold much as analysis of an individual interview's transcript. The key difference between individual and focus group interview analysis, however, is the element of interaction. Based on agreement or disagreement relative to a given statement, the researcher might be able to discern which statements the participants felt the most strongly about and, consequently, which statements can be considered with more confidence. Is a comment an isolated comment, or is it a comment emphatically echoed by a number of participants? If the latter, more weight might be given to considering that comment as codes are determined. Individual statements by participants serve as data in the same manner as in an individual interview, but the added element of interaction might allow the researcher to draw a stronger, more substantiated, conclusion.

4.8.2. Coding

Research studies in music education commonly describe their analysis procedures for focus groups as analyzing transcripts for codes and categories. At other times, researchers might only listen to the focus groups initially, as part of the overall analysis procedure. Yourn (2000) wrote: "Analysis was carried out initially by listening to the tape recordings of the focus groups, discussing perspectives with mentor teachers and carefully annotating field notes that were verified with the student teachers." In the case of studies that contain several focus group interviews, Morgan (1988) suggests that the researchers begin with a detailed analysis of one group, to begin building a coding structure, and then use this as a basis for analysis of additional focus group interviews.

Additionally, the focus group and its analysis may play a role in the larger picture of the research design, such that the focus group itself is a form of analysis, as described by Conway, Eros, Hourigan, and Stanley (2007, 45): "Individual interviews and email surveys had been analyzed previous to the focus group meeting so the focus group provided an opportunity for a 'collective analysis' and member check." Robinson (2005) discussed how focus group discussions were used after the primary data set had been analyzed: "These discussions . . . helped to either clarify previous points or to extend my interpretations of comments made by various individuals at other times" (52).

Ruthmann (2008, 47) described his focus group interview analysis, including the use of coding, as follows:

> The data were coded, transcribed when salient and analyzed throughout the study using a constant comparative method looking for places of resonance and tension among participants' experiences and perceptions. The techniques of member check and peer-debriefing (Lincoln & Guba, 1985), along with data reflective of the

teacher's, students', and researcher's perspectives, were further analyzed through a process of "crystallization" (Richardson, 2000). This process involved viewing and vetting data and interpretations through collecting data from multiple perspectives. This process enables the researcher to transfer the focus from the data as objective and discrete to that of the situated understandings and meanings reflected in the data and as seen through multiple facets of lived experience.

4.8.3. Technology

Until recently, focus groups required coordinating a face-to-face meeting of several people. However, the ever-changing factor of technology allows for other options in coordinating focus group interviews. Conference calls, online chat rooms, and discussion boards, while available for quite some time, have not been used to a great degree in music education. In a general discussion of the role of technology in focus groups, Stewart (2005) examined the use of online focus groups, using a close analysis of two scenarios, one real-time (synchronous) and one not (asynchronous). Recently, videoconferencing devices such as the platform created by Skype have made it possible for participants to see and interact with one another without being physically present. Videoconferencing is being used with increasing frequency in research in music education (Dammers 2009; Riley 2009). Riley (2009) used videoconferencing as a means to enable undergraduate music education majors in the United States to work with students in Mexico. Dammers (2009) used Skype and webcams to hold individual lessons between a trumpet professor and a student. The implications for music education research are significant, as the focus group methodology might not have been an option previously for certain participant populations. For example, due to distance considerations, a focus group of five rural music educators might have been extremely difficult to coordinate, to say nothing of the potential for international research.

However, other issues must be considered. All participants would need access to appropriate computers and webcams, all in good working order and with reliable Internet connections. Also, confidentiality becomes even more difficult to account for. Without the researcher being able to directly regulate the setting, it is impossible to know if anyone else is in the room with a participant while the discussion is taking place. This becomes an issue for all of the participants and must certainly be described in detail in the informed consent documentation. On the general topic of virtual focus groups, Galloway (2011) suggests that, "Depending on the medium used and nature of the network, evaluators may be limited in their ability to guarantee that someone who is a nonapproved participant cannot access the focus-group discussion" (49–50).

Additionally, the essential element of interaction will not be the same as an in-person focus group. Dammers (2009) remarked that in his study: "although the [trumpet] instructor and student clearly established a good rapport, it became apparent that this format creates some challenges to establishing a positive interpersonal dynamic." For a device such as a focus group interview, in which rapport and interaction are substantial factors, this must be considered. It will be difficult if not impossible for the participants and the researchers to maintain awareness of body language, gestures, etc. Participants might also attempt to multitask and not give their full attention to the focus group, again compromising the potential for spontaneous interaction and comment.

Even with its disadvantages, it is valuable to acknowledge synchronous technology as an additional tool. Provided the researcher is aware of, and describes, the inherent limitations, videoconferencing may certainly be employed. Clearly, this is an area ripe for exploration by researchers in music education.

4.9. Conclusion

The focus group is a device that can generate rich data, and can also play a strong role as an element of validity in an overall research design. The fundamental aspect of interaction is a natural fit for the field of music education, in which interaction plays such a fundamental role. Indeed, P–12 students interact with one another in classes and ensembles, and music teachers share many common threads (such as levels and disciplines taught, as well as musical and educational backgrounds and settings) that can form the basis of interaction.

Moreover, the area of focus group research is ripe for exploration in ways unique to music education. As one possibility, an intersection of focus groups and Arts-Based Research might be explored. Instead of a discussion prompt, a music education focus group interview might begin with a performance of a piece of music, or perhaps an improvisation. Although the primary data produced from focus group interviews is typically the recordings and transcripts of the discussions, focus group interviews in music education settings have the potential to generate data in arts-based forms, such as musical improvisations and compositions (Beegle 2010). This would have further ramifications for the presentation of findings.

Further research possibilities are numerous. More traditional focus groups might be used for research into music teachers' experiences and perceptions of events in their careers, such as entering the field, or aspects of their teaching practice, such as score study or lesson planning. Others might explore ways to investigate music-making, such as composition and improvisation, or ensemble performance by student groups. With its potential for generating rich data, combined with its potential for a variety of presentations of findings (arts-based and otherwise), the focus group interview is a powerful data collection device for research in music education.

References

Beegle, A. A. 2010. "Classroom-Based Study of Small-Group Planned Improvisation with Fifth-Grade Children." *Journal of Research in Music Education* 58 (3): 219–39.

Brenner, M. E. 2006. "Interviewing in Educational Research." In *Handbook of Complementary Methods in Education Research*, 3rd ed., edited by J. L. Green, G. Camilli, and P. B. Elmore, 357–70. Hillsdale, NJ: Lawrence Erlbaum Associates.

Byrne, C., and R. A. R. MacDonald. 2002. "The Use of Information and Communication Technology (I&CT) in the Scottish Music Curriculum: A Focus Group Investigation of Themes and Issues." *Music Education Research* 4 (2): 263–73.

California State University, East Bay. 2011. Focus Group Consent Form. http://www20.csueastbay.edu/orsp/irb/forms.html.

Conway, C. M. 2000. "Perceptions of Beginning Music Teachers, Their Mentors, and Administrators Regarding Preservice Music Teacher Preparation." *Journal of Research in Music Education* 50 (1): 20–36.

Conway, C. M. 2003. "An Examination of District-Sponsored Beginning Music Teacher Mentor Practices." *Journal of Research in Music Education* 51 (1): 6–23.

Conway, C., J. Eros, R. Hourigan, and A. M. Stanley. 2007. "Perceptions of Beginning Teachers Regarding Brass and Woodwind Instrument Techniques Classes in Preservice Education." *Bulletin of the Council for Research in Music Education* 173: 39–54.

Conway, C., J. Eros, K. Pelligrino, and C. West. 2010a. "Instrumental Music Education Students' Perceptions of Tensions Experienced during Their Undergraduate Degree." *Journal of Research in Music Education* 58 (3): 260–75.

Conway, C., J. Eros, K. Pelligrino, and C. West. 2010b. "The Role of Graduate and Undergraduate Interactions in the Development of Preservice Music Teachers and Music Teacher Educators: A Self-Study in Music Teacher Education." *Bulletin of the Council for Research in Music Education* 183: 49–64.

Conway, C. and T. M. Hodgman. 2008. "College and Community Choir Member Experiences in a Collaborative Intergenerational Performance Project." *Journal of Research in Music Education* 56 (3): 220–37.

Dammers, R. J. 2009. "Utilizing Internet-Based Videoconferencing for Instrumental Music Lessons." *Update: Applications of Research in Music Education* 28 (1): 17–24.

Eros, J. 2009. "A Case Study of Three Urban Music Teachers in the Second Stage of Their Teaching Careers." PhD diss., University of Michigan.

Galloway, K. L. 2011. "Focus Groups in the Virtual World: Implications for the Future of Evaluation." *New Directions for Evaluation* 131: 47–51.

Gouzouasis, P., J. Henrey, and G. Belliveau. 2008. "Turning Points: A Transitional Story of Grade Seven Music Students' Participation in High School Band Programmes." *Music Education Research* 10 (1): 75–90.

Hyman, H. H. and W. J. Cobb, J. J. Feldman, C. W. Hart, and C. H. Stember. 1954. Chicago: University of Chicago Press.

Kamberelis, G., and G. Dimitriadis. 2005. "Focus Groups: Strategic Articulation of Pedagogy, Politics, and Inquiry." In *The Sage Handbook of Qualitative Research*, 3rd ed., edited by N. K. Denzin and Y. S. Lincoln, 887–907. Thousand Oaks, CA: Sage Publications.

Krueger, R. A. 1994. *Focus Groups: A Practical Guide for Applied Research*. 2nd ed. Thousand Oaks, CA: Sage Publications.

Lee, R. 2010. "The Secret Life of Focus Groups: Robert Merton and the Diffusion of a Research Method." *American Sociologist* 41 (2): 115–41.

Mantie, R., and L. Tucker. 2008. "Closing the Gap: Does Music-Making Have to Stop upon Graduation?" *International Journal of Community Music* 1 (2): 217–27.

Marshall, N. A., and D. J. Hargreaves. 2007. "Crossing the Humpback Bridge: Primary-Secondary School Transition in Music Education." *Music Education Research* 9 (1): 65–80.

Merriam, S. B. 2009. *Qualitative Research: A Guide to Design and Implementation*. 4th ed. San Francisco, CA: Jossey-Bass.

Merton, R. K. 1987. "The Focussed Interview and Focus Groups: Continuities and Discontinuities." *The Public Opinion Quarterly* 51 (4): 550–66.

Merton, R. K., M. Fiske, and P. L. Kendall. 1956. *The Focused Interview: A Manual of Problems and Procedures*. New York: The Free Press.

Merton, R. K., and P. L. Kendall. 1946. "The Focused Interview." *American Journal of Sociology* 51: 541–57.

Morgan, D. L. 1988. *Focus Groups as Qualitative Research*. Newbury Park, CA: Sage Publications.

Morgan, D. L., ed. 1993. *Successful Focus Groups: Advancing the State of the Art*. Newbury Park, CA: Sage Publications.

Morgan, D. L. 2001. "Focus Group Interviewing." In *Handbook of Interview Research: Context and Method*, edited by J. F. Gubrium and J. A. Holstein, 141–60. Thousand Oaks, CA: Sage Publications.

Morgan, D., C. Fellows, and H. Guevera. 2008. "Emergent Approaches to Focus Group Research." In *Handbook of Emergent Methods*, edited by S. N. Hesse-Biber and P. Leavy, 189–296. New York: The Guilford Press.

NVIVO. http://www.qsrinternational.com/products_nvivo.aspx.

Papageorgi, I., E. Haddon, A. Creech, F. Morton, C. de Bezenac, E. Himonides, J. Potter, C. Duffy, T. Whyton, and G. Welch. 2010a. "Institutional Culture and Learning I: Perceptions of the Learning Environment and Musicians' Attitudes to Learning." *Music Education Research* 12 (2): 151–78.

Papageorgi, I., E. Haddon, A. Creech, F. Morton, C. de Bezenac, E. Himonides, J. Potter, C. Duffy, T. Whyton, and G. Welch. 2010b. "Inter-Relationships between Perceptions of the Learning Environment and Undergraduate Musicians' Attitudes to Performance." *Music Education Research* 12 (4): 427–46.

Patton, M. Q. 2002. *Qualitative Research and Evaluation Methods*. 3rd ed. Thousand Oaks, CA: Sage Publications.

Riley, P. E. 2009. "Video-conferenced Music Teaching: Challenges and Progress." *Music Education Research* 11 (3): 365–75.

Robinson, M. 2005. "The Impact of Beginning Music Teacher Assessment on the Assessors: Notes from Experienced Teachers." *Bulletin of the Council for Research in Music Education* 164: 49–60.

Roulston, K., R. Legette, M. DeLoach, C. Buckhalter-Pittman, L. Cory, and R. S. Grenier. 2005. "Education: Mentoring and Community through Research." *Research Studies in Music Education* 25 (1): 1–22.

Ruthmann, S. A. 2008. "Whose Agency Matters? Negotiating Pedagogical Experiences and Creative Intent during Composing Experiences." *Research Studies in Music Education* 30 (1): 43–58.

Seidman, I. 2006. *Interviewing as Qualitative Research: A Guide for Researchers in Education and the Social Sciences*. 3rd ed. New York: Teachers College Press.

Skype. www.skype.com.

Stewart, K., and M. Williams. 2005. "Researching Online Populations: The Use of Online Focus Groups for Social Research." *Qualitative Research* 5 (4): 395–416.

Yourn, B. R. 2000. "Learning to Teach: Perspectives from Beginning Music Teachers." *Music Education Research* 2 (2): 181–92.

CHAPTER 5

GENERATING AND ANALYZING MULTIMODAL AND MULTIMEDIA DATA

EVAN S. TOBIAS

5.1. Introduction

THIS chapter addresses collecting, generating, and analyzing data contextualized through two key aspects of contemporary society and research: (1) the notion of multimodality as a way of expanding beyond text as the sole or primary way of situating, recording, and analyzing data; and (2) the mediation of research through digital media and technology. To understand multimodality one must first acknowledge the multiple modes at play in a given context. Modes are resources for or ways of making meaning, such as speaking or gesturing, that are expressed through or made into form as media, such as what a music educator says or how students respond (Dicks, Soyinka, and Coffee 2006; Kress and Van Leeuwen 2001). Jewitt (2011) identifies four overarching theoretical assumptions of multimodality: (1) language is a part of a multimodal ensemble; (2) each mode in a multimodal ensemble is understood as realizing different communicative work; (3) people orchestrate meaning through their selection and configuration of modes; and (4) meanings of signs fashioned from multimodal semiotic resources are, like speech, social (14–15). Multimodality is thus a framework for recognizing and understanding the use, meaning, and interaction of multiple diverse modes. International researchers such as Dicks, Soyinka, and Coffee (2006), Jewitt (2011), Kress and Van Leeuwen (2001), and Norris (2011) have developed a strong foundation for research and thinking in this vein. Multimodal scholarship often focuses on analyzing meanings of modes and media through frameworks such as semiotics. This chapter situates multimodality more comprehensively, while recognizing that different media afford varied types of meaning.

Conducting research through a multimodal framework accounts for how participants communicate and engage with the world through diverse modes. One's data and analysis thus ought to convey what is specific to particular modes (Dicks et al. 2006). Dicks, Soyinka, and Coffee (2006) suggest that "multimodal representation implies the need for careful consideration of the particular kinds of meaning afforded by different media" (92). They encourage researchers to consider multiple media in terms of data and how these data are represented. The types of modes at play in a study, modal density or when multiple modes of communication and action occur simultaneously (Norris 2011), and how modes work together as an ensemble (Kress and Van Leeuwen 2001) ought to inform one's approach to collecting and generating data. This chapter looks specifically at methodological approaches accounting for multiple modes and media with a focus on collecting, generating, and analyzing data.

The following sections situate qualitative research as occurring within an increasingly digitized society, where even phenomena and data unconnected to technology might be understood through digitally mediated research methods. In some cases the approaches and techniques discussed draw specifically upon affordances of technology. Consequently, the chapter advocates a convergence or "bringing together of a whole range of new *and* old technologies in ways that can further the traditional yet also enable new approaches to conducting qualitative enquiry" (Brown 2002, 2).

5.2. Generating and Collecting Multimodal and Multimedia Data

Generating multimodal and multimedia data affords researchers ways to observe, analyze, and understand phenomena that might not otherwise be possible. This is partially due to how multimedia and digital tools assist in generating overlapping data to provide thick and rich description (Geertz 1973) beyond what one observes and records in field notes (Flewitt 2006). Generating and recording the range and density of data that one might address when observing participants create or perform music requires concentration, coordination, analysis, and decision-making to determine what data to generate and the most appropriate process for doing so.

While researchers are often the sole investigators in a study, sometimes assistants, team members, or participants generate data. Researchers ought to consider the benefits and challenges associated with recording data on their own or having others do so, given the importance that decisions made while generating data have to a study. Communicating with collaborators before, during, and after recording data is critical in guiding research (Tobin and Hsueh 2007).

Multimedia data can be collected and generated through a continuum of stationary to mobile sources. Whereas an application installed in a computer to record data is a stationary source, moving through a site with a video camera is more mobile. Such approaches and tools may be used in overlapping combinations based on what is most appropriate for particular sites and studies. The following section outlines processes for generating multimodal and multimedia data and decisions that may ensue when involved in such research. For additional information related to observing and video recording, see volume 2, chapter 2 of this *Handbook*.

5.2.1. Generating Data through Video and Audio Recording

Generating digital video and multimodal data is useful for analyzing the varied phenomena encompassed by music education research. Barrett (2007) suggests that digital video affords qualitative researchers the ability to "work directly with sound, events, and talk in close proximity and without losing nuance through transcription into another form" (431). Video data is particularly useful when researching participants' interactions in the field given the difficulty for even the most skilled researchers to focus on and record every detail of the multiple modes at play (Barrett 2007). Additionally, video recording interviews provides context and nonverbal data ranging from facial reactions to gestures unavailable in audio recordings.

Unlimited viewing of video records allows for increased detail in constructing data (Barron and Engle 2007). This affordance is key when analyzing multimodal data in music teaching and learning contexts. Barrett (2007) highlights how video data assisted graduate student researchers in analyzing relationships between choral singers' discussion of music they were singing and their performance throughout a rehearsal. Reviewing video records can aid researchers' analysis of rich and complex data inherent in such musical engagement. The ability to slow down (S. Goldman and McDermott 2007) and pause video data to capture still frames (Jacobs, Kawanaka, and Stigler 1999) supports researchers' capacity to see and hear details not possible while in the field.

Video records' degree of detail make them rich data sources but introduces challenges given the magnitude of data generated and researchers' roles in its generation (Ash 2007; Barron 2007). Including video data in qualitative research adds significantly to a researcher's responsibilities. One must consider what type and how many video cameras to use (Hall 2007), where and how they should be placed and positioned (Barron 2007), who should record the footage (Tobin and Hsueh 2007), what to record, and how the video should be recorded. These decisions may require adjustments on-site and play an important role in obtaining and analyzing data.

5.2.2. Choosing and Operating Recording Devices

Specific attributes of one's study and research questions ought to guide choices regarding what types of data and recording devices are needed for a particular study and whether equipment is used in a stationary, mobile, or combined manner. Before beginning data generation, researchers might ask themselves questions such as: What types of recording devices do I need for this study? What is the internal audio quality of the device? What types of audio input does a particular video-recording device allow? Is it most advantageous to acquire one or more pro-level video cameras, semi-pro wearable cameras, or lower-quality video-recording devices? What types of recording formats do the devices allow and to what extent are they compatible with the computer and software allocated for this study? Does the recording device contain zoom functionality? What equipment is necessary to support and secure recording devices?

Logistical concerns such as budgets, physical layouts of research sites, participants' use of space, and quality of recording device also factor in one's decisions. Generating video data in settings where participants stand on risers and an educator remains on a podium may require a different approach than one where students create music throughout a classroom with the teacher moving between groups. While a basic image is sometimes sufficient, high-quality video and audio data that afford fine-grained visual detail may be required. A blurry image obscuring details of artifacts such as notated music or composition software can limit one's ability to analyze data accurately.

Deciding how many recording devices to use and their implementation in the field are important elements of one's design (Derry 2007). Though in some studies one stationary video camera may be acceptable to generate data needed for fruitful analysis, when used alone a fixed video-recording device may exclude valuable data. The ability to move recording devices when needed is ideal. In settings where numerous participants engage with music individually or in groups, two or more portable cameras might be incorporated to generate data from several perspectives. Using multiple video-recording devices supports including a range of multimodal data, varied points of view, and foci that may not be possible when confined to one camera, but presents logistical and analytical challenges to researchers.

When using multiple recording devices, one camera might provide a wide-angled or global perspective, with other devices focused on individuals or small groups of participants (Barron 2007). For example, providing a comprehensive sense of a large ensemble setting might include placing one camera at the back of a room recording the entire ensemble and music educator, another camera at the front of the room focused on all ensemble members, and a third camera at a room's side focused on a row of ensemble members' profiles. Incorporating multiple cameras is pivotal if participants are spread across a space or simultaneously located in different spaces.

Combining a tripod and dolly with wheels can help maintain continuous steady footage when recording while moving a device. Recording of some music settings may call for nimble movement, so that recording devices must be handheld. Tripods and supportive devices that can be clipped onto surfaces or attached to objects such as music stands allow one to move and secure recording devices as needed. This may be critical when participants move frequently or a researcher is multitasking. Researchers interested in recording data from participants' or their own perspective while maintaining free use of their hands might find wearable cameras helpful. Small recording devices worn on one's head or around/in one's ear, just as a Bluetooth earpiece, can provide data that might otherwise be difficult to record. Just as Wiggins (1994) had students in a music class wear lapel microphones attached to tape recorders to generate data unobtrusively, researchers might have participants wear small video-recording devices to better understand what they see and hear while engaging with music. When participants' points of view contribute to understanding their musical engagement, wearable cameras may be most appropriate.

Researchers ought to consider how they collect audio data along with or as a part of video data. Generating audio data specific to individuals or groups of participants in settings where numerous people are performing can be challenging. Knowing video-recording devices' specifications, types of audio input possible, and what might be needed to expand beyond basic audio can inform one's recording strategies. If a high degree of audio fidelity is needed beyond video cameras' capabilities, researchers might incorporate external microphones that can input to video cameras (Ash 2007; Barron 2007) or cameras that accept microphones via XLR cables. Wireless microphones may sometimes assist in capturing audio that might be unclear if only using the built-in microphone of the video camera (Barron 2007). Mobile devices with audio-recording capabilities or the internal audio input of a laptop may also be used in place of or in addition to video-recording devices for data generation.

5.2.3. Addressing Participants' Use of Computers and Digital Devices On-Site

Paricipants' use of technology in research settings presents challenges for fully encompassing the density of data involved in their interactions with computers, other participants, and their surroundings. When participants engage with combinations of analog, electronic, digital, Musical Instrument Digital Interface (MIDI), and computer instruments or devices, it is ideal to record multiple streams of data (Ruthmann 2006; Tobias 2010). Using a single video camera positioned behind participants exclusively or one set up solely in one part of the room might exclude details of their interactions with computers along with the sound and image needed to determine what is occurring.

Ruthmann (2006) leveraged a multi-camera setup to record key informants working in a music lab by including two cameras placed at selected students' stations and a third camera recording the entire class from the music educator's perspective at the front of the room. By positioning cameras at computer stations, Ruthmann generated data related to "social interactions, ambient audio, audio from a students' computer and synthesizer, as well as the computer screen and keyboard use of different students throughout the class" (88). Tobias (2010) combined the use of a video camera, tripod and dolly, laptop, and computer screencasting software to generate audio and video data of students creating, recording, and producing music on computers while performing on acoustic and electric instruments or MIDI controllers throughout multiple rooms. The nature of these studies required flexibility in generating data that encompassed the richness of participants' multimodal musical engagement with technology.

Generating audio data related to participants' interaction with technology presents unique challenges. Recording equipment's limitations, a computer or mobile device's audio setup, and whether participants use speakers or headphones can determine one's capability of recording audio from computers or other technology. When participants listen to the audio output of computers, electronic devices, or instruments with headphones, researchers might request that headphone amplifiers and splitters be used. This equipment amplifies and splits a single audio output into additional outputs, permitting one to listen in with headphones or connect the output to recording devices. When analog audio devices or instruments are used in conjunction with computers, a mixer from which the output can be recorded before being input to the computer along with the computer and other audio might be required.

Though one can record participants' computer work with audio- and video-recording devices, such resources may be inadequate to capture digital data with a high degree of fidelity needed for certain types of analysis. In some situations one might leverage computer video cards to record participants' work with music software (Kirkman 2010). Screencasting software such as Screenflow or Camtasia allows one to record all video and audio within a computer, external audio such as participants' dialogue, and video of what occurs in front of the computer. Using screencasting software, Tobias (2010) was able to analyze students' recording and producing processes in computer environments with a high degree of detail and fidelity of audio and video data.

Given the range of existing and emerging music technologies, researchers might be interested in generating data relevant to technology beyond audio and video media. MIDI data provides precise information related to musical parameters and can benefit observation and analysis of participants' use of and interaction with music technology (Hickey 1997; Kirkman 2010). MIDI data can be collected by connecting a MIDI interface to the originating device or computer outputting the MIDI and a computer running software to record the MIDI data in real time. Open Sound Control (OSC) data, a protocol used to control music software and devices, can also be recorded but may first need to be converted to MIDI data through applications such as OSCulator. Besides recording such data in real time, researchers might collect iterative saved files of participants' musical engagement with computers (Hickey 1997; Stauffer 2001). Knowing the parameters necessary to encapsulate all information related to participants' work when saving or exporting files and the technology needed to access the saved data once off-site is essential.

5.2.4. Coordinating and Synchronizing Data

Including multiple data sources demands strategies for coordinating and synchronizing recorded data. Locating specific information or identifying and piecing together a particular event across varied formatted data recorded by multiple devices is challenging but viable when a system for organizing, archiving, and logging data is employed. Time-stamping media records while recording is a simple but valuable technique that facilitates this process.

Time-stamping field notes can assist in marking significant events or points of time that a researcher wants to remember when analyzing across data streams during analysis (Derry 2007). Maintaining an overarching sense of what took place along with significant events during each site visit by keeping a log, spreadsheet, or other type of organizational structure can assist in retrieving particular data from digital records (Barron 2007). For instance, a researcher observing groups of students creating music might time-stamp field notes on a tablet or laptop computer while simultaneously recording participants' work with recording devices. While observing and recording a group creating music, the researcher might notice students stop their work, listen to another group's music, discuss its similarity to a popular song, and then incorporate aspects of that song in their own music. In such a scenario, generating a memo with a time stamp would assist the researcher in remembering to look at that particular moment across the data records at a later point in time. Using time stamps in combination with logs or spreadsheets containing information about each site visit would also assist the researcher in finding such significant events in each data record.

While software such as Final Cut Pro X or PluralEyes can synchronize video clips generated by numerous devices, precisely aligning multimedia recordings from different sources is difficult if the synchronization does not occur simultaneously with recording. Though visible or audible signals such as hand claps or clapper boards can aid in aligning digital recordings, achieving precise synchronization necessitates technical solutions. This is difficult when setting up multiple recording devices, taking field notes, and avoiding interfering with the setting. Kirkman's (2010) study of young people creating music in the United Kingdom employed a synchronous multiple video (SMV) system enabling him to record and synchronize multiple data streams of video footage, audio, and MIDI information from computers and wireless microphones (111–12). This system included a multi-input audio/video capture card in a desktop computer, a video signal converter, and a MIDI interface to transfer MIDI data from the desktop to a laptop. Kirkman was thus able to generate data providing a view of the classroom, students working on specific computers, video of the computer itself with audio of students' dialogue, and MIDI from their computer work. This unique approach offers a potential model for music educators interested in generating synchronized multimedia data including computers, video-recording devices, and MIDI controllers. When such technological solutions are not possible, researchers can use contextual information across data streams such as listening for the same audio or aligning visual information to synchronize the media.

5.2.5. Collecting and Digitizing Analog Artifacts and Data

Collecting artifacts and objects that are meaningful to participants or significant to the study, sometimes referred to as material culture, is an important method for generating data. Atkinson and Delamont (2005) bemoan the lack of material culture in ethnographic fieldwork, urging researchers to "pay systematic attention to the physical embodiment of cultural values and codings" (827). Artifacts such as music curricular and policy documents or examples of students' work may be essential to one's study, though sometimes inaccessible to the researcher. Obtaining such artifacts may require contacting people beyond the immediate sample of participants, such as site staff or administrators. Researchers ought to consider and address these issues when drafting IRB permissions forms. Though artifacts ranging from sheet music to students' compositions might be collected physically, it may be necessary to record material culture that cannot be removed from a site, such as trophies and banners in a band room. Researchers might also employ artifacts to obtain additional data. A list of participants' favorite music, for example, might inform searches for related recordings or videos.

5.2.6. Incorporating Participant-Generated Data

Many of the strategies addressed thus far also apply to including audio, video, and other artifacts generated and recorded by participants. Whether text-based artifacts such as reflective journal entries or multimedia recordings, participant-generated data can provide information and perspectives that might otherwise be inaccessible to or missed by a researcher and potentially more representative of participants' worlds and experience than those generated by researchers (Clark-Ibáñez 2007; Mannay 2010). Additionally, participant-generated data can serve as a triangulation measure to researchers' interpretations of their own observations (Russell 2007).

Including participant-generated photos, sometimes referred to as auto-driven visual research, can involve participants generating photographs collaboratively (Kaplan and Howes 2004) or independently (Samuels 2007). Kaplan and Howes's (2004) international research speaks to the rich data that photographs can provide and how such data might be generated collaboratively. Music education researchers might provide groups of students with digital cameras or mobile devices to photograph aspects of their musical engagement such as when, where, and how they do music. Researchers can alternatively request that participants refrain from sharing what they intend to photograph with each other (Samuels 2007). Providing parameters as to what participants might photograph may be important to one's research design. Samuels (2007) found more success when asking his participants to photograph specific aspects of their lived experience in terms of topics such as "something that captures the essence of Buddhism" (200) than when using a more open-ended approach that simply specified participants to photograph "ten things they like[d]" (202). Providing criteria that are too specific, however, may limit the type of data participants generate based on a researcher's preconceived idea of what should be included. It is thus incumbent on one to strike the best balance of specificity and openness with what participants might photograph and a study's focus. Researchers might learn much from participants' photographs of what is meaningful in terms of their musicianship or musical engagement.

Processes for including participant-generated video data parallel aforementioned video research approaches and techniques of auto-driven visual research. Additional techniques such as having participants record video diaries, similar to reflective journals, may benefit a study. Holliday (2007), whose research in the United Kingdom exemplifies this particular use of video data, argues that "video diaries afford participants the potential for a greater degree of reflection than other methods through the process of watching, recording, and editing their diaries before submission" (262). Having participants create video diaries can be particularly beneficial for generating data related to musical engagement that researchers are unable to observe or participants' reflections beyond the context of interviews.

Video confessionals, consisting of someone looking at and speaking directly to the camera (Holliday 2007), may be familiar to participants given this format's presence on television shows that adopt documentary techniques. Rowe (2009), a researcher from the United Kingdom, makes a similar observation regarding video diaries and reality television shows. Holliday (2007), in discussing the value of video confessionals, suggests that they be paired with follow-up interviews since they present a one-way conversation (277). Researchers might elicit video confessionals during or after rehearsals, project work, and other settings by providing participants with recording devices or placing them on-site. Video diaries and confessionals may also be useful for obtaining data related to participants' musical engagement or perspectives in settings outside of a researcher's immediate purview.

Creating and using other visual artifacts such as concept maps or mind maps provides a mechanism for displaying participants' knowledge, understanding, and perspectives of particular phenomena (Novak and Cañas 2006; Wheeldon and Faubert 2009). While some use the terms "concept maps" and "mind maps" interchangeably, others differentiate between the two approaches. According to Novak and Cañas (2006), concept maps "show the specific label (usually a word or two) for one concept in a node or box, with lines showing linking words that create a meaningful statement or proposition" (177). Using Novak and Cañas's approach, concept maps are arranged hierarchically and contain statements and visual information demonstrating relationships between the concepts (177). Mind maps, however, according to Novak and Cañas, typically "lack one or more of the above characteristics" (177) of concept maps. Having participants create such maps provides them with a creative process to engage their own thinking and researchers with visual representations of participants' perspectives and understanding of particular topics or phenomena (Wheeldon and Faubert 2009). Butler (2001) analyzed preservice music educators' concept maps of "effective teaching" created at initial and final stages of a study. Including concept maps assisted Butler in analyzing students' conceptual understanding of what it means to be an effective teacher.

Participant-generated visual data can extend to other types of maps, drawings, representations of music, and self-portraits. Music educators have used listening maps or visual representations of music as a means of students' musical engagement and data for research (Blair 2008; Kerchner 2000). Incorporating artifacts such as drawings, artworks, and self-portraits provides participants with opportunities to share their insights through artistic means beyond text-based or verbal responses to researchers' questions (Mannay 2010; Russell 2007). Mannay's (2010) and Russell's (2007) research demonstrates how participants' drawings can communicate multiple meanings and perspectives that might otherwise be missed. Though the aforementioned artifacts may be more open to interpretation than textual data and in some cases constrained by participants' artistic ability and technical skill (Mannay 2010), when combined with accompanying text and/or discussion they provide entry points to participants' thinking and experience. Thompson and Campbell (2003), for example, incorporated pre-service educators' drawings with accompanying descriptions to analyze their teaching metaphors.

5.2.7. Eliciting Data from Data

Researchers can use existing artifacts such as notated music, instruments, or musical recordings; data generated on-site such as media recordings of participants engaged in music-making; or artifacts and media generated by participants such as mind maps or video diary entries, to elicit additional data from participants. Discussions that ensue when engaged in this process can be recorded as additional data and part of the triangulation process. It is critical, however, that researchers distinguish between data used to elicit additional data and the information generated in this process (Russell 2007). Photo and video elicitation will be outlined in the following, though the strategies can be applied to the range of data discussed throughout this chapter.

Photo elicitation is a methodological approach whereby one incorporates photographs as prompts, foci, references, and other means for generating data through dialogue and interviews extending beyond a solely verbal-oriented process (Harper 2002; Samuels 2007). Auto-driven photo elicitation, in which participants discuss photographs they generated, brings to focus what they find relevant and meaningful (Clark-Ibáñez 2007; Samuels 2007). This can assist researchers in clarifying potential misinterpretations (Mannay 2010). In music education, photographs of participants engaged in music-making or participant-generated photographs of meaningful musical experiences can serve as springboards for discussing music and research foci.

Video elicitation consists of participants viewing and discussing specific excerpts, or moments of video that they or researchers select. Video-stimulated recall involves having participants view video data of themselves to recall and discuss what they were thinking at the particular moment that they observe on the video footage. Though for some, video-stimulated recall encompasses participants commenting on aspects of what they were doing, it is the reliving of experience that is most characteristic of this approach (Rowe 2009; Smith 2008).

Tochon (2007) traces how the use of stimulated recall has "shifted from a focus on reconstructing past thinking ... toward a focus on constructive, shared reflections on present and future actions" (60–61). Tochon suggests that researchers abandon the notion of stimulated recall when "dealing with video-based prospective knowledge construction," which she terms "video-based shared reflection" (VBSR) (60). Rather than having students "relive" the prior experience to recall what they were doing and thinking at the time they were recorded, video-based shared reflection engages participants in "constructive, shared reflections" from their present perspective by discussing video data with the researcher or other participants (Tochon 2007, 61).

Participants might be encouraged to treat VBSR similar to commentary provided as extra content when watching films on DVD or other media. This approach can generate information that may not be verbalized during interviews or observations. For example, Tobias's (2010) incorporation of VBSR led to a participant discussing for the first time how he and his partner accommodated for each other's guitar skills throughout their creative process. This was spurred by the participant observing himself changing a strumming pattern while practicing an original song with his partner.

5.3. Analyzing Multimodal and Multimedia Data

Given the spectrum of possible approaches and frameworks for analyzing multimodal and multimedia data, this section focuses on overarching or meta-approaches. Keeping in mind that theoretical frameworks, prior research, and participants' perspectives will inform analysis of data ranging from photographs to participants' self-portraits, this section addresses multimedia data specifically by highlighting issues of transformation and transcription and discussing bricolage as an analytical strategy.

Analyzing multimodal and multimedia data incrementally and/or recursively may assist researchers in making strategic decisions throughout their study (Ash 2007; Green, Skukauskaite, Dixon, and Cordova 2007; Rich and Patashnick 2002). While most approaches share analytical transformations of data such as indexing, transcribing, creating narrative accounts, creating intermediate representations of data, and coding, these techniques are not necessarily performed in the same order. The theoretical and methodological frameworks from which one operates will influence how one proceeds with analysis (Ash 2007; R. Goldman, Erickson, Lemke, and Derry 2007).

Goldman et al. (2007) suggest that video researchers make analytical decisions based upon inductive, deductive, or narrative evolving approaches to data selection. In an inductive approach the researcher starts with broad questions without a strong orienting theory guiding data selection. Through repeated viewings the researcher might make use of transcripts and intermediate representations of data, such as diagrams, graphs, and matrices, to determine significant events and themes (22). A deductive approach makes use of a strong theory and clear research questions to identify and create a representative set of video cases from which to sample systematically to answer the research questions (22). In a narrative evolving approach, data may be selected during and after the recording process to construct a narrative for answering research questions. This approach often includes collaboration with participants (22–23).

Rich and Patashnick (2002) demonstrate an inductive process consisting of viewing video records with minimum manipulation, logging the visual and audio narrative aspects of the records in multiple passes, and creating transcripts. Transcripts are then coded and analyzed for "conceptual model building" (256). Both Green et al. (2007) and Ash (2007) move back and forth through layers of analysis recursively. Whereas Green et al. (2007) begin with locating points in the data significant to the study, Ash (2007) first transcribes video records. Both approaches then make extensive use of intermediate representations of data such as maps (Green et al. 2007) and flow charts (Ash 2007) to analyze, find relationships between, and apply theoretical frameworks to the video data. Ash (2007) and Green et al. (2007) then conduct detailed discourse analyses on the identified significant events before moving to a macro level of analysis to contextualize and make sense of the data.

Rostvall and West (2005) take a more deductive approach, beginning with an analytical framework based on research concepts; transcribing speech, gesture, and music into text; and coding data using a concept matrix based on their analytical framework. This is followed by coding based on an additional set of conceptual frameworks. Engle, Conant, and Greeno (2007) suggest a process of progressive refinement of hypotheses wherein a researcher starts with a question and hypothesis about a particular phenomenon. After viewing video through multiple iterations at various degrees of detail, significant events are identified, coded with pre-specified categories, and compared to test various hypotheses. Codes are then applied to build categories and eventually a model explaining the central phenomenon, which is tested against specific cases and aspects of the video data through using transcripts and content logs.

5.3.1. Preparing and Processing Multimedia Data

Viewing and indexing multimedia data before and during the transformation and transcription of data can greatly assist with analysis (Hall 2007). Along with viewing and cataloging video (Barron 2007), indexing can include coordinating time-stamped field notes with video records. During multiple viewings of a record, researchers might focus on particular aspects of the video and adjust the speed of footage, gaining different perspectives (Barron 2007).

Creating content logs of video data by outlining the media content provides researchers with an indexing mechanism for reviewing specific events or aspects of the data at later points in time (Barron and Engle 2007). In contrast to the concision of content logs (Flewitt 2006), narrative accounts of video data consist of generating detailed and comprehensive descriptions of the entire video recording (Angelillo, Rogoff, and Chavajay 2007). Narrative accounts represent multimodal data through rich description, communicating what occurred to someone who was not present (Angelillo et al. 2007; Barron 2007).

5.3.1.1. *Transforming and Transcribing Multimedia Data*

When working with multimedia data, the researcher performs as instrument through transforming, making sense of, and making decisions in relation to data (Barrett 2007). Issues of data transformation and analysis are thus embedded within data generation processes and are influenced by a researcher's interests and principles, a point echoed by UK researchers Bezemer and Mavers (2011). Video footage is initially transformed to data through indexing or transcription (Angelillo et al. 2007; Barron and Engle 2007). Researchers might choose to transcribe only particular events and instances in the video record (Spiers 2004) or entire records. Given the analytical decisions inherent in transforming and transcribing multimodal and multimedia data (Barron and Engle 2007), researchers ought to consider the ramifications of having others transcribe data before delegating this process to assistants or team members.

A multimodal paradigm accounts for analyzing data ranging from speech and actions to participants' embodied expressions such as gestures and gaze (Flewitt 2006; West 2011). Sound and music also play important roles as data, as do various visual representations of music. Challenges abound when determining whether to transform or transcribe one mode to another and the most appropriate process for doing so (Bezemer and Mavers 2011; Kress and Van Leeuwen 2001). Music, for instance, can be transformed from its original recorded format to descriptive text, standard notation, MIDI data, waveforms, iconic notation, spectrograms, or notation devised specifically for the purposes of a particular study. It is thus necessary to be deliberate about the notational convention one uses to represent data (Baldry and Thibault 2010).

The ability to generate a composite transcript of varied modes such as speech, gestures, music, and other information is critical when events or interactions involve a high density of multimodal data or constant shifts between modes (Rostvall and West 2005; West 2011). Rostvall and West's (2005) detailed transcript of an instrumental lesson in Sweden provides a close look at the complexity of transcription when considering multimodal aspects of data. Whether focusing on one mode at a time over multiple iterative passes through data or transcribing the gestalt of multimodal data, it is important to consider that multiple communicative modes can become incoherent and lose meaning when viewed and listened to independently of one another (Tobias 2010; West 2011). West (2011) highlights how when studying one-on-one music lessons, participants communicated through multiple modes that transformed from one to another such as "from spoken language into gesture and music" (290). Tobias (2010) noted similar movement between, and overlap of, modes when students worked on recording and producing music. Participants would often point to a computer screen, manipulate digital content in the computer environment, hum or sing, speak, and play instruments as they collaborated on their music. In both studies, focusing solely on a single mode would obscure the larger meanings of what occurred.

Working exclusively within linguistic-focused transcription frameworks can limit one's ability to analyze the richness and complexity of multimodal data (Flewitt 2006). Flewitt's (2006) research in the United Kingdom of young participants' interactions provides a strong rationale for addressing multimodal data. Approaches to address multimodal data range from creating separate transcripts for each mode to composite transcripts with columns designated for each mode (Rostvall and West 2005). Including speech, actions, and other data in the same transcript mediates analysis and helps researchers make sense of individual modes and how they work together.

5.3.2. Analysis through Bricolage

While coding is one way of making sense of data, applying montage or bricolage to juxtapose and put varied data into conversation can lead to interesting analyses and insights (Denzin and Lincoln 2005; Kincheloe and Berry 2004). Employing montage as an analytical approach might be characterized by "many different things . . . going on at the same time—different voices, different perspectives, points of views, angles of vision" (Denzin and Lincoln 2005, 5). While bricolage does not require using computers, technology affords layering, hyperlinking, and creating multimedia as a form of analysis and in some cases representations of data (Lemke 2007). Researchers might juxtapose and shift their attention between written descriptions of students' musical engagement, researcher memos, recordings of participants' music, video clips of their process, and audio excerpts of related interviews. Such techniques encourage researchers to extend beyond linear, chronological, or hierarchical approaches when analyzing data.

Processes such as selecting and reordering "clips" with video-editing applications can be extremely helpful in organizing events in video records for detailed analysis (Barrett 2007; Spiers 2004). Barret (2007) explained how graduate student researchers marked significant segments of video footage, grouped the segments together, and organized the clips to create an overview of a choral rehearsal. This aided the researchers in "mov[ing] back and forth from the entire excerpt to segments of interest and back again to the whole" (428). Similar analytical approaches might be applied to data ranging from iterative recordings of students' original music or performances to significant events throughout a setting where people engage with music.

Along with using video-editing software, researchers might leverage visual-editing applications to combine digital photos or still images of video with annotations, text such as interview data, timelines, concept maps, or other artifacts to gain insight and make connections between data (Flewitt 2006). Using a combination of software, one can weave together interview data, journal entries, photographs, video clips, audio excerpts, researcher memos, and other data to understand one's research in ways that are not possible when coding exclusively. This process is particularly helpful when specific aspects of data relate to one another but are spread across multiple points in time in varied formats from different sources. For instance, a researcher can leverage technology to compile all occurrences in which a participant references a particular band, whether in speech, through his original music, or on a t-shirt worn on-site. These disparate data recorded at different moments can be juxtaposed visually and/or conceptually through a creative writing or multimedia process of bricolage to reveal connections that may be key to the study.

5.4. Future Developments and Directions in Qualitative Research Data Collection and Generation

Online research and digital ethnographic methods are hardly new but are not yet widely present in music education. Given the ubiquity of social media and networks, emerging web-based technologies, and ways people engage with music online, music education research ought to account for web-based data. Fieldwork now encompasses digital and hybrid spaces. While studies of online music communities are emerging internationally (Partti and Karlsen 2010; Waldron and Veblen 2008), music education researchers might also incorporate data such as YouTube videos and associated comments, participants' blog posts or Facebook updates, and microblogging or Twitter messages. Searching through and across such digital media may generate valuable data; however, ethical and methodological issues primarily relating to privacy must be negotiated and reconciled. Addressing new technologies, media, and modes of communication is critical to studying musical engagement as society evolves.

The use of large-scale databases to archive and share data for secondary analyses, while fairly common in the sciences, is largely missing from music education research. Pea and Lemke (2007) suggest that providing access to video data allows for "making it possible to subject claims based on the data to scholarly debate" and "enabl[es] other researchers to benefit from the time—and in many cases public money—invested in acquiring the data (42). The ability for peer researchers to access, engage with, and analyze archived data ranging from visual and sonic representations of students' original music to video clips of people discussing their musical identities could provide opportunities for collaborative, iterative, and longitudinal investigations of phenomena across music education.

Strategic planning is needed to address the diversity of data content and formats as well as how this content might be shared. Including metadata or information embedded within the data, in addition to appropriate web-based schemas that can be read and searched within web browsers, can increase the likelihood of data being found and accessed by researchers (Pea and Lemke 2007). Though individuals can create online archives and websites using open source content management and archiving systems, collaborative efforts may assist in broadening beyond analyses "isolated in data islands that can only be used and understood within the tools and projects in which they are created" (Pea and Lemke 2007, 42). This necessitates developing standardized systems to format and label data for use in databases and spaces online ranging from determining what types of meta information should be attached to participants' original music to the digital format of those files. Music education research might benefit from researchers, institutions, and organizations collaborating to develop and maintain the infrastructure, policies, and knowledge necessary to share and access data and analysis across digital networks.

5.5. Conclusion

Integrating multimedia and multimodal data in qualitative research offers a way to encompass the varied modes of communication at play in music teaching and learning. This chapter focused on collecting, generating, transforming, and analyzing such data, particularly in relation to those digital or digitized. The complexities inherent when integrating multimedia and diverse artifacts were also highlighted, along with issues related to developing systems and strategies for generating, archiving, organizing, accessing, and analyzing data ranging from video clips to participant-created imagery. As technology develops, musical engagement evolves, and data sources or formats diversify, one might draw upon the strong foundation of qualitative research methods and issues discussed throughout this chapter to inform work on future studies. Music education researchers might thus involve the scope of modes and media applied throughout music teaching.

References

Angelillo, C., B. Rogoff, and P. Chavajay. 2007. "Examining Shared Endeavors by Abstracting Video Coding Schemes with Fidelity to Cases." In *Video Research in the Learning Sciences*, edited by R. Goldman, R. Pea, B. Barron, and S. J. Derry, 189–206. Mahwah, NJ: Lawrence Erlbaum.

Ash, D. 2007. "Using Video Data to Capture Discontinuous Science Meaning Making in Nonschool Settings." In *Video Research in the Learning Sciences*, edited by R. Goldman, R. Pea, B. Barron, and S. J. Derry, 207–226. Mahwah, NJ: Lawrence Erlbaum.

Atkinson, P., and S. Delamont. 2005. "Analytic Perspectives." In *The Sage Handbook of Qualitative Research*, 3rd ed., edited by N. K. Denzin and Y. S. Lincoln, 821–40. Thousand Oaks, CA: Sage Publications.

Baldry, A., and P. J. Thibault. 2010. *Multimodal Transcription and Text Analysis*. London: Equinox.

Barrett, J. R. 2007. "The Researcher as Instrument: Learning to Conduct Qualitative Research through Analyzing and Interpreting a Choral Rehearsal." *Music Education Research* 9 (3): 417–33.

Barron, B. 2007. "Video as a Tool to Advance Understanding of Learning and Development in Peer, Family, and Other Informal Learning Contexts." In *Video Research in the Learning Sciences*, edited by R. Goldman, R. Pea, B. Barron, and S. J. Derry, 159–87. Mahwah, NJ: Lawrence Erlbaum.

Barron, B., and R. A. Engle. 2007. "Analyzing Data Derived from Video Records." In *Guidelines for Video Research in Education: Recommendations from an Expert Panel*, edited by S. J. Derry, 24–33. Chicago: Data Research and Development Center.

Bezemer, J., and D. Mavers. 2011. "Multimodal Transcription as Academic Practice: A Social Semiotic Perspective." *International Journal of Social Research Methodology* 14 (3): 191–206.

Blair, D. V. 2008. "Do You Hear What I Hear? Musical Maps and Felt Pathways of Musical Understanding." *Visions of Research in Music Education* 11: 1–23.

Brown, D. 2002. "Going Digital and Staying Qualitative: Some Alternative Strategies for Digitizing the Qualitative Research Process." *Forum: Qualitative Social Research* 3 (2): 1–17.

Butler, A. 2001. "Preservice Music Teachers' Conceptions of Teaching Effectiveness, Microteaching Experiences, and Teaching Performance." *Journal of Research in Music Education* 49 (3): 258–72.

Clark-Ibáñez, M. 2007. "Inner-City Children in Sharper Focus: Sociology of Childhood and Photo Elicitation Interviews." In *Visual Research Methods: Image, Society, and Representation,* edited by G. C. Stanczak, 167–196. Thousand Oaks, CA: Sage Publications.

Denzin, N. K., and Y. S. Lincoln. 2005. "Introduction: The Discipline and Practice of Qualitative Research." In *The Sage Handbook of Qualitative Research*, 3rd ed., edited by N. K. Denzin and Y. S. Lincoln, 1–32. Thousand Oaks, CA: Sage Publications.

Derry, S. J., ed. 2007. *Guidelines for Video Research in Education: Recommendations from an Expert Panel.* Chicago: Data Research and Development Center.

Dicks, B., B. Soyinka, and A. Coffee. 2006. "Multimodal Ethnography." *Qualitative Research* 6 (1): 77–96.

Engle, R. A., F. R. Conant, and J. G. Greeno. 2007. "Progressive Refinement of Hypotheses in Video-Supported Research." In *Video Research in the Learning Sciences*, edited by R. Goldman, R. Pea, B. Barron, and S. J. Derry, 239–54. Mahwah, NJ: Lawrence Erlbaum.

Flewitt, R. 2006. "Using Video to Investigate Preschool Classroom Interaction: Education Research Assumptions and Methodological Practices." *Visual Communication* 5 (1): 25–50.

Geertz, C. 1973. *The Interpretation of Cultures.* New York: Basic Books.

Goldman, R., F. Erickson, J. Lemke, and S. J. Derry. 2007. "Selection in Video." In *Guidelines for Video Research in Education: Recommendations from an Expert Panel*, edited by S. J. Derry, 15–23. Chicago: Data Research and Development Center.

Goldman, S., and R. McDermott, R. 2007. "Staying the Course with Video Analysis." In *Video Research in the Learning Sciences*, edited by R. Goldman, R. Pea, B. Barron, and S. J. Derry, 101–113. Mahwah, NJ: Lawrence Erlbaum.

Green, J., Skukauskaite, A., C. Dixon, and R. Cordova. 2007. "Epistemological Issues in the Analysis of Video Records: Interactional Ethnography as a Logic of Inquiry." In *Video Research in the Learning Sciences*, edited by R. Goldman, R. Pea, B. Barron, and S. J. Derry, 115–32. Mahwah, NJ: Lawrence Erlbaum.

Hall, R. 2007. "Strategies for Video Recording: Fast, Cheap, and (Mostly) in Control." In *Guidelines for Video Research in Education: Recommendations from an Expert Panel*, edited by S. J. Derry, 4–14. Chicago: Data Research and Development Center.

Harper, D. 2002. "Talking about Pictures: A Case for Photo Elicitation." *Visual Studies* 17 (1): 13–26.

Hickey, M. 1997. "The Computer as a Tool in Creative Music Making." *Research Studies in Music Education* 8: 56–70.

Holliday, R. 2007. "Performances, Confessions, and Identities." In *Visual Research Methods: Image, Society, and Representation*, edited by G. C. Stanczak, 255–79. Thousand Oaks, CA: Sage Publications.

Jacobs, J. K., T. Kawanaka, and J. W. Stigler. 1999. "Integrating Qualitative and Quantitative Approaches to the Analysis of Video Data on Classroom Teaching." *International Journal of Educational Research* 31: 717–24.

Jewitt, C. 2011. "An Introduction to Multimodality." In *The Routledge Handbook of Multimodal Analysis*, edited by C. Jewitt, 14–27. New York: Routledge.

Kaplan, I., and A. Howes. 2004. "'Seeing through Different Eyes': Exploring the Value of Participative Research Using Images in Schools." *Cambridge Journal of Education* 34 (2): 143–55.

Kerchner, J. L. 2000. "Children's Verbal, Visual, and Kinesthetic Responses: Insight into Their Music Listening Experience." *Bulletin of the Council for Research in Music Education* 146: 31–50.

Kincheloe, J. L., and K. Berry. 2004. *Rigour and Complexity in Educational Research*. New York: Open University Press.

Kirkman, P. R. 2010. "Exploring Contexts for Development: Secondary Music Students' Computer-Mediated Composing." *Journal of Music, Technology, and Education* 3 (2–3): 107–24.

Kress, G., and T. Van Leeuwen. 2001. *Multimodal Discourse: The Modes and Media of Contemporary Communication*. London: Arnold.

Lemke, J. 2007. "Video Epistemology In-and-Outside the Box: Traversing Attentional Spaces." In *Video Research in the Learning Sciences*, edited by R. Goldman, R. Pea, B. Barron, and S. J. Derry, 39–51. Mahwah, NJ: Lawrence Erlbaum.

Mannay, D. 2010. "Making the Familiar Strange: Can Visual Research Methods Render the Familiar Setting More Perceptible?" *Qualitative Research* 10 (1): 91–111.

Norris, S. 2011. "Modal Density and Modal Configurations: Multimodal Actions." In *The Routledge Handbook of Multimodal Analysis*, edited by C. Jewitt, 78–90. New York: Routledge.

Novak, J. D., and A. J. Cañas. 2006. "The Origins of the Concept Mapping Tool and the Continuing Evolution of the Tool." *Information Visualization* 5: 174–84.

Partti, H., and S. Karlsen. 2010. "Reconceptualising Musical Learning: New Media, Identity and Community in Music Education." *Music Education Research* 12 (4): 369–82.

Pea, R., and Lemke, J. 2007. "Sharing and Reporting Video Work." In *Guidelines for Video Research in Education: Recommendations from an Expert Panel*, edited by S. J. Derry, 34–46. Chicago: Data Research and Development Center.

Rich, M., and J. Patashnick 2002. "Narrative Research with Audiovisual Data: Video Intervention/Prevention Assessment (VIA) and NVivo." *Social Research Methodology* 5 (3): 245–61.

Rostvall, A., and T. West. 2005. "Theoretical and Methodological Perspectives on Designing Video Studies of Interaction." *International Journal of Qualitative Methods* 4 (4): 1–26.

Rowe, V. C. 2009. "Using Video-Stimulated Recall as a Basis for Interviews: Some Experiences from the Field." *Music Education Research* 11 (4): 425–37.

Russell, L. 2007. "Visual Methods in Researching the Arts and Inclusion: Possibilities and Dilemmas." *Ethnography and Education* 2 (1): 39–55.

Ruthmann, S. A. 2006. "Negotiating Learning and Teaching in a Music Technology Lab: Curricular, Pedagogical, and Ecological Issues." PhD diss., Oakland University, Rochester, MI.

Samuels, J. 2007. "When Words Are Not Enough: Eliciting Children's Experiences of Buddhist Monastic Life through Photographs." In *Visual Research Methods: Image, Society, and Representation*, edited by G. C. Stanczak, 197–224. Thousand Oaks, CA: Sage Publications.

Smith, J. 2008. "Compositions of Elementary Recorder Students Created under Various Conditions of Task Structure." *Research Studies in Music Education* 30 (2): 159–76.

Spiers, J. A. 2004. "Tech Tips: Using Video Management/Analysis Technology in Qualitative Research." *International Journal of Qualitative Methods* 3 (1): 1–8.

Stauffer, S. L. 2001. "Composing with Computers: Meg Makes Music." *Bulletin of the Council for Research in Music Education* 150: 1–20.

Thompson, L. K., and M. R. Campbell. 2003. "Gods, Guides and Gardeners: Preservice Music Educators' Personal Teaching Metaphors." *Bulletin of the Council for Research in Music Education* 158: 43–54.

Tobias, E. 2010. "Crossfading and Plugging in: Secondary Students' Engagement and Learning in a Songwriting and Technology Class." PhD diss., Northwestern University, ProQuest Dissertations and Theses (3402496).

Tobin, J., and Y. Hsueh. 2007. "The Poetics and Pleasures of Video Ethnography of Education. In *Video Research in the Learning Sciences*, edited by R. Goldman, R. Pea, B. Barron, and S. J. Derry, 77–91. Mahwah, NJ: Lawrence Erlbaum.

Tochon, F. V. 2007. "From Video Cases to Video Pedagogy: A Framework for Video Feedback and Reflection in Pedagogical Research Praxis." In *Video Research in the Learning Sciences*, edited by R. Goldman, R. Pea, B. Barron, and S. J. Derry, 53–65. Mahwah, NJ: Lawrence Erlbaum.

Waldron, J. L., and K. K Veblen. 2008. "The Medium is the Message: Cyberspace, Community, and Music Learning in the Irish Traditional Music Virtual Community." *Journal of Music, Technology, and Education* 1 (2–3): 99–111.

West, T. 2011. "Music and Designed Sound." In *The Routledge Handbook of Multimodal Analysis*, edited by C. Jewitt, 284–92. New York: Routledge.

Wheeldon, J., and J. Faubert. 2009. "Framing Experience: Concept Maps, Mind Maps, and Data Collection in Qualitative Research." *International Journal of Qualitative Methods* 8 (3): 68–83.

Wiggins, J. H. 1994. "Children's Strategies for Solving Compositional Problems with Peers." *Journal of Research in Music Education* 42 (3): 232–52.

CHAPTER 6

MUSIC-MAKING AS DATA

Collection and Analysis

KRISTEN PELLEGRINO

> Music making... lies at the heart of what *music* is and music making is a matter of musical knowledge-in-action.
>
> (Elliott 1995, 72)

USING music-making as data is a potentially rich but underexplored topic in American music educational research. If music-making is a matter of musical knowledge-in-action, as Elliott believes, then it makes sense that music education researchers would collect and analyze music-making data to provide important insights into the music learning process as well as the very nature and impact of music-making. However, music education researchers who plan to use music-making data are largely left to their own devices, as this is seldom addressed as a separate topic in research books. The purpose of this chapter is to explore the uses of music-making as data in qualitative research in American music education and to offer suggestions about how to collect and analyze music-making data.

This chapter begins with an overview of Arts-Based Educational Research (ABER) and music's place in this field. The second section presents a more comprehensive discussion about collecting music-in-the-moment data, differentiating between collecting (1) *process-of-music-making* data; (2) *product-of-music-making* data; and (3) *meanings-of-music-making* data. The third section explores how music education researchers analyzed music-making data, including (1) verbal and nonverbal interactions; (2) musical and nonmusical responses; and (3) social interactions/connections. Then, music therapy research is examined to inspire ways to broaden analysis categories to include individual responses to music-making, perceptions of others' responses to music-making, and understanding music or music education itself. The chapter concludes with suggestions for future research studies that may benefit from using music-making data and encourages music education researchers to use music-making data collection and analysis models presented here as well as to continue to explore and create new models.

6.1. Arts-Based Educational Research (ABER)

6.1.1. A Brief Overview of ABER

ABER developed from the use of Arts-Based Research (ABR). McNiff (1992, 1998, 2008) was one of the pioneers of ABR. As a creative-arts therapist, he aimed to integrate practice and research in his field. Since creative-arts therapists believe that the arts provide valuable ways of communicating and expressing oneself, he decided to experiment by using art as research. This idea was adopted by educational researchers, and a new branch of research emerged.

According to Barone and Eisner (2006, 2011), the purpose of ABER is the enhancement of perspectives. They believe that it offers "a unique means for enhancing the educational perspectives of audience members by successfully communicating the ineffable dimensions of experiences within schools" (2006, 101). Although arts-based research has become more common in fields such as art and theater, it has scarcely been used in American music education research (Bresler 2008; Daykin 2009; Leavy 2009; Sefton and Bayley 2012). However, Leavy (2009) writes that "music-based methods can help researchers access, illuminate, describe, and explain that which is often rendered invisible by traditional research practices" (101).

The American Educational Research Association (AERA) has 175 Special Interest Groups (SIGs), and "Arts-Based Educational Research" was the ninth to be created. The stated purpose of this SIG is "To provide a community for those who view education through artistic lenses, who use a variety of arts-based methodologies, and who communicate understandings through diverse genres" (http://www.aera.net/tabid/11093/First/A/Last/G/Default.aspx). These diverse genres include connecting knowledge gained through the arts to other areas, such as researching, teaching, learning, or including an artistic expression as a representation of the research itself.

6.1.2. Music and ABER

Literature about ABER often mentions the use of music within the framework of research methodologies but offers little specific advice about how to collect or analyze music-making data. Leavy (2009), however, has created a Checklist of Considerations:

> When considering using music in your research, consider the following questions:
> What is the purpose of the study and how can music serve as a medium to shed light on this topic?

What is my conception of music? In this study, is music conceptualized as a text, as an object, as a sign system, as a performance, or as some combination of these? Am I interested in the textual form of music, music at the moment of articulation, or both?

What form will the musical data be in? For example, are the data in the form of compositions, scores, and lyrics, or am I interested in the performative, audible aspects of music? In terms of the latter, will live performances be recorded, or will audiotapes be used? Will the physical performance serve as data, or only the music itself?

What is the analysis strategy? For example, will the music alone be analyzed or will data be gathered regarding people's subjective experience of the musical performance via interviews or other methods? In terms of the latter, what do I want to learn from the research participants (e.g., their process of creating meaning out of the music, their identity negotiations, their experiences of resistance or community-building, transcendental qualities of the performance)?

If using music as a model for conducting qualitative research, how will I pay attention to dynamics, rhythm, texture, and harmony during my observations and interviews? How will my understanding of form affect my writing process? How will I adapt these principles in order to attend to issues of difference and diversity? What form will my writing/representation take? (116)

Examples of music inspiring the writing process and using music as a model for conducting qualitative research include Bresler (2008, 2009), who compared the process of music-making to the process of researching, and Daykin (2009), who used her own process of music-making and performing to inspire her writing process. For example, Bresler (2008) compared the intensified engagement of giving a music performance with that of performing live research presentations, whereas Bresler (2009) described her approach to teaching doctoral-level research to music education students. First, Bresler discussed connecting knowledge that is documented and "out there" with personal knowledge and connecting the communication between performer or researcher and the audience. To this second point, Bresler wrote:

> The teaching and learning of research, I suggest in this paper, calls for learning to perceive, listen and improvise, all of which are crucial to establish connection. Focusing on how these processes can be addressed in teaching research, I discuss the important and unexamined contributions that musicianship can offer to research education. (8)

Bresler also likened music and qualitative research in terms of temporal and fluid realities. Even though there are many possible uses of music in ABER, the remainder of this chapter will focus on the uses of what Leavy (2009, 116) referred to as "music at the moment of articulation," "audible aspects of music," and "people's subjective experiences" of music in the moment in qualitative research in the field of music education.

6.1.3. Music Education Research and ABER

6.1.3.1. *Exploring One Study in Depth*

Because there are so few examples of musical performance representing research, this section will examine one work (Sefton and Bayley 2012) in depth. In this autoethnographic and ABER study, Sefton and Bayley explored their experiences of teaching in a "faculty of education while attempting to claim space and recognition for performance as research, and for their professional identity as musicians" (321). The purpose of this investigation was to uncover issues of identity for performing musicians who also teach in faculties of education.

Sefton and Bayley juxtaposed their work with other ABER, writing that "Arts-based research has often used art as a means of researching non-art subjects, using art as a metaphor, medium, or process, by researchers who have limited skills or knowledge of art" (326). However, these skilled and knowledgeable musicians and music teachers explored their own art-making and used ABER as a strategy for their research study. They also used identity as a theoretical framework and described their own music-making experiences:

> The experience was uncanny—there was an immediate feeling of ease and communication between us. We began to meet regularly. As our work progressed, we also talked about what it meant to us, personally and professionally. Making time to work seriously with another musician started to open up not only a revitalized sense of self as musician, but also started to raise areas of friction and conflict with our "other" job as university faculty. (328)

The authors spoke and wrote about their own music-making as "an escape and an embrace," but they also referred to it as an "act of resistance against the institutional expectations and social meanings of our disciplinary group identity" (331).

The researchers explained that they considered performing for the research audience during the presentation session but decided against it "due to the logistical problems of transporting instruments" (329). They presented video clips of their rehearsals and journal entries, which revealed their thoughts about music-making, their identities, and how this research developed. In a completed version of the paper, the authors wrote:

> Our intention was to extend the research into the academic conference as a site of performance, reception, and dialogue. While a video of performance is less immediate than a live performance, it activates a responsive relationship with the spectator . . . during our session of four papers, every presentation talked *about* music education and performance; only our presentation included performance, albeit in video form. (329)

During the presentation, the video clips seemed to be data as opposed to representing the study, as claimed, but that might be a distinction for future researchers to consider.

The paper addressed personal and professional revelations and possible implications for students' learning. Findings included: (1) Sefton felt more present, something he felt only when music-making; (2) Bayley felt rejuvenated and enjoyed "a return to a higher level of music making" (331); and (3) both explored how they were coming to terms with their professional identity. The authors wrote about the adage "Those who can, do; those who cannot, teach" (332) and explored some of the differences between studio professors, who work in schools of music, and music education professors, some of whom work in faculties of education. They also posed questions and included thoughts about undergraduate and graduate students. For instance, they asked, "What message do we send to teacher candidates about the importance of creativity and how it can be nurtured through the arts if the practice of the arts is absent or invisible within the walls of faculties of education?" (332). They wrote that "The potential benefit of education professors engaging in creative activity goes beyond modeling and mentoring; it opens up spaces of possibility for informal learning resulting from the curiosity and self-motivation of the student" (333).

6.1.3.2. *Possible Issues with Musical Performance as Research*

I attended the conference presentation at which the preceding study was explained, and after reading the paper two years later, my impression was that the paper was better developed. This is not surprising, though, as at the conference the authors were presenting something new and experimenting with how best to represent themselves and their research. Their excitement was palpable and the idea intriguing, but the paper might do more to act as a catalyst for future researchers to use these new methods within the field than the presentation itself.

Their presentation did spark conversation, and I continued to consider why I reacted with less enthusiasm than I would have expected. Perhaps it has to do with the fact that music can be understood in many ways: as art, as something that evokes emotion, as something that conveys a message or tells a story, or as something that reifies a moment in time. Meanings of music-making can be explored for individuals, communities, or cultures, and music-making can be used as a form of therapy or a way to form social connections. How each person receives and interprets music is not universal, however. This poses a potential problem for representing research in a musical performance and may account for one reason that researchers shy away from musical performance as research and music in ABER.

Another reason might be the preferred status of language within the research tradition (Sefton and Bayley 2009) and possible confusion about the difference between musical research and a concert. This last statement might be confounded by another factor. Perhaps music education researchers have an unspoken or unexamined desire to have their scholarship look similar to other "core subject" educational research to help legitimize the scholarship, as well as to set it apart from other music faculty members' scholarship, which consists of concertizing. These issues might be important when searching for a job or when applying for tenure. However, researchers in other fields have successfully included ABER as part of their research portfolios, and presentation opportunities are available through conferences. For example, Sefton and Bayley's work was accepted by blind peer review and presented at prestigious conferences, which should make this an acceptable form of scholarship in the view of their institution.

The paper is beautifully written and insightful, and it stands alone as an excellent research document, even though the authors wrote about their motivations as being musical and writing the paper as being secondary. They chose to perform in a recital as well as to present their research. Although they said that they used music-making to represent the study in their presentation, their paper used music-making as data and as a catalyst to write about their thoughts and feelings while music-making and about their music-making. This can be related to other music education research that has used music-making as data.

6.2. Music in the Moment: Collecting Music-Making Data

Collecting music-in-the-moment data, referred to in this chapter as *music-making data*, refers to capturing the auditory production of music. The use of music-making as data can be varied, but it can be separated into categories. In this chapter, *process-of-music-making, product-of-music-making, and meanings-of-music-making* all refer to types of music-making data. Each type of data can be collected alone or combined. For instance, if we consider Sefton and Bayley's work as using music-making as data, they would have included the *process-of-music-making* as well as *meanings-of-music-making*. If they had continued their research study to include their performance, then they would have utilized all three data-collection techniques.

6.2.1. Differentiating between Process-of-Music-Making and Product-of-Music-Making Data

Differentiating the nature of data derived from the *process* of music-making from data derived from the *product* of music-making is an important methodological consideration, made more complex by the fine line that separates the two. The process of music-making might consist of rehearsals, lessons, the act of composing a new piece of music, and any other in-the-moment work of being a musician. Of course, any of these processes may be recorded for later analysis, but the researcher's focus would remain on the musicians' course of action during the episode of music-making rather than on what resulted later from this course of action. The *product-of-music-making* is an end result: formal performances, polished recordings, or completed compositions. Some researchers collect data on both *process-of-music-making* and *product-of-music-making* data (Kratus 1989), and others choose one or the other (McNair 2010; Stanley 2008).

Kratus (1989) collected process- and product-of-music-making data in his study of children's musical composition. Process data included children composing music in the moment (10-minute recordings of their compositional process as they worked on the pieces) as well as the product, their finished pieces (recordings of their performances, played twice for the researcher). He examined both types of data for children's musical use of exploration, development, repetition, and silence. He used the term "closure" to represent the point at which the child's active, experimental music-making came to a point of completion:

> Distinguishing between process and product can be confusing, because the word *composition* refers to both process (the activity of composing) and product (the resulting music) ... if one cannot replicate an original melody, then it can be inferred that there is no closure, and the music does not exist as a composed product. (7–8)

Therefore, Kratus's description of the term "closure" helps distinguish between composition as *process-of-music-making data* or *product-of-music-making data*.

Stanley (2008) used *process-of-music-making data* to examine the collaboration between two young violinists who played duets together for fun after school. Stanley was interested in the way these violinists collaborated in the moment, and how their rehearsals might result in shared understandings that might in turn enhance their individual musical knowledge. Stanley analyzed the video recordings of her participants practicing their music together and found they featured creativity, turn-taking, problem-solving, and rich verbal and nonverbal communication. Had Stanley videotaped and analyzed the "closure" of these efforts—say, a public performance of their violin duo—the data may not have yielded a full depiction of the nature of their collaboration.

McNair (2010) used *process-of-music-making data* to examine the nature of joint music attention between toddlers and herself, as the researcher-participant and the toddlers' early childhood music teacher. Multiple data sets were collected, including (1) videos of the six toddler music-play sessions; (2) the researcher's observations and reflections immediately after each session; (3) the assistant researcher's observations and reflections immediately after each session; (4) open-ended video observation forms filled out by the researcher, lead teacher, assistant teacher, and two music specialists; and (5) individual think-aloud interviews with two teachers and two music specialists, as they viewed one selected music-play session video with McNair.

The first data set was the videos of the six toddler music-play sessions (*process-of-music-making data*), which were recorded from multiple angles.

> An assistant investigator video recorded the music play sessions and was instructed to focus a Flip video camera on the music teacher and those toddlers who were directly interacting with the music teacher. Additionally, I positioned a stationary Flip video camera prior to teaching each music play session so that there were two videos taken from different angles in each of the six music play sessions. (42)

McNair also collected *meanings-of-music-making data*, which will be described in the next section; her method of data analysis will be explored in the third section of this chapter.

6.2.2. Meanings-of-Music-Making Data

Although *meanings-of-music-making data* can be derived without collecting "music in the moment data" or music-making data, some researchers choose to collect music-making data in conjunction with *meanings-of-music-making data*. Therefore, **meanings-of-music-making data** are often combined with **process-of-music-making data** or **product-of-music-making data**, but the *purpose* of the music-making is to derive the meanings that participants make of the music-making in the moment. McCarthy (2009), McNair (2010), Pellegrino (2010, 2014, 2015a, 2015b, 2015c), and Wu (2010) all observed **process-of-music-making data**, and McCarthy (2009) and Wu (2010) also observed **product-of-music-making data**. Again, even though they collected music-making data, the purpose was to use the music-making data as a catalyst to understanding the meanings of music-making. Two benefits of combining these data-collection techniques were to provide shared experiences between participants and researcher (McCarthy 2009; McNair 2010; Pellegrino 2010, 2014; Wu 2010) and, in Pellegrino (2010, 2014, 2015b), also a shared experience between participants.

In "Exploring the Spiritual in Music Teacher Education: Group Musical Improvisation Points the Way," McCarthy (2009) used process- and product-of-music-making data when observing five rehearsals and three performances. In addition, McCarthy observed a Contemplative Practice Seminar and interviewed a faculty member and four Jazz and Contemplative Studies college music students involved in the University of Michigan's Creative Arts Orchestra, who described their experiences with music-making in this group. This is an example of *meanings-of- music-making data*.

McCarthy described the surroundings while observing the music-making as well as her thoughts while and after observing the music-making. McCarthy artfully intertwined her narrative, the quotes from the participants, and philosophical literature. McCarthy found four prevalent elements of their experience that could be applied to music teacher education: attention (getting in the moment), intention (an honest reaction to music), relationship ("meeting in the One"), and community ("Democracy . . . a community that is always in the making") (15–19). In this way, McCarthy seemed inspired by process-of-music-making data as well as the meanings her participants constructed based on their music-making, which helped her come to new understandings and then apply them to teacher education.

Revisiting McNair's (2010) examination of the nature of joint music attention between toddlers and the researcher, one of the many data sets included *meanings-of-music-making data* in the form of four think-aloud interviews with two teachers who were present at the time the video was taken and two music specialists who were not involved in the session. McNair defines the purpose of these interviews:

> Ericsson and Simon (1993) noted that a think-aloud interview conducted while viewing a video of an event stimulates recollection of thought processes that occurred during the actual event and also enables observations of occurrences that were not noticed at the actual time of the event. (42)

The same verbal instructions were given to each of the four teachers prior to the think-aloud interviews:

> I simply asked them to view the video and to comment out loud on their observations of joint music attention. I had given them a printed definition of joint music attention, complete with a glossary of pertinent terms, on the instructions for the video observation form, Appendix D. They each had the printed definition in front of them during the think-aloud interview. As I interviewed each of the four teacher participants separately, I encouraged them to think aloud as they simultaneously viewed the video, offering their comments on observations of joint music attention. I video recorded the think-aloud interviews of all four participants. (43)

How McNair analyzed the data will be explored in the third section of this chapter.

Wu (2010) studied eight second-generation teenage Chinese American string students who participated in both school and community youth orchestras. Wu observed 38 rehearsals and concerts over a five-month period and interviewed the participants, their parents, and their music teachers. In the Findings section, Wu included observations that often described the students' appearance and actions, the students' and teachers' words, and, to a lesser extent, musical analysis (intonation, tone, dynamics, etc.). The music and music-making itself was not the dominant theme, though. The purpose of this study was to examine second-generation Asian identity by understanding meanings of playing their string instruments and being part of the orchestra. Although Wu interviewed the participants, their parents, and their music teachers, she also felt compelled to observe 38 rehearsals and concerts, trying to glean meaning from their music-making and describe her observations of her participants while music-making.

In Box 6.1, I explain how I have collected music-making data in my research.

Collecting music-making data can serve many purposes. In the studies discussed in this section, music-making data included videotaping participants while music-making (while composing or playing their instruments, during child-play sessions, etc.), observing rehearsals and concerts, videotaping participants while music-making to be viewed together in talk-aloud interviews, videotaping participants while music-making in order to discuss what they experienced, and music-making to stimulate conversation about the meanings of music-making during a focus-group interview. When considering the appropriateness of this data set or practical issues concerning the collection of music-making data, these ideas can inform the researcher's choices but should not limit them. This is a newly explored topic, so finding new techniques and reasons to collect music-making data is strongly encouraged.

Box 6.1 Collecting Music-Making Data

I have used music-making data in multiple studies (2010, 2014, 2015a, 2015b, 2015c). For example, the purpose of my (2010) phenomenological case study was to examine the meanings and values of music-making in the lives of string teachers and to explore the intersections of music-making and teaching. Music-making in the moment was used as two data sets for two different purposes. First, four string teachers were videotaped while music-making on their primary instruments inside the classroom (*process-of-music-making data*). Then, teacher participants and I watched the video together so that participants could explain why they chose to make music on their instrument at that moment, what they thought their students were learning from their music-making models, and what they noticed about their students' reactions (*meanings-of-music-making data*).

Music-making was also used during a focus-group interview. Participants were asked to bring music that had special meaning to them, that would be sight-readable, and that would be appropriate for a string quintet or string orchestra to play. The participants' music-making was a catalyst to talk about past and present music-making experiences: how participants felt when they played the music, why these chosen pieces were important to each participant, and how meanings may have remained consistent or changed over time. This time, the act of music-making with other participants during the interview was used as a shared experience that formed the basis of discussing the meanings of music-making in their lives.

In both of these ways, music-making in the moment helped participants come to new realizations about their own music-making. Watching the videotapes of participants making music in the classroom with their students helped participants realize how their own music-making impacted their own teaching and their students' learning. Similarly, bringing a piece of music that had meaning to them and then playing the music in the moment with other participants helped them come to new understandings about the connections between past and present music-making and sparked storytelling that had not been shared during three previous individual interviews that did not include their own music-making in the moment. It also helped participants who did not all know each other form a relationship through music-making at the beginning of the focus-group interview, something one of my participants spoke about during the focus-group interview and later to me alone. In both instances, I collected both *process-of-music-making data* and *meanings-of-music-making data*.

6.3. ANALYSIS OF MUSIC-MAKING DATA

This section examines how music education researchers have analyzed music-making data in qualitative research. The main analysis category has been to analyze verbal and nonverbal interactions (Conway, Pellegrino, and Stanley 2011), but these interactions can be further analyzed into musical and nonmusical responses or social interactions/connections.

6.3.1. Verbal and Nonverbal Interactions

Verbal and nonverbal interactions (Barrett 2006; Berg 1997; Custodero 2005, 2007; King 2004; St. John 2010; Weeks 1996) provide different perspectives on musical endeavors. This distinguishes between verbal output that might accompany music-making (i.e., what the musicians say aloud) and the nonverbal communication also inherent in music-making. King (2004) analyzed the *verbal and nonverbal interactions* contained in the process of music-making data during rehearsals, looking for the "musical collaboration that might arise explicitly through verbal negotiation of technical or interpretative ideas" as well as the musical collaboration that "may also occur implicitly during play, through eye contact, bodily gestures . . . and in the subtle shaping of sound" (14). Analyzing the verbal interactions may provide more information on musicians' thought processes as well as their social interactions. Analyzing nonverbal interactions may enable the researcher to closely examine the nonverbal cues shared between people as well as musical interactions.

Looking at the *verbal interactions*, Berg (1997) examined two small chamber ensembles composed of high school students in order to better understand the nature of peer collaboration. Two chamber-music groups were observed in rehearsal, coaching, and concert settings over a five-month period. Research questions included: (1) Do identifiable patterns of musical thought and action exist within the ensembles? If so, how do these patterns compare and contrast in the two ensembles? and (2) How do these patterns of musical thought and action reveal ways that students assist each other in moving through the "zone of proximal development" (ZPD) (Vygotsky 1978) to construct an interpretation of music? Over a period of five months, Berg observed 33 independent group rehearsals or coaching sessions. Using an ethnographic analysis of interaction procedure, Berg evaluated the videotapes of the rehearsals and conducted formal and informal interviews with the students.

Analyzing verbal and nonverbal interactions, Berg found that students took turns assisting one another through the Vygotskyan ZPD. Berg's verbal interactions led to the finding that group patterns of thought and action occurred most often when quartet members arrived at decisions on more objective matters—rhythm, tempo, and articulation—rather than interpretation of phrasing, dynamics, and tone color. In some cases, Berg found that quartet members seemed not to resolve differences, but settled for a peer's or a coach's suggested interpretation. Berg characterized this as a reluctance to engage in conflict and a premature end to consideration of all the musical options. Berg also found that nonmusical social participation structures stemming from students' roles in larger sociocultural systems (the school orchestra, the high school, the community) also had an impact on students' ability to engage together in music-making.

Looking at the *nonverbal interactions*, Weeks (1996) sought to "gain insight into the ongoing accomplishment of collective music" (205), i.e., the way seven members of a chamber-music group performed a piece of music together. Specifically, Weeks was interested in finding out how the musicians restored synchrony after two members made musical errors that resulted in a momentary lapse in musical coordination for the group. Weeks analyzed the musical maneuvers made by either the erring musician or another musician in order to bring the group back together. He called this the constant "split second constitution of synchrony and its restoration despite disruptions" (215). Weeks pointed out that these minute adjustments are generally not created or accessible through talk. In an attempt to make the musical group "members' practices recoverable from the observable details in the recordings and the transcripts [visualized sounds in graphic form]," Weeks uses the captured sound (recordings) as "docile data" to be mined over and over again until, as an informed musician listener, he could demonstrate, by using details of the musical data, the intent and orientation of the performers.

Outside the United States, some researchers have also found that analyzing both verbal and nonverbal interactions of music-making data results in a vivid description of a musical endeavor. For example, Barrett (2006) *combined verbal and nonverbal data analysis* for a fuller picture of young children's creativity in music-making. First, Barrett collected all three types of music-making data. Data included video footage and transcriptions of children's musical processes and products as composers and songmakers (known and invented); researcher transcriptions of children's music-making; and children's notations of compositions and songs (known and invented): "The generation and analysis of observational and verbal data in conjunction with musical and notational data provided rich insight into children's musical thought and activity as composers, songmakers, and notators" (209).

6.3.1.1. *Musical and Nonmusical Responses*

Data can be further delineated into *musical and nonmusical responses*. For example, Reynolds (2006) analyzed videotaped sessions ($N = 9$) of the opening segment (3–10 minutes) of early childhood music classes in order to describe the types and frequencies of adults' and young children's vocal interactions. Participants were eight children (age 18–36 months) and their caregivers (seven mothers and one grandmother). Data were analyzed to find *the musical and nonmusical responses*. The nine types of vocal events found included (1) greeting song; (2) greeting pattern; (3) tonal patterns without words; (4) purposeful silences; (5) songs without words; (6) melodic with words; (7) rhythmic without words; (8) harmonic without words; and (9) talking, which is considered nonmusical in this study.

Custodero (2007) collected both process-of-music-making (paired improvisation sessions of two late-career adult composers and two seven-year-old children [four sessions]) and meanings-of-music-making data (unstructured group interviews/discussions) in order to explore the *musical responses* and human processes of improvisations of children and adults. Custodero used the phenomenological lenses of time, space, and responsivity to examine the "origins of spontaneous musical creativity associated with childhood dispositions and the musical expertise gained from practice, training and experience." In an effort to document "the improvisational process in an authentic way," Custodero sought to discover "how the collaborations were musically responsive and receptive to the musical cues of the performing partner" (84–85). Further analysis included

Responsivity to the musical instruments, to the general milieu, and to performing partners contributed to the improvisational process and hence the content; it is explored through three experiential lenses viewing the musician at play, the musician in motion, and the musician in communication, respectively. (89)

The purpose of St. John's (2010) study was to investigate the trail of interactions in preschoolers' pretend play during musical instrument exploration to aid in concept discovery and musical understanding. Eight three- to five-year-old children were enrolled in an independent music class that met once a week for 15 weeks during the fall. St. John acted as a participant-observer as she videotaped her students and herself in six consecutive 45-minute instrumental exploration sessions. St. John invented *three combinations of nonverbal, verbal, musical, and nonmusical analysis* (nonverbal musical, nonverbal communication, and verbal communication analysis of the musical events that were shared among students). Analysis of the session included a narrative description of these musical, nonmusical, verbal, and nonverbal exchanges that resulted in 50 hours of coding.

6.3.1.2. *Social Interactions/Connections*

Finally, in addition to musical and nonmusical analysis, social interactions/connections become another important analysis category used in music education research (Custodero 2005; McNair 2010; St. John 2006). Although all of these researchers used additional codes as well as the flow experience and/or Vygotskyan theory as lenses with which to view the data, the common analysis category was *social*.

In an effort to better understand the developmental implications of flow indicators, Custodero (2005) examined four groups of students ranging in age from seven months to eight years old in "naturally occurring contexts where musical instruction was an established routine" (190). Participants in each group were eight infants (7–23 months) in a university laboratory facility with four caregivers; ten toddlers (25–34 months) in a university laboratory facility with four caregivers; six violin students (5–6 years old) with one teacher; and five Dalcroze students (6–8 years old) with one teacher in an afterschool program. Sessions were videotaped over a two-month period, and two videotaped sessions per group were randomly chosen to be analyzed. Descriptive analysis was based on clearly observable behavior, and three main analysis categories were (1) challenge-seeking indicators (self-assignment, self-correction, gesture); (2) challenge-monitoring indicators (anticipation, expansion, extension); and (3) *social context indicators* (awareness of adults and peers). Custodero defined social context:

Music is both perceived and produced in a social milieu and it is the interpersonal context that provides meaning. . . . For the present study, the awareness of peers and adults were recorded separately, and defined as "Any observable interactions that involve prolonged gaze, head turning, or physical movement toward another person. Attempts to engage another person physically or verbally were especially noteworthy." (196)

St. John (2006) observed 12 young children (4 to almost 6 years old) in order to examine collaborative efforts of collective music-making. The teacher presented children with music materials to manipulate and transform. St. John found that the role of others was fundamental as children made "in-the-moment" adjustments based on their perception of challenge presented and requisite skill. Combining two theoretical frameworks, flow experience and Vygotskyan theory, and analyzing the process of music-making data, three themes emerged: *the power of social influence*, the children's transforming behaviors, and the provision of temporal space to explore the music content. Findings included that "Discovering where to situate themselves and with whom, the 12 children... 'played off of' each other, much like jazz musicians improvising, and intensified their experience through shared ideas" (238).

McNair (2010) used process-of-music-making data to examine the nature of joint music attention between toddlers and the researcher, who was their early childhood music teacher. This qualitative case study used theoretical frameworks of Gordon's music learning theory, Vygotsky's sociocultural learning theories, and Bruner's joint attention theories. McNair used both *musical interactions* and *social interactions* to analyze her data. McNair identified and defined three initial codes to analyze the data: "The three joint music attention cultural domains, *shared music focus, shared music interaction, and shared music understanding*, were each characterized by social interaction between the toddlers and me as we made music together" (71). From here, McNair found the following themes: (1) physical proximity influenced joint music attention; (2) the toddlers and the researcher each initiated reciprocal music-making; (3) a social and music-making history was necessary for joint music attention; (4) purposeful silences encouraged joint music attention; (5) objects were useful for achieving joint music attention; and (6) play and playfulness encouraged joint music attention. Additionally, McNair included many subcategories and provided vignettes of joint music attention.

6.3.2. Broadening Analysis Categories

Since analyzing music-making data is a newly explored topic, using these ideas as models and/or finding new ways to analyze music-making data is equally encouraged. Music education researchers might learn about music-making data from music therapy researchers. Music therapy is the use of music and all of its facets to achieve therapeutic goals in the physical, behavioral, mental, emotional, social, and spiritual domains (Bruscia 1998). Music education researchers might analyze music-making data to explore areas of interest to music therapists, such as perceptual awareness (using and heightening the senses), physical and psychological stimulation (motivation and stimulation of music-making helps develop greater engagement with people and the greater world), communicative ability, emotional expression, cognitive abilities, social behavior, and individual resources and capacities (Wigram, Pedersen, and Bonde 2002, 170–72). In addition, if music therapy terms are converted to music education terms (such as "patient" changed to "student" and "therapist" changed to "teacher"), another list of coding ideas for analyzing music-making data might include (1) the nature of the student-teacher relationship; (2) the student's personal experience of music-making; (3) the teacher's personal experience of music-making; (4) changing quality of music-making in the dynamic interaction over time; (5) perception of others (parents, relatives, other teachers, or students) regarding the student's music-making; (6) how music education works; and (7) the relationship between music-making and the student or teacher as a whole person (222–23).

6.4. Conclusion

Although using music-making as data has not often been addressed as a separate topic in American music educational research, it has been used as a data set in several qualitative studies. This chapter offers an opportunity to consider the uses of this data set as well as several examples of the ways music education researchers have collected and analyzed music-making data. Some reasons for collecting data included examining musical learning, rehearsal techniques, composing, musical interactions, social interactions, and the nature of collaboration, as well as learning more about what music-making means to people and its connection to identity. These reasons influenced decisions about which types of music-making data were collected: *process-of-music-making data, product-of-music-making data,* or *meanings-of-music-making data.* Data analysis categories included *verbal and nonverbal interactions, musical and nonmusical responses,* and *social interactions/connections* and may be broadened to include categories suggested by music therapy researchers, such as *individual responses, perceptions of others' responses to someone's music-making,* and *an understanding of music or music education itself.* By categorizing ways music education and music therapy researchers have used music-making data, I hope this chapter becomes a catalyst for more frequent use of music-making data in new research studies. Although previous research can offer models for music-making data collection and data analysis techniques, researchers are also encouraged to create new models in the future.

Whether using ABER methodologies or more common qualitative research methods, analyzing music-making data might bring new insights into topics such as pedagogy, curriculum, student learning, student well-being, student identity, and music teacher identity (in-service, preservice, and teacher educator). Research topics that may benefit from using music-making data include examining the use of music teachers' music-making in the classroom and its impact on student learning or examining the impact of preservice music teachers' music-making during teaching episodes on (1) their perceptions of their teaching during fieldwork and/or student teaching experiences and (2) their students' and cooperating teachers' perceptions of the preservice music teachers' teaching. I would imagine that collecting process-of-music-making data and meanings-of-music-making data from both the preservice or in-service music teachers and their students would be appropriate. Other ideas include examining the musical, social, and individual ways music-making impacts student music-makers, music teacher music-makers, or music teacher educator music-makers; the impact of students' music-making on targeted audiences (parents, peers, administrators, school board members, etc.); or the music-making choices of music students or music teachers outside the classroom. Music education researchers may wish to examine classroom teachers' use of music-making and the impact of musical programs arranged by classroom teachers on their audiences (parents, peers, administrators, school board members, etc.). Other research study ideas include examining verbal, nonverbal, and musical interactions of chamber musicians or examining the nonverbal interactions of professional musicians of all types and how they relate to audience members' meanings-of-music-making. These suggestions are not meant to limit music education researchers' interest in using music-making data, but rather to begin to spark an interest in the varied topics for which music-making data may be useful.

References

Barone, T., and E. W. Eisner. 2006. "Arts-Based Educational Research." In *Handbook of Complementary Methods in Education Research*, edited by J. Green, G. Camilli, and P. Elmore, 93–107. New York: Lawrence Erlbaum Associates.

Barone, T., and E. W. Eisner. 2011. *Arts-Based Research*. Thousand Oaks, CA: Sage Publications.

Barrett, M. S. 2006. "Inventing Songs, Inventing Worlds: The 'Genesis' of Creative Thought and Activity in Young Children's Lives." *International Journal of Early Years Education* (14) 3: 201–20.

Berg, M. H. 1997. "Social Construction of Musical Experience in Two High School Chamber Music Ensembles." PhD diss., Northwestern University.

Bresler, L. 2008. "The Music Lesson." In *Handbook of the Arts in Qualitative Research: Perspectives, Methodologies, Examples, and Issues*, edited by J. G. Knowles and A. L. Cole, 225–50. Thousand Oaks, CA: Sage Publications.

Bresler, L. 2009. "Research Education Shaped by Musical Sensibilities." *British Journal of Music Education* 26 (1): 7–25.

Bruscia, K. E. 1998. *Defining Music Therapy*. 2nd ed. Gilsum, NH: Barcelona.

Conway, C., K. Pellegrino, and A. M. Stanley. 2011. "Music-Making as Data in Qualitative Research: A Discussion of Method and Analysis." Session presented at the 2011 Biennial Qualitative and Ethnographic Conference in Cedarville, OH, May.

Custodero, L. A. 2005. "Observable Indicators of Flow Experience: A Developmental Perspective on Musical Engagement in Young Children from Infancy to School Age." *Music Education Research* 7 (2): 185–209.

Custodero, L. A. 2007. "Origins and Expertise in the Musical Improvisations of Adults and Children: A Phenomenological Study of Content and Process." *British Journal of Music Education* 24: 77–98.

Daykin, N. 2009. "Music and Qualitative Research." In *Method Meets Art: Arts-Based Research Practices*, edited by P. Leavy, 101–34. New York: Gilford Press.

Elliott, D. 1995. *Music Matters: A New Philosophy of Music*. New York: Oxford University Press.

Ericsson, K. A., and H. A. Simon. 1993. *Protocol Analysis: Verbal Reports as Data*. Cambridge, MA: MIT Press.

King, E. C. 2004. "Collaboration and the Study of Ensemble Rehearsal." Paper presented at the Eighth International Conference on Music Perception and Cognition, Evanston, IL, August.

Kratus, J. 1989. "Time Analysis of the Compositional Processes Used by Children Ages 7 to 11." *Journal of Research in Music Education* 37 (1): 5–20.

Leavy, P. 2009. *Method Meets Art: Arts-Based Research Practices.* New York: Gilford Press.

McCarthy, M. 2009. "Exploring the Spiritual in Music Teacher Education: Group Musical Improvisation Points the Way." *The Mountain Lake Reader: Conversations on the Study and Practice of Music Teaching,* 12–22. http://digital.watkinsprinting.com/publication/?i=16158andp=1.

McNair, A. A. 2010. "Joint Music Attention between Toddlers and a Music Teacher." PhD diss., University of South Carolina.

McNiff, S. 1992. *Art as Medicine: Creating a Therapy of Imagination.* Boston, MA: Shambhala.

McNiff, S. 1998. *Art-Based Research.* London: Jessica Kingsley.

McNiff, S. 2008. "Arts-Based Research." In *Handbook of the Arts in Qualitative Research: Perspectives, Methodologies, Examples, and Issues,* edited by J. G. Knowles and A. L. Cole, 29–40. Thousand Oaks, CA: Sage Publications.

Pellegrino, K. 2010. "The Meanings and Values of Music-Making in the Lives of String Teachers: Exploring the Intersections of Music-Making and Teaching." PhD diss., University of Michigan.

Pellegrino, K. 2015a. "Becoming Music-making Music Teachers: Connecting Music Making, Identity, Wellbeing, and Teaching for Four Student Teachers." *Research Studies in Music Education,* 37 (2): 175–194. doi: 10.1177/1321103X15589336.

Pellegrino, K. 2015b. "Student, Cooperating, and Supervising Teacher Perceptions of Educational and Musical Interactions during Student Teaching." *Journal of Music Teacher Education,* 24 (2): 54–73. doi: 10.1177/1057083713508653.

Pellegrino, K. 2015c. "Becoming a Music Teacher: Preservice Music Teachers Describe the Meanings of Music-Making, Teaching, and a Tour Experience." In Advances in Music Education Research, vol. 6, edited by L. Thompson and M. Campbell, 69–96. Charlotte, NC: Information Age Publishing, Inc.

Pellegrino, K. 2014. "Examining the Intersections of Music-Making and Teaching for Four String Teachers." *Journal of Research in Music Education,* 62, 128–47. doi: 10.1177/0022429414530433.

Reynolds, A. M. 2006. "Vocal Interactions during Informal Early Childhood Music Classes." *Bulletin of the Council for Research in Music Education* 168: 35–49.

Sefton, T., and J. G. Bayley. 2012. "The Performing Professor: Conflicts of Identity and Work in Faculties of Education." *Personhood and Music Learning: Connecting Perspectives and Narratives* 5: 319–37.

St. John, P. 2006. "Finding and Making Meaning: Young Children as Musical Collaborators." *Psychology of Music* 34 (2): 238–61.

St. John, P. 2010. "Crossing Scripts and Swapping Riffs: Preschoolers Make Musical Meaning." In *Vygotsky and Creativity: A Cultural-Historical Approach to Play, Meaning Making, and the Arts,* edited by C. Connery, V. P. John-Steiner, and A. Marjanovic-Shane, 63–81. New York: Peter Lang.

Stanley, A. M. 2008. "Rose and Giancarlo: Evidence of and for Musical Collaboration." In *Sociological Explorations: Proceedings of the 5th International Symposium on the Sociology of Music Education,* edited by B. A. Roberts, 337–52. St. John's, Newfoundland: Binder's Press.

Weeks, P. A. D. 1996. "Synchrony Lost, Synchrony Regained: The Achievement of Musical Co-Ordination." *Human Studies* 19: 199–228.

Wigram, T., I. N. Pedersen, and L. O. Bonde. 2002. *A Comprehensive Guide to Music Therapy: Theory, Clinical Practice, and Training*. Philadelphia, PA: Jessica Kingsley.

Wu, Chi-Hwa. 2010. "Meanings of Music Making Experiences among Second-Generation Chinese American String Students." DMA diss., Arizona State University.

Vygotsky, L. S. 1978. *Mind in Society*. Cambridge, MA: Harvard University Press.

CHAPTER 7

SOFTWARE TO INTERROGATE QUALITATIVE DATA IN MUSIC EDUCATION

PETER R. WEBSTER

7.1. INTRODUCTION

QUALITATIVE data analysis is becoming a prominent paradigm of choice for many music education/therapy researchers. An accounting of the many doctoral dissertations submitted to the ProQuest database in music education/therapy in a recent review revealed that over one-third of the studies completed used some sort of qualitative methodology. This compares to less than 10 percent of the dissertations completed in 1994, the year of the first Qualitative Conference in Music Education at the University of Illinois. A recent study of the curricula at doctoral programs in the United States and Canada found that of the 52 responding schools, 38 required a course in qualitative methodology (Rutkowski, Webster, and Gossett 2012). All of the major research journals in the field of music education now publish qualitative studies, including the *Journal of Research in Music Education*. The attention now paid to qualitative empirical work in music teaching and learning in the United States has taken a long time to develop compared to other fields of education, but nonetheless remains a remarkable achievement for our maturing profession. This very *Handbook* is testimony to the growing interest in qualitative inquiry as a full partner to quantitative, historical, and philosophical studies.

What remains unclear is the extent to which the profession is using all of the tools at its disposal to accomplish the best qualitative work possible. What qualitative work we have prior to 1985 was often accomplished with scattered field notes, cumbersome tape recordings, and interview transcripts that were laboriously created and studied, often without the benefit of carefully crafted theoretical models or little technological support.

The development of affordable and increasingly powerful personal computers in the decades at the end of the twentieth century to the present day supported much early work in qualitative research. Database, word processing, and spreadsheet software supported and continue to support qualitative work. More specialized programs such as idea organizers (e.g., *Mindmeister* (http://www.mindmeister.com/education) and a large assortment of more generalized media production software for audio and video content have played a role in organizing the complexity of qualitative work.

But starting in the mid-1980s, some of the first software products especially designed for the qualitative researcher began to emerge (Davidson and di Gregorio 2011, 630–31). The rationale for such specialized products was based on the obvious need for scholars to organize, code, and interpret many forms of observed data in ways that more completely supported research goals. A general-use word processing or spreadsheet program did not easily provide the ability for a researcher using digitally rendered content to "see" and clearly document interconnections and associations. By the end of the next decade, much more sophisticated programs of this sort emerged that not only allowed for text retrieval, but provided ways to manage other data types in an organized whole. Flexibility was offered for viewing, juxtaposing, and reflecting on data. In more recent times this same software has embraced video and audio data sources and has provided links to multimedia files as well as possible geo-coding of media objects. Today, hyperlinking between project components has become common, and researchers are allowed to place reflective memos connected to data sources where appropriate. Interestingly, such developments mirror the development of recent Internet affordances offered by blogs, wikis, and other social networking elements to an extent that they may be partners with specialized qualitative analysis software (Davidson and di Gregorio, 2011, 637).

This kind of software, designed particularly for qualitative researchers to "interrogate" qualitative data, has been labeled either Computer Assisted Qualitative Data Analysis Software (CAQDAS) or Qualitative Data Analysis Software (QDAS). Its use by music education researchers is relatively rare, but is growing quickly. The major purpose of this chapter is to review some of the features of this software that might be of interest to music education researchers. I will also summarize some of the frequently cited concerns about such software and note why, even within the larger qualitative community, such software is seen as less than desirable. Sample studies in music education that have successfully used these products in the last 10 years will be reviewed and some speculation for the future will be offered. The chapter is designed as a partner to Tobias's chapter 5 in this volume, which describes more custom solutions for multimodal and multimedia data.

7.2. What Are QDAS Programs?

A good place to start in understanding such software is to identify qualitative data and its analysis. For most music education researchers, qualitative data are in non-numeric form and often include: (1) text sources such as interview transcripts, field notes, documents (reports, meeting minutes, e-mails), (2) still images, (3) video, (4) audio, and (5) music scores.

> Such data usually involve people and their activities, signs, symbols, artefacts [sic] and other objects they imbue with meaning. The most common forms of qualitative data are what people have said or done.... Qualitative Data Analysis (QDA) is the range of processes and procedures whereby we move from the qualitative data that have been collected into some form of explanation, understanding or interpretation of the people and situations we are investigating. QDA is usually based on an interpretative philosophy. The idea is to examine the meaningful and symbolic content of qualitative data. (Taylor and Gibbs 2010)

Such analysis usually entails the "interrogation" of data by exploring, organizing, integrating, and interpreting information.

> These four components require that researchers retrieve, rethink, compare subsets, and identify patterns and relationships. Various QDAS program features support analysis tasks including linking and grouping, annotating and searching, writing and making connections, and incorporating references and combining or converting findings. These are the same tasks researchers using traditional methods perform except that without the power of the computer, it is difficult to retrieve data, so you are limited in comparing subsets and identifying patterns, which then have a limiting effect on your ability to rethink data. (Davidson and di Gregorio 2011, 628)

Lewins and Silver (2007) have written extensively about qualitative research software and have identified main tasks of analysis that work well with a wide variety of QDAS programs on the market today. Table 7.1 is adapted from their writing and provides a workflow that might be useful for the reader in thinking about the adoption of a QDAS program for possible use with a music education project. Chapters in their book are useful in guiding researchers through stages of use with software programs.

It should be clear from Table 7.1 that an important function of QDAS programs is to act as a content manager—a kind of command central for the many pieces of the puzzle the researcher must face as the goals for analysis are met. A large-scale "project" is identified, boundaries are established, and work can begin with the aid of digitization. The work becomes portable and shareable as well, so that collaboration is facilitated and approaches to trustworthiness are enhanced. Depending on the program's design, databases can be internal to the program or linked to outside resources that can be accessed for analysis. Multiple projects can also be accomplished if a large array of data needs be studied with different methodologies. Modern QDAS programs are not necessarily designed to favor one methodology, such as an ethnography as opposed to multiple case studies, or grounded theory. Researchers must come into the process of use with their thinking clearly established as to how the QDAS resources will be used for their purposes.

Table 7.1 Main Tasks of Analysis Using QDAS Resources

Task	Analytic Rationale
Planning and managing a project	Keep together the different aspects of work. Aid continuity, and build an audit trail. Later, illustrate the process and rigor.
Reading, marking, and commenting on data	Discover and mark interesting aspects in the data.
Searching (for strings, words, phrases, aspects of audio and video files)	Explore data according to their content, discovering how content differs, how it helps with understanding.
Writing analytic memos	Manage the developing interpretations by keeping track of ideas as they occur, and building on them as progress is made.
Developing a coding schema	Manage ideas about data, in themes, concepts, etc. Structure and function may depend on methodology and style.
Coding	Capture what is going on with the data. Bring together similar data according to themes, concepts, etc. Generate codes from the text level or according to existing ideas as necessary, define the meaning and application of codes—especially in light of multimedia sources of data.
Retrieval of coded segments	Revisit coded data to assess similarity and difference, to consider how coding is helping analysis, and "where to go next"
Hyperlinking	Link data to other data segments and/or to other files to track process, contradiction, etc.
Recoding	Recode into broader or narrower themes or categories if appropriate and necessary. Perhaps bring data back together and think about them differently.
Organization of data	Organize data according to known facts and descriptive features to allow consideration of how these aspects play a role in understanding.
Mapping	Manage analytic processes by visualizing connections, relationships, patterns, processes, ideas.
Searching the database and the coding schema	Test ideas, interrogate subsets for similarity and difference, or generate another level of coding.
Generating output	Report on different aspects of progress and the project at any stage. Save as files to capture status at an analytic stage, or to work in other applications. Print out materials to get away from the computer and think and work in more "traditional" ways.

Adapted from Lewins and Silver (2007, 9).

7.3. Major QDAS Programs: Their Use and Special Features

At this writing, there are seven major QDAS programs that are worth consideration by music education researchers. Each, with the exception of Transana, provides the basic functionality that is portrayed in the preceding, including all of the steps in analysis that are noted in Table 7.1. Transana is included here because of its extensive support for video and audio analysis. It is worth noting that programs of this sort are in constant change as each vendor strives to respond to feedback from users. Table 7.2 provides a comparative analysis of basic information as of the date of publication and readers are encouraged to check the website for each software program for changes that are the result of new versions of each product. The website for each product provides ample displays of user interfaces and offers comment on the strengths of each offering. Unfortunately, a careful survey of independent analyses of each product from published sources does not provide a contemporary perspective that is current. Researchers will need to download the trial versions of each program and decide for themselves as to the product's worthiness for their research needs.

Each program provides its own special strengths for methodological approaches. For example, MAXQDA, QDAMiner, and Qualrus offer interesting options for mixed methods approaches since they include statistical functionality and ways to export data to quantitative tools. MAXQDA, for example, supports the importing of data from interviews, focus groups, online surveys, web pages, images, audio and video files, spreadsheets, and RIS data that use specialized tags. QDAMiner 4 offers integrated statistical and visualization tools, such as clustering, multidimensional scaling, heat maps, correspondence analysis, and sequence analysis. None of these software products offers the statistical capabilities of major quantitative packages such as R or SPSS, but they do offer excellent support for the integration of mixed approaches if the discoveries warrant such an approach.

For certain requirements in discourse analysis, search features offered by QSRNVivo, including "fuzzy" searches, might be of interest. For example, if investigating dense text that might contain multiple ways of expressing an idea, a fuzzy search strategy that uses wildcard characters can be used to maximize the likelihood of a hit.

Because of the requirements of multiple data sources in ethnography, the multiple data types allowed in ATLAS.ti, HyperRESEARCH, and Qualrus could be compelling. ATLAS.ti offers extensive flexibility in coding segments of video and audio that can be seen in relation to text files. Certainly for detailed work with video and audio, Transana is worth a careful look, perhaps in tandem with other more text-based/mixed methods programs such as Qualrus.

If a methodology requires strong collaboration capabilities, QSRNVivo and ATLAS.ti might be important because of tools designed for collaborative work and the offering of the software in many languages (German, French, Spanish, Japanese, and Chinese).

Table 7.2 Descriptive Information for QDAS Programs

Software	Website	OS Support	Cost (US)	Download Trial	Multimedia Data Types in Addition to Text	Modeling/Visualization	Collaboration
ATLAS.ti 7	www.atlasti.com/	Win[a]	$99 student $670 education	Yes	Yes	Yes	Yes
HyperRESEARCH 3.5	www.researchware.com/	Mac/Win	$199 student $495 education	Yes	Yes	Yes	Limited
MAXQDA 11	www.maxqda.com/	Win	$99 student $620 education	Yes	Yes	Yes	Yes
QDA Miner 4	http://provalisresearch.com/products/qualitative-data-analysis-software/	Win	$590 education	Yes	Images only	No	Yes
QSRNVivo 10	http://www.qsrinternational.com/default.aspx	Win	$670 education $215 student	Yes	Audio only	Yes	Yes
Qualrus	http://www.ideaworks.com/qualrus/index.html	Win	$399 education $179 student	Yes	Yes	Yes	Limited
Transana 2.5	http://www.transana.org/index.htm	Mac/Win	$65 education discount Wisconsin-based institution	Yes	Video and audio only	No	Yes

[a] Windows-only software will run on Macintosh platform when the Win OS is installed as an option.

Major QDAS titles are moving toward shared server spaces in the "cloud" so that teams of researchers might be able to assemble and code data in various parts of the world. As of this writing, two web-based qualitative platforms that feature collaboration were identified (Saturate (http://www.saturateapp.com/) and dedoose (http://www.dedoose.com/)). Such programs might be very useful for teams of music education researchers investigating problems concurrently. Use of these web-based approaches might be especially attractive when used in combination with the more sophisticated, stand-alone applications.

In addition, support for multiple platforms such as iPads and other mobile devices can be found in ATLAS.ti and other software. With the continued use of more powerful mobile devices in the field, this trend will likely continue in coming years.

Cost and platform support can be determining factors in choice. In all cases, educational pricing is available and student prices are available as options. Video demos of the software can be found both at the website for the product and online in the expected outlets such as YouTube. Trial versions vary in their capability but most are fully functional for a trial period and technical support from the vendor is offered for nearly all products noted here.

A caution about use of such software is important to note: in all cases, QDAS packages that are profiled in this chapter are not always immediately intuitive. In fact, they are complicated programs that will require some time to learn. Much like an extensive music notation program or a full-featured music sequencing package, the options are many and the paths to follow in their use are varied. For these reasons, support in the form of video demos, manuals, and training courses is important. The decision on the part of the researcher to use such software should be coupled with a willingness to invest time and effort in understanding the complexities. Investment of time and effort might be well worth it given the quality of return. The software will of course not interpret the findings and derive meaning for the research being done, but may well open pathways to the complexity of phenomena that might not otherwise be found.

7.4. QDAS Programs Used by Music Education Researchers

A study of the published literature in music education in the United States reveals that some researchers have used QDAS programs in their work. This section reviews a sampling of these studies in order to offer the reader a profile of their use. This is not meant as a comprehensive listing but does provide useful information for how researchers in our field have begun to use this kind of specialized software. Regrettably, not all accounts of the research in published form provide detail on how the particular software was used; a personal contact with the researcher might be necessary to answer more detailed questions about the options employed for the analysis. Researchers in music education might be advised to be more complete in their description of how QDAS programs were used in order to help readers understand the work accomplished and to add to their research creditability.

7.4.1. QSRNVivo

Carlow (2004) used QSRNVivo in a dissertation study completed at the University of Maryland. The purpose of the study was to explore the musical experiences of immigrant students in an American high school choral classroom. Data collection methods included: semi-structured and in-depth interviews, student and teacher surveys, observations, focus groups, and dialogue journal writing collected over a 10-month period. She imported Microsoft Word files into QSRNVivo and coded text to discover themes. In a study of young students' music preferences, Roulston (2006) used QSRNVivo in a similar way. She used the results of field notes and transcripts of interviews with children and parents to create codes that led to the identification of themes that were reported in the findings. Hunt (2009) studied the voices of rural and urban music teachers in order to develop a model of cultural awareness for music teaching. Interview data were coded in what appears to be a similar fashion to other researchers noted earlier.

Turner (2009) completed a dissertation at Teachers College, Columbia University, that offered more detail in her use of QSRNVivo. In this case study of mentoring music educators in gospel music, Turner describes the way she used the coding options to create hierarchies of coding structure and explained the use of researcher memos to help clarify her data.

> Using a computer program to code large amounts of data has both benefits and problems. . . . All files were imported and coded electronically, thereby eliminating the use of paper; this advantage saved space and was environmentally-friendly. I was able to find a file or code by searching for a word in the title. The memos feature was one of the most-used aspects of the program. I captured my thoughts midstream without having to exit NVivo 8 to use another program. Also I could refer back to the memo at a later time and continue my thoughts or revise and use the text for later inclusion in my dissertation. All memos and data files could be exported as Microsoft Word documents, which allowed me to access them without having to own NVivo 8. (92–93)

Tsugawa's (2009) work at Arizona State University on meaning construction in two New Horizon Band ensembles chronicles his decision to use QSRNVivo after struggling with more conventional ways to keep track of qualitative data. The purpose of this study was to investigate music learning, motivation, and meaning construction among members of two senior adult music ensembles. A qualitative, multiple case study design was used. His use of codes was similar to other researchers, but this study is more explicit on the codes used and how they formed the results.

Keeping data organized throughout the coding process proved to be a difficult task. Given the large amount of data, distilling the data and codes into broader categories and themes became time consuming as I electronically copied and moved scraps of data from the raw transcripts to various folders and subfolders on my computer. In order to manage the large volume of data collected in this study, I used NVivo 8, a qualitative data analysis software program. My initial data management and coding procedure allowed me to label data by specific categories. I was able to code, label, and categorize particular informant statements within the context of each individual informant's transcript. In order to compare and analyze individual informant statements with similar statements from other informants, I made multiple copies of each statement and placed these statements in separate NVivo files labeled by category, group, and participant. NVivo allowed me to expedite the analysis process by quickly organizing and connecting data by site, informant, and theme. (69–70)

7.4.2. Atlas.ti

Six studies were identified that used the Atlas.ti software in music education (Jaramilloa 2008; D. Kokotsaki 2011; D. Kokotsaki and Hallam 2007; D. Kokotsaki and Hallam 2011; Norgaard 2011; Walls 2008). All six of these studies simply indicated that they used the software and provided no details in how the features were used beyond the coding of text. This is disappointing because the software is quite powerful and provides a number of tools and techniques that can be used for good advantage in music education research.

7.4.3. HyperRESEARCH

Studies by Teachout (2004), Freer (2009), Barnes (2010), and Koops (2011) all used HyperRESEARCH for their data analysis. Again, few details were provided about how the software was used other than to suggest that codes were assigned to assist in analysis. Kelly-McHale (2011) completed a dissertation at Northwestern University on the subject of music identity in a general music classroom. Her use of HyperRESEARCH involved the recoding of transcriptions, adding definitions for each code, and checking this against literature. She added memos as needed. She used a report feature of HyperRESEARCH to provide a summary of the coding process before proceeding to the final solution.

7.4.4. HyperRESEARCH and Transana

One study was identified that used multiple QDSA programs, an approach that allowed the desirable qualities of each product to be used effectively. Tobias (2010) completed a Northwestern University study that examined the musical engagement and learning of secondary students in a songwriting and technology class that focused on the creation, performance, recording, and production of original music. His use of HyperRESEARCH was similar to Kelly-McHale, using codes and memos to help establish a report that could be studied. His use of Transana, however, was somewhat more complicated:

> The second analytical layer, transcription, focused on transcribing video and screencast data. Transana . . . was used to create two types of transcripts, one focusing on discourse and the other on actions. . . . Video data were first viewed with minimal manipulation to create a narrative transcript of gestures, forms of engagement, interactions, and events. In cases where little dialogue took place, discourse such as unstructured interviews between myself and the participant or conversation between participants was combined with the narrative transcript. The transcripts served as text-based descriptions or transformations of the digital video/audio data. Interviews were videotaped and treated the same as other video data with the focus on discourse except for situations when a particular action or visual cue was integral to the meaning of the discourse. (127)

In addition, Tobias used a number of additional software programs throughout his dissertation to explicate his data and to report findings. These included iMovie, Audacity, ScreenFlow, MindManager, DEVONThinkPro, and OmniFocus. This use of a number of software titles to complement QDSA products is an excellent model for researchers to consider, especially if their use enhances the theoretical and methodological intent.

7.5. Decision to Use QDAS

Clearly, qualitative music education researchers have been slow in adopting the use of QDAS. There are probably a wide range of reasons for this that relate to how such tools are somehow not in the "spirit" of the qualitative culture—that somehow the use of such tools makes one too quantitative. This, of course, is nonsense. Qualitative work is difficult, messy, and enormously challenging to do. Tools that bring order are not only desirable, but absolutely essential.

Are such programs necessary for all qualitative work? The simple answer is "no." Berg and Lind (2003) completed a qualitative study of preservice music teachers and portfolio use for reflective practice that used no such software. Blair (2007) used musical maps as narrative inquiry and Ellis (1996) used a layered analysis technique with video in studying children with special needs. These studies were completed without the reported aid of any QDAS assistance, but this does not preclude the fact that complicated sources of data do present themselves in many studies and the aids that QDAS provide could be a welcomed approach.

One view is that software of this sort gives the illusion of "doing the analysis" and that the products tend to channel the researcher into methodologies that are not intended. Davidson and diGregorio (2011) take a decidedly different tack:

We recognize that there is strong resistance to the notion that elements of analysis are common among diverse methodological approaches to qualitative research. This resistance is a residue, we believe, of the tough battles of legitimacy qualitative researchers fought to gain a position in academic and other circles. It is time, however, to put this one to rest. As the pressure for participation in the digital world increases, it is critical that qualitative researchers get beyond these artificial and self-imposed barriers they have erected and get on with more important tasks. (639)

QDAS programs are tools to assist in analysis and are not meant to dictate analytical solutions. Some aspects of certain programs might be more suited to one sort of methodology or another, as was noted earlier, but the decisions to use the features of software are always in the hands of the researcher.

Perhaps part of the reason that such software programs are not more often considered is that the teaching of qualitative research in our field typically does not include it. As younger professors who have more experience with technology in general and with QDAS programs in particular move into positions of authority as teachers of qualitative research, this may change.

Finally, QDAS software remains expensive and, in some cases, challenging to use. As social networking becomes a driving force for greater sharing, more collaboration, and enhanced creative thinking, the vendors of QDAS may well improve interfaces and reduce cost. Cloud-based solutions are likely to emerge and the use of smaller and more powerful hardware devices will become prevalent. The large emphasis on text analysis will be balanced with much more evidence based on audio and video records—thus changing and improving the functionality of the software and its use in the study of the arts in particular. Researchers studying the complexities of music teaching and learning and who imagine approaching their problems qualitatively in some form are encouraged to consider such software for organizing, managing, and finding meaning.

References

Barnes, G. 2010. "Teaching Music: The First Year." *Bulletin of the Council for Research in Music Education* 185 (Summer): 63–76.

Berg, M., and V. Lind. 2003. "Preservice Music Teacher Electronic Portfolios Integrating Reflection and Technology." *Journal of Music Teacher Education* 12 (2): 12–28. doi:10.1177/10570837030120020104.

Blair, D. 2007. "Musical Maps as Narrative Inquiry." *International Journal of Education and the Arts* 8 (15): 1–19. http://www.ijea.org/v7n9/.

Carlow, R. 2004. "Hearing Other's Voices: An Exploration of the Musical Experiences of Immigrant Students Who Sing in High School Choir." University of Maryland, College Park, ProQuest Dissertations Publishing. 3152852.

PhD diss., ProQuest Dissertation and Theses Database. UMI No. 3152852.

Davidson, J., and S. di Gregorio. 2011. "Qualitative Research and Technology." In *Sage Handbook of Qualitative Research*, edited by N. Denzin & Y. Lincon, 4th ed., 627–43. Thousand Oaks, CA: Sage Publications.

Ellis, P. 1996. "Layered Analysis: A Video-Based Qualitative Research Tool to Support the Development of a New Approach for Children with Special Needs." *Bulletin of the Council for Research in Music Education* 130: 65–74.

Freer, P. 2009. "Boys' Descriptions of Their Experiences in Choral Music." *Research Studies in Music Education* 31 (2): 142–60. doi:10.1177/1321103X09344382.

Hunt, C. 2009. "Perspectives on Rural and Urban Music Teaching: Developing Contextual Awareness in Music Education." *Journal of Music Teacher Education* 18 (2): 34–47. doi:10.1177/1057083708327613.

Jaramilloa, M. 2008. "The Music Educator's Professional Knowledge." *Music Education Research* 10 (3): 347–59. doi:10.1080/14613800802280084.

Kelly-McHale, J. 2011. "The Relationship between Children's Musical Identities and Muisc Teacher Beliefs and Practices in an Elementary General Music Classroom." Northwestern University, Evanston, IL, PhD, UMI No. 3456672.

Kokotsaki, D. 2011. "Student Teachers' Conceptions of Creativity in the Secondary Music Classroom." *Thinking Skills and Creativity* 6 (2): 100–113.

Kokotsaki, D., and S. Hallam. 2007. "Higher Education Music Students' Perceptions of the Benefits of Participative Music Making." *Music Education Research* 9 (1): 93–109. doi:10.1080/14613800601127577.

Kokotsaki, D., and S. Hallam. 2011. "The Perceived Benefits of Participative Music Making for Non-Music University Students: A Comparison with Music Students." *Music Education Research* 13 (2): 149–72. doi:10.1080/14613808.2011.577768.

Koops, L. H. 2011. "Perceptions of Current and Desired Involvement in Early Childhood Music Instruction." *Visions of Research in Music Education* 17 (1): 1–22.

Lewins, A., and C., Silver. (2007). *Using Software in Qualitative Research: A Step-by-Step Guide*. London: Sage Publications.

Norgaard, M. 2011. "Descriptions of Improvisational Thinking by Artist-Level Jazz Musicians." *Journal of Research in Music Education* 59 (2): 109–27. doi:10.1177/0022429411405669.

Roulston, K. 2006. "Qualitative Investigation of Young Children's Music Preferences." *International Journal of Education and the Arts* 7 (9): 1–22. http://ijea.org/v7n9/.

Rutkowski, J., P. Webster, and J. Gossett. 2012. "A Further Examination of Doctoral Programs in Music Education." Presented at the meeting of the Biennial Music Educators National Conference, St. Louis, MO.

Taylor, C., and G. Gibbs. 2010. *What Is Qualitative Data Analysis (QDA)?* http://onlineqda.hud.ac.uk/Intro_QDA/what_is_qda.php.

Teachout, D. 2004. "Factors Affecting Individuals' Decisions to Enter Music Teacher Education Doctoral Programs." *Action, Criticism, and Theory for Music Education* 3 (3): 1–25.

Tobias, E. 2010. "Crossfading and Plugging in: Secondary Students' Engagement and Learning in a Songwriting and Technology Class." Northwestern Univeristy, Evanston IL, PhD, ProQuest Dissertation and Theses Database. UMI No. 3402496.

Tsugawa, S. 2009. "Senior Adult Music Learning, Motivation, and Meaning Construction in Two New Horizons Ensembles." Arizona State University, Tempe, AZ, DMA, ProQuest Dissertation and Theses Database. UMI No. 3392131.

Turner, P. E. 2009. "Mentoring Music Educators in Gospel Music Pedagogy in the Classroom." Teachers College, Columbia University, EdD, ProQuest Dissertation and Theses Database. UMI No. 3391753.

Walls, K. 2008. "Distance Learning in Graduate Music Teacher Education Promoting Professional Development and Satisfaction of Music Teachers." *Journal of Music Teacher Education* 18 (1): 55–66. doi:10.1177/1057083708323137.

CHAPTER 8

CHANGING THE CONVERSATION

Considering Quality in Music Education Qualitative Research

MITCHELL ROBINSON

> The validity of experimental methods and quantitative measurement, appropriately used, was never in doubt. Now, qualitative methods have ascended to a level of parallel respectability. That ascendance was not without struggle and sometimes acrimonious debate and, to be sure, there are still backwaters where the debate lingers, but among serious methodologists and practitioners, the debate is, for all practical purposes, over.
>
> (Patton 2002, 265)

THE establishment of criteria for quality in qualitative research in music education has existed as a problematic issue within our profession for many years. The range of opinions and beliefs concerning "goodness" criteria for qualitative research is vast, and encompasses multiple belief systems, paradigm orientations, and research stances. The purpose of this chapter is to briefly review the conversation in our profession with respect to establishing and modifying evaluative criteria in qualitative research over the past several decades, to provide alternative approaches to considering issues of evaluation in qualitative inquiry in music education, and to extend the conversation as we consider our future as a research community.

8.1. REVIEWING THE CONVERSATION

As in our sister discipline of general education, scholars in music education have approached the issue of evaluative criteria when conducting qualitative research in multiple ways. The choice of what terms to use when discussing evaluative criteria reveals much about our professional conversation when it comes to these matters.

8.1.1. Words Matter

The words we use to describe our actions and intentions as researchers are powerful tools. These words do more than provide information about content and structure; they offer clues as to our beliefs about the profession, our research, and our view of the world. The conversation regarding qualitative inquiry—and among inquirers—in music education is characterized by fascinating literary turns and plot twists along the way, denoting our growth as scholars, and perhaps our self-esteem as a scholarly community.

The earliest examples of qualitative publications in music education professional journals are characterized by a notable brevity of methodological description. For example, a 1981 case study of a chromesthetic by Haack and Radocy in the *Journal of Research in Music Education* (*JRME*) includes only the following methodological information: "four interviews and testing sessions (were) conducted during the period 1974–79. Consistency of response to identical stimuli throughout the period was sought and documented as a means of internal validity. This was accomplished by means of structured interviews and testing sessions wherein responses were recorded via audio tape and data assessment forms for comparative analyses over time" (86–87).

Other early examples of qualitative work in music education scholarship are characterized by the use of quantitative evaluative terminology, such as *validity, reliability*, and *generalizability*. Reviewers and readers were comfortable with these terms, understood their meaning from their own experiences and knowledge base, and were able to apply them to what was a new and sometimes confusing approach to research. Authors of this period may have felt that using these terms was part of the "game" of doing publishable research, or may have learned these terms in their own research classes as graduate students. The following plaintive passage from the general education literature in an article by Finlay is especially pertinent, and expresses the ambivalence of many qualitative music education scholars regarding this issue:

> I sometimes worry that our preoccupation with evaluation criteria simply reflects our insecurities about the scientific status of our work as qualitative researchers. Does the mission to find and use appropriate criteria pander to the positivists? Aren't we just playing their game? Can't we be valued on our own terms? But then I see the other side of the argument. The reality is that we work in a competitive world where quantitative experimental methodology forms the bedrock of the dominant positivist paradigm. We have to play the "science game" if we have a hope of competing. It comes down to politics and PR. After all, there are many people out there who still need to be convinced: funding bodies, ethics committees, sceptical supervisors and examiners, to say nothing of the qualitative researchers themselves who have a stake in seeing high quality studies being disseminated. So it is with mixed feelings that I write this paper on "criteria," recognising it is both a game and a serious undertaking. (Finlay 2006, 321)

Even when qualitative evaluation strategies were employed, they were often applied in rather quantitative ways. For example, Baldridge (1984) used ethnographic observation strategies to make "qualitative comparisons" (81) between teacher-reported classroom behaviors and those teachers' responses to survey items in a study of listening activities in the elementary general music classroom, and then used a "Pearson intercorrelation" formula (81) to determine the statistical relationship between the two criteria.

Krueger's (1987) article in the *JRME* represents an important milestone for qualitative work in our discipline, advancing a more secure and sophisticated approach to describing the methodological traditions of the qualitative enterprise. Written as a sort of ethnographic "primer," this article offers a clear explanation of qualitative data collection, analysis, and evaluation strategies and techniques, while still framing the discussion with decidedly positivist terminology. Indeed, the headings for this discussion are parallel to their counterparts in quantitative design (i.e., reliability, validity, generalizability), perhaps in an attempt to assuage the "critics" Krueger refers to in the article.

For instance, in the "reliability" section of the article, Krueger acknowledged that critics of "field research" argued that "external reliability" was a major concern with this form of scholarship, and suggested the following strategies for addressing these concerns, after Le Compte and Goetz (1982):

(1) identification and description of the researcher's role;
(2) description and background of the subjects;
(3) descriptions of settings in which observations take place;
(4) identification of methods for data collection and analysis; and
(5) explanation and outline of the theoretical framework guiding the study. (Krueger 1987, 73)

Perhaps more notable, and even provocative for its time, was Krueger's assertion that "validity," rather than being a liability of qualitative inquiry, was "a major strength of qualitative research, since the flexibility of data collection and interviews allows the researcher to examine the knowledge and meanings construed by the participant" (73–74).

In any event, these positivist terms were an awkward and unsatisfactory "fit" for the paradigm and frameworks being used in these studies, and researchers began to suggest new sets of criteria. The eminent qualitative scholars Lincoln and Guba (1985) proposed four criteria for what they termed "naturalistic" research, and due to the significance of their contribution to this discussion, I have summarized these criteria, and the primary techniques used for each, in the following in some detail.

- **Credibility**: Involves establishing that results of qualitative research are credible or believable from the perspective of the participant in the research. Since the purpose of qualitative research is to describe or understand the phenomena of interest from the participant's eyes, the participants are the only ones who can legitimately judge the credibility of the results. (Techniques: member checks; prolonged engagement in the field; data triangulation.)

- **Transferability**: Refers to the degree to which the results of qualitative research can be generalized or transferred to other contexts or settings. Transferability is primarily the responsibility of the one doing the generalizing. Can be enhanced by doing a thorough job of describing the research context and the assumptions that were central to the research. The person who wishes to "transfer" the results to a different context is then responsible for making the judgment of how sensible the transfer is. (Techniques: thick description of setting and/or participants.)
- **Dependability**: The traditional view of reliability is based on the assumption of replicability or repeatability, concerned with whether we would obtain the same results if we could observe the same thing twice. But this is impossible—by definition if we are measuring twice, we are measuring two different things. Dependability, on the other hand, emphasizes the need for the researcher to account for the ever-changing context within which research occurs. The researcher is responsible for describing the changes that occur in the setting and how these changes affected the way the research approached the study. (Techniques: audit trail; researcher's documentation of data, methods, and decisions; researcher triangulation.)
- **Confirmability**: Each researcher brings a unique perspective to the study. Confirmability refers to the degree to which the results could be confirmed or corroborated by others. There are a number of strategies for enhancing confirmability. The researcher can document the procedures for checking and rechecking the data throughout the study. Another researcher can take a "devil's advocate" role with respect to the results, and this process can be documented. The researcher can actively search for and describe *negative instances* that contradict prior observations. And, after the study, one can conduct a *data audit* that examines the data collection and analysis procedures and makes judgments about the potential for bias or distortion. (Techniques: audit trail and reflexivity.)

While the preceding set of criteria was clearly structured as "parallel terms" to traditional quantitative notions of internal validity, external validity, reliability, and objectivity, they provided an important and useful bridge for qualitative scholars. Later, Guba and Lincoln (1989) added a fifth set of criteria to their list, "authenticity," that was unique to constructivist assumptions and could be used to evaluate the quality of the research beyond the methodological dimensions.

By 1989, a discernible shift in both language use and methodological descriptiveness in our professional literature can be noticed. DeLorenzo's article on sixth-grade students' creative music problem-solving processes includes the following methodological statement: "The following steps were taken to ensure consistency and credibility in data collection and analysis" (191). Note the use of alternative terms (i.e., *consistency* rather than *reliability*, and *credibility* rather than *validity*), a signal that paradigm-specific language was beginning to find acceptance in our professional literature—albeit sparingly. DeLorenzo's article is also noticeably more descriptive in terms of the protocols followed throughout the research process, including nearly two pages of information on participants ("sample," 192), an audit trail ("procedures," 192), and data-collection techniques.

Schleuter's 1991 study on student teachers' pre-active and post-active curricular thinking represents another important evolutionary step in the language and thinking surrounding qualitative research in music education; in this case, regarding the notion of "generalizability" in the qualitative paradigm. The author cites Shulman's definitions of two forms of "generalizability": *across-people*, "not appropriate for ethnographic research" (48), and *across-situations*, which was deemed pertinent to the study at hand. While still appropriating largely positivist terminology, the contribution here was to prod our collective thinking in respect to a basic tenet of research in music education—that in order for results to be meaningful, they must be applicable broadly; to other students, schools, or populations. Schleuter goes on to suggest that rather than being concerned with the ability to widely generalize the results of the findings, a primary goal of ethnographic work was to construct new understandings from observing the actions and behaviors of participants, and that these understandings were, by definition, subjective rather than objective. She includes a warning regarding generalizing the results of the study: "generalizability of these findings should be made only to situations most like the ones described in this study" (58).

Creswell (2007, 20–22) provides another set of guidelines for qualitative authors, consisting of techniques and strategies for ensuring the "goodness" of one's study design and write-up. While not in the form of evaluative criteria per se, these suggestions are offered as helpful reminders to those engaged in qualitative work:

- **Employ** rigorous data collection, using multiple forms of data, summarized and presented in various ways (tables, charts, graphs).
- **Frame** the study with a qualitative approach, acknowledging evolving design, multiple truths, the researcher as primary data collection instrument, and a strong focus on the voice(s) of participant(s).
- **Use** a tradition of inquiry, demonstrating a full and complete knowledge of the design's history and philosophical foundations.
- **Begin** with a single focus, starting with a single idea or problem, not a relationship among variables or comparisons of groups.
- **Include** detailed methods, using established and multiple data-collection, analysis, and verification procedures.
- **Write** persuasively, so that the reader is drawn into the research setting, scene, or situation.
- **Analyze** data in multiple levels, moving from particular to general layers of abstraction.
- **Writing** should be clear, engaging, and full of unexpected ideas.

8.1.2. The Narrative "Turn"

At this point the conversation is still functioning as though firmly rooted in a scientific world, and the discussion is being conducted using the terms and tools of the academician. This traditional approach to research has been dominated in large part by a modern, positivist viewpoint—a viewpoint that may have been useful for the "business" of doing research (gaining acceptance from reviewers, having pieces approved for publication, obtaining promotion and tenure), but was still somewhat at odds with the very nature of the questions being asked and the forms of knowledge being sought.

The "narrative turn" in qualitative inquiry reflects an awareness among those in the broader scholarly community that our goals can be more expansive, and our gaze can be lifted.

> The narrative turn moves away from a singular, monolithic conception of social science toward a pluralism that promotes multiple forms of representation and research; away from facts and toward meanings; away from master narratives and toward local stories; away from idolizing categorical thought and abstracted theory and toward embracing the values of irony, emotionality, and activism; away from assuming the stance of the disinterested spectator and toward assuming the posture of a feeling, embodied, and vulnerable observer; away from writing essays and toward telling stories. (Bochner 2001, 134–35)

A study by Wiggins (1994) shows a further development of qualitative evaluation strategies and terminology. With children's compositional problem-solving strategies as the focus of her study, the author devotes nearly four pages of the manuscript to a detailed discussion of the research process, paying special attention to issues of "participant selection" (including the identification of two "target children"), data collection and sources, and an elegant explication of her "role as researcher." In terms of evaluative criteria, Wiggins provides information on data and participant triangulation techniques and provisions for establishing credibility based on suggestions from Lincoln and Guba (1985), including "prolonged engagement, persistent observation, and negative case analysis" (237).

Wiggins' article is one of the first music education research publications to adopt completely the qualitative terminology that many scholars now accept as common, and to use it comfortably and fluently to describe the uniqueness of the qualitative research process. Her thick descriptions of classroom activities, copious use of students' music notation examples, snippets of dialogue, and the weaving in of interpretive musings throughout the discussion paint a vivid picture of both her classroom and the research process, and welcome the reader into the setting in which the study was conducted.

Like Schleuter, Wiggins warns that "it would be inappropriate to draw broad generalizations to the field or to imply that these findings have implications outside the realm of my own classroom" (250). However, she continues, "Whether other children in other class settings would use similar strategies in solving compositional problems remains to be seen. I hope, however, that this discussion of findings as they relate to my own music classroom might help others gain insight into their situations." We see here the recognition that "generalizability," or *credibility* as Wiggins employs the term, is about giving the reader enough information to make her or his own decisions regarding what and what not to believe, and that the knowledge gained here was primarily local—with the recognition that it may have implications for others in similar situations.

An article by Della Pietra and Campbell (1995) shows a further solidification of qualitative evaluation strategies at work. In a study exploring the influence of improvisation training in a college music methods course, the authors demonstrate a fluency and comfort with the tools of qualitative inquiry through their use of techniques and terms such as "think-aloud protocols," "data and investigator triangulation," and "informants." As in Wiggins's writing, this article draws the reader into the "classroom culture" established through the research activities, and allows the audience to compare and contrast their own experiences with those of the participants.

8.1.3. A New Vocabulary

As alternative approaches to constructing evaluative criteria continued to emerge, researchers became bolder in asserting new metaphorical and conceptual foundations for establishing evaluative criteria. Polkinghorne (1983) emphasized the artistic possibilities inherent in narrative work. He suggests that qualities such as *vividness, accuracy, richness*, and *elegance* (Polkinghorne 1984) are useful criteria for judging the trustworthiness of phenomenological interpretation:

> Is the research vivid in the sense that it generates a sense of reality and draws the reader in? Are readers able to recognise the phenomenon from their own experience or from imagining the situation vicariously? In terms of richness, can readers enter the account emotionally? Finally, has the phenomenon been described in a graceful, clear, poignant way? (Finlay 2008, 12)

In art education, Eisner further crystallizes this dialectical turn in both our evaluative terminology and our very orientation to the research enterprise: "Educational research is now a species of scientific inquiry using the language of propositions.... The realities of the classroom are an array of qualities for which meanings are construed and will always present more than propositional language can capture. We need a language capable of conveying qualities" (1984, 447).

Eisner argues for our adoption of the language of criticism and metaphor, and to turn toward the humanities for frameworks of reference and language. As Eisner's notions of educational connoisseurship and criticism begin to coalesce into a viable research mode, he predicts the emergence of a new dialogue regarding our evaluative "moves" as researchers:

> Over time, descriptive language becomes less mechanical, more incisive and increasingly literary or poetic as students try to get at the essence of what is occurring.... [This] requires ... not only sensitivity to the emerging qualities of

classroom life, but also a set of ideas, theories and models that enable one to distinguish the significant from the trivial. (1985c, 221)

Richardson (1992) also proffers an offering of literary, rather than solely scientific, dimensions for our consideration in evaluating qualitative study: *substantive contribution; aesthetic merit; reflexivity; impact*; and *expression of a reality*. Advocating for the use of poetry and other literary forms in scholarly writing, Richardson suggests that "increasingly ethnographers desire to write ethnography which is both scientific—in the sense of being true to a world known through the empirical senses—and literary—in the sense of expressing what one has learned through evocative writing techniques and form. More and more ways of representing ethnographic work emerge" (1992, 253).

Finlay leaves us with the following thought:

> Qualitative criteria offer a way for researchers to move beyond accounting for their evidence in terms of scientific criteria. Instead, the criteria direct us to address the **special qualities** of qualitative research and to explore the broader impact and social relevance of a particular project. Criteria also help us explore both strengths and weaknesses. For instance, a particular piece of research may be poorly evidenced or lack rigour, but it might still have value in its power and relevance. Alternatively, a particularly rigorous study, while lacking literary force, may carry its validation through its claims to "science." The challenge lies in selecting the criteria which best suits the research being conducted.

The next section of this chapter will engage in a discussion of alternative criteria for judging our work as qualitative music education scholars.

8.2. Alternative Approaches to Establishing and Selecting Evaluative Criteria in Qualitative Inquiry in Music Education

In considering approaches to evaluative criteria in qualitative music education, we are reminded of similar challenges in the related disciplines of historical musicology and ethnomusicology. Efforts to make value judgments on music's worth, quality, and "goodness" across genres and styles are fraught with peril and doomed to failure. There is not a single set of evaluative criteria, for instance, for judging the merit of a Renaissance motet against that of a Western African drumming performance. Each genre is distinguished by its emphasis on specific musical elements, qualities, and techniques, not to mention each genre's situatedness in widely different communities of musical, social, and cultural practices.

8.2.1. Choosing Our Words

In an effort to stimulate this conversation, I provide the following discussion based on Patton's (2002) alternative criteria for evaluating qualitative studies. As Patton points out, the goal of this discussion is both illustrative and pragmatic:

> With what perspectives and by what criteria will our work be judged by those who encounter and engage it? By understanding the criteria that others bring to bear on our work, we can anticipate their reactions and help them position our intentions and criteria in relation to their expectations and criteria, a dialogue I find that I spend a great deal of time engaged in. (Patton 2002, 7)

Patton advances five alternative sets of criteria for judging quality and credibility of qualitative research based on the major stages of development in qualitative inquiry, as suggested by Denzin and Lincoln (2000):

- Traditional scientific research criteria;
- Social construction and constructivist criteria;
- Artistic and evocative criteria;
- Critical change criteria; and
- Pragmatic utilitarianism.

In the following section, I will flesh out the specific evaluative techniques, strategies, and stances employed within each of the preceding sets of criteria and qualitative approaches, informing the discussion with brief examples from a seminal study from the music education research literature that is situated within each approach. Due to space constraints, only short snippets from each study can be included in the following text; for further information, I encourage the reader to find each of the cited articles to read in their entirety.

8.2.1.1. *Traditional Scientific Research Criteria*

Given the preponderance of quantitative research in our history as a scholarly discipline, some authors have chosen to adopt the terms and stances of the scientific paradigm in their qualitative work, while conducting their inquiries using ethnographic techniques, such as interviews and observations, as data collection strategies. Their goals here are accuracy, objectivity, and minimizing observer bias, all of which reference the priorities placed on the strictures of traditional scientific inquiry.

In "Prediction of Performer Attentiveness Based on Rehearsal Activity and Teacher Behavior," Yarbrough and Price (1981) provide an excellent example of this approach to data collection and analysis. The purpose of this descriptive study was to examine the attentiveness of student musicians in relation to their teachers' rehearsal techniques and behaviors. The authors collected the data by observation and video recordings of subject responses, and coded the data through time-sampling the recordings into 5- and 10-second intervals. The video recordings were taken by two "media technicians (who) ... surrounded the group during the recorded rehearsals," and "two trained observers" (211) who reviewed the videotapes for instances of student off-task behaviors and teacher eye contact. The procedures outlined here confirm the tenets of this approach as conveyed by Patton:

> Those working within this tradition will emphasize rigorous and systematic data collection procedures, for example, cross-checking and cross-validating sources during fieldwork. In analysis it means, whenever possible, using multiple coders and calculating inter-coder consistency to establish the validity and reliability of pattern and theme analysis. (2002, 266–67)

Rigorous reporting procedures and mandates in the health care industry have also influenced our colleagues in music therapy to adopt the language and protocols found in medical research to the smaller sample sizes and client-focused settings common in the field of music therapy research, forging a unique hybrid of small-scale design analyzed through a scientific and statistical lens.

8.2.1.2. *Social Construction and Constructivist Criteria*

Following Lincoln and Guba, constructivists and interpretivists have forged a new lexicon of terms to explain their approaches to conducting research in naturalistic settings. Rather than relying on words like "validity" and "reliability" to describe their data, constructivist researchers talk about the "credibility" of their findings, acknowledge the subjectivity of their results, and employ triangulation strategies to represent multiple perspectives from stakeholders.

In "Painting a Big Soup: Teaching and Learning in a Second Grade General Music Classroom," Wiggins and Bodoin (1998) looked at the ways in which students and teachers in an elementary music classroom made meaning and reflected on their mutual learning. In keeping with their social constructivist approach to research, the authors made use of strategies such as data triangulation, negative case analysis, and member checks to analyze the data and represent the beliefs and understandings of both students and teachers. The attention to detail and the rich, thick descriptions of teaching-learning interactions woven throughout the narrative are indicative of the constructivist's perspective:

> They view the social world (as opposed to the physical world) as socially, politically and psychologically constructed, as are human understandings and explanations of the physical world. They triangulate to capture and report multiple perspectives rather than seek a singular truth. Constructivists embrace subjectivity as a pathway deeper into understanding the human dimensions of the world in general as well as whatever specific phenomena they are examining. (Patton 2002, 8)

8.2.1.3. *Artistic and Evocative Criteria*

Exploring the boundaries between the arts and sciences has long been at the core of the creative experience. The acceptance of research that blurs these boundaries has faced rather more scrutiny in the academic community. Patton asserts that artistic criteria are legitimate evaluative tools for assessing the quality of research, a suggestion that should find an appreciative audience in the qualitative music education community.

According to Patton,

> Artistic criteria focus on aesthetics, creativity, interpretive vitality, and expressive voice. Case studies become literary works. Poetry or performance art may be used to enhance the audience's direct experience of the essence that emerges from analysis. Artistically-oriented qualitative analysts seek to engage those receiving the work, to connect with them, move them, provoke and stimulate. Creative nonfiction and fictional forms of representation blur the boundaries between what is "real" and what has been created to represent the essence of a reality, at least as it is perceived, without a literal presentation of that perceived reality. (10)

In "Second Chair: An Autoethnodrama," Saldaña offers a deft, heartbreaking, and poignant glimpse into the world of the high school band experience. The author casts the play as "a metaphor for the feelings of lesser status experienced by the marginalized individual in a competitive mainstream society" (2008, 277), and uses his own experiences as a high school clarinetist to explore issues of race, ethnicity, gender, and sexual orientation.

Saldaña uses the metaphor of "first chair–second chair" status to represent issues of discrimination and marginalization, framing these concepts in a context that is easily understandable to his audience of music teacher educators:

> The autoethnodramatic format provides me with a forum for sharing messages of personal and vital importance to fellow artists and educators. If musicians can understand the feelings accorded to someone of "second chair" status, they can hopefully understand the feelings of the marginalized individual in a competitive mainstream society: ". . . it's always feeling and sometimes being treated as lesser than, second best, like playing a cheap-ass plastic Bundy when you'd rather be playing an ebony wood Selmer with a glass mouthpiece. (2008, 13)

Patton suggests that artistic criteria include being provocative, connecting with and moving one's audience, expressing your message in a distinct "voice," and conveying a "true," "authentic," or "real" sense of purpose to the reader. In my review of Saldaña's autoethnodrama, I wrote the following:

> Comparing the strength and depth of my recollected feelings to my relatively subdued response to merely reading the play makes me wonder if the very power of the actual performance is indeed a form of arts-based trustworthiness for the value of ethnodrama as narrative inquiry. As a music teacher educator, I wonder if we

might "transform" the typical Introduction to Music Education class assignment of writing one's musical autobiography by having students perform these stories as autoethnodramas? How much more powerful and transformative would these stories become if they were dramatized, and shared with one's classmates? (Robinson 2008, 207)

8.2.1.4. *Critical Change Criteria*

One of the hallmarks of the traditional research design process is the neutral, detached stance the researcher is expected to take in respect to the subjects or sample population, and the sense of objectivity maintained throughout the research process. In direct contrast to this position, "Critical theorists set out to use research to critique society, raise consciousness, and change the balance of power in favor of those less powerful" (Patton 2002, 11). Critical scholars such as Patti Lather (critical feminist theory), Paulo Freire (pedagogy of the oppressed), and Tom Barone (emancipatory educational story-sharing) have broken new ground in educational research, proposing activist strategies designed to redress injustices and improve social and learning conditions for marginalized populations.

Koza (2002), in "A Realm without Angels: MENC's Partnerships with Disney and Other Major Corporations," turns her attention to the relationship between the Music Educators National Conference (MENC) (now the National Association for Music Education) and the Walt Disney Company, as well as MENC's relationship with other major corporations, and the implications that these partnerships may have on school funding and other issues. As Patton tells us, "Those engaged in qualitative inquiry as a form of critical analysis aimed at social and political change eschew any pretense of open-mindedness or objectivity; they take an activist stance" (2002, 11).

Koza begins the article with what is sometimes referred to as a "bias dump," or what LeCompte and Preissle (1993) term as "coming clean":

> My interest in partnerships between the MENC and major corporations such as Disney dates back to 1996 when I was invited to attend a free premiere screening of the movie, *Mr. Holland's Opus*. . . . I did not like the film much even though I agreed with its message that public schools and public school music should be adequately funded, and I was sorry that MENC had entered into a partnership to promote it. . . . I soon discovered that the film itself was but one small part of a much larger story about MENC's deepening involvement in educational/business partnerships. (Koza 2002, 72)

The rest of the article reads much like a well-researched investigative report, focusing on the relationship between financial incentives, tax breaks, and other special considerations given to major corporations, collectively known as "corporate welfare" (Koza 2002, 73), and the damage caused by these concessions to the financial infrastructure of the public schools—and, by extension, to public school music programs. The author examines public tax records, corporate financial reports, and studies conducted by business/industry watchdog groups, and uses this information to provide a richly detailed case study of one company's corporate practices and the complicated impact that these practices have on the finances of public education. Koza's work here is an excellent example of what Patton defines as the most important goal of this form of inquiry: "While the term 'critical' gets used in many different ways and contexts in relation to research and theory, what it almost always connotes is an interest in and commitment to social change" (2002, 12).

8.2.1.5. *Pragmatic Utilitarianism*

There is a long-standing tradition of using qualitative methods in the field of educational program evaluation, where the techniques of the ethnographer are applied to gathering data regarding the efficiency and effectiveness of teaching methods, pedagogical approaches, and teachers. As Patton states: "The focus is on answering concrete questions using practical methods and straightforward analysis while appreciating that those who use evaluations apply both 'truth tests'—are the findings accurate and valid?—and 'utility tests'—are the findings relevant and useful?" (2002, 12).

Conway (2002), in "Perceptions of Beginning Teachers, Their Mentors and Administrators Regarding Preservice Music Teacher Preparation," used multiple forms of data (i.e., questionnaires, individual and focus group interviews, classroom observations, teacher journals, researcher's log) from various stakeholders to present a portrait of the strengths, weaknesses, and challenges inherent in the music teacher preparation curriculum at "Big Ten University," or "BTU" (21). The author triangulated the data by seeking information from the beginning teachers, their assigned mentors, and the building administrators responsible for evaluating these novice educators. By turning the reflective lens to her own institution's program, Conway addressed both local and professional goals: "I sought to improve the preservice music teacher education program at BTU for the students and faculty involved in that program. In addition, I attempted to gather information about preservice music teacher education that might have relevance for preservice preparation programs that are similar to the one provided by BTU" (4).

The pragmatic criteria used to evaluate this form of scholarship allow the researcher to "engage in straightforward qualitative inquiry answering concrete questions aimed at largely descriptive answers, e.g. what do participants in programs report as strengths and weaknesses, without locating the inquiry within some major philosophical, ontological, or epistemological tradition. Grassroots practitioners have concrete questions and information needs that can be answered in straightforward ways through qualitative inquiry and they judge the answers pragmatically by their utility, relevance, and applicability" (Patton 2002, 12).

8.3. Continuing the Conversation

8.3.1. Listening to Other Voices

In her Senior Researcher Award acceptance speech in 1996, Cornelia Yarbrough suggested, "The goal of all research in music should be a product that contributes to knowledge about music and musical behavior" (190). It is our challenge and our responsibility as scholars to recognize if our goal for a specific research project is "knowing that," "knowing of," or "knowing more."

Perhaps we need to concern ourselves not just with the goals of our research, but with its potential impact on teaching and learning. The disconnect between theory and practice is a consistent and long-maligned theme in educational research. According to Bresler, applied research is concerned primarily "with the improvement of practice and of materials," while basic research is "concerned with deep understanding and the generation of theory" (1996, 6).

Eisner (1985a, 255–68) asks the question even more bluntly: "can educational research inform educational practice?" His answer: "We study education through social science disciplines which were originally meant for rat maze learning. . . . We have built a technology of educational practice . . . of commando raids on the classroom. . . . So often what is educationally significant, but difficult to measure, is replaced with that which is insignificant, but easy to measure" (Eisner 1985b, 12). To illustrate his point, Eisner notes that 10 studies in the 1981 American Educational Research Journal reported on a range of experimental treatments, with a "median exposure time per student" of a little more than an hour. "Data were collected during these brief visits and processed back at the research 'laboratory,' then decently buried in obscure journals" (in Swanwick 1996, 18).

Bresler (1996, 12) posits the following: "Central to any disciplined inquiry is the issue of trustworthy criteria. Some criteria are important to all research, quantitative and qualitative, whereas others are more specific to a particular paradigm, or to applied or basic orientations. In consideration of merit, it seems that the most important criterion for any research is that it is about something important to researchers as well as readers."

8.3.2. Changing the Conversation

In many ways, our conversation has been stuck—stuck in a false debate between notions of realism and relativism. As Kerlinger (1979) said, "the procedures of science are objective, not the scientists. Scientists, like all men and women are opinionated, dogmatic, ideological . . . that is the very reason for insisting on procedural objectivity; to get the whole business outside of ourselves" (264).

With the growing knowledge that the empiricists' dualism of subject and object was impossible, much energy has been expended in the past several decades on first working around this duality in ways that would allow for claims of "knowing reality," and then with creating elaborate sets of knowledge points—or criteria—that would serve to judge claims of truth or empirical quality. While this realist approach may have "worked" so long as we adopted the traditional tools and processes of the scientific method, these criteria have proven to be an awkward fit for those of us engaged in more relativist forms of inquiry.

Many scholars have struggled with a "quasi-foundationalist" approach (Smith and Deemer 2000, 880), functioning in a nether-world of conundrums. "Any elaboration of criteria must take place within the context of . . . ontological realism on the one side and, on the other, their realization that they are obligated to accept a constructivist epistemology" (880). For these authors, the challenge has been to try to fit the "square peg" of work informed by a postmodern worldview into the "round hole" of positivist criteria and publishing requirements designed to accommodate traditional research products. Even when we are "successful" at reconciling these contradictory belief systems, we are left to wonder if the end result is worth the bargain.

Music education research journal editors and review board members also struggle with this issue in the context of their responsibilities as "gatekeepers" in the publication arena. Using one set of guidelines or criteria to make judgments about the merits of two submissions, one carried out as an experimental study with a sample size of 200, and the other conducted as an ethnographic case study of a single informant, would seem a dubious proposition at best. At many of our institutions the differences between quantitative and qualitative research are recognized by the existence of separate review boards and evaluative criteria. As research teachers and advisors, we would not presume to guide these two projects in the same way, and yet our professional publications have resisted the establishment of specific sets of criteria for particular methodological approaches.

In a 1987 article in the *American Educational Research Journal*, Smith made the following observation:

> The policy of the *AERJ* editors to encourage the submission of qualitative research will be welcomed by qualitative researchers of all types. Such a policy can only mean that editors will use different criteria to judge and select such studies from those they use for experiments and surveys. Editors should also understand that different ideologies exist within the discipline of qualitative research. To send a manuscript submitted by an interpretivist to a systematist (or vice versa) is more likely to provoke unresolvable methodological debate than meaningful criticism or fair editorial recommendations. The editors must become ethnographers of the culture of qualitative research. Then reviews can be fairly solicited and properly understood. (Smith 1987, 182)

Perhaps as we listen to the many different voices that have contributed to our discussions about criteria, it is time we change the conversation from one that emphasizes *discovery* and *finding*, to one that stresses *constructing* and *making* (Smith and Deemer 2000). Rather than spending our time as scholars, advisors, reviewers, and editors attempting to judge work with a "one size fits all" set of guidelines, we need to better acquaint ourselves with the options at our disposal. Denzin (1997) suggests that we have entered the era of the "new ethnography," and that "the stories ethnographers will tell to each other will change, and the criteria for reading stories will also change" (87).

I will close the chapter by asking the reader to consider the following questions, and suggest that our answers should provoke further conversation with our colleagues, especially those with whom we disagree:

- Is it our goal to know a specific thing (i.e., the effect of one variable upon another, or the relationship between two or more musical or education constructs), or to explore a group, a phenomenon, a happening, or an occurrence so as to further our understanding of what is happening in these settings?
- Is it our goal to measure the effectiveness of a particular teaching method or approach against another, or to know more about the choices and beliefs of a group of teachers, students, or community members?
- Is it our goal to test a hypothesis of a predicted interaction, or to work toward change when we perceive inequity, unfairness, or a lack of justice?
- Is it the goal of "all" research to produce a product or measure a behavior, or sometimes simply to begin a conversation?
- Is it our task to provide an answer, or to provoke a thought?

To paraphrase Gombrich (2000), artists do not paint what they can see, they see what they can paint. Perhaps in respect to research in music education, we do not sing what we can hear, we hear what we can sing.

References

Baldridge, W. R., II. 1984. "A Systematic Investigation of Listening Activities in the Elementary General Music Classroom." *Journal of Research in Music Education* 32 (2): 79–93.

Bochner, A. P. 2001. "Narrative's Virtues." *Qualitative Inquiry* 7: 131–57.

Bresler, L. 1996. "Basic and Applied Qualitative Research in Music Education." *Research Studies in Music Education* 6 (1): 5–17.

Conway, C. 2002. "Perceptions of Beginning Teachers, Their Mentors, and Administrators Regarding Preservice Music Teacher Preparation." *Journal of Research in Music Education* 50 (1): 20–36.

Creswell, J. W. 2007. *Qualitative Inquiry and Research Design: Choosing among Five Approaches*. 2nd ed. Thousand Oaks, CA: Sage Publications.

Della Pietra, C. J., and P. S. Campbell. 1995. "An Ethnography of Improvisation Training in a Music Methods Course." *Journal of Research in Music Education* 43 (2): 112–26.

DeLorenzo, L. C. 1989. "A Field Study of Sixth-Grade Students' Creative Music Problem-Solving Processes." *Journal of Research in Music Education* 37 (3): 188–200.

Denzin, N. K. 1997. *Interpretive Ethnography: Ethnographic Practices for the 21st Century*. Thousand Oaks, CA: Sage Publications.

Denzin, N. K., and Y. S. Lincoln. 2000. "Introduction: The Discipline and Practice of Qualitative Research." In *Handbook of Qualitative Research*, 2nd ed., edited by N. Denzin and Y. S. Lincoln, 1–28. Thousand Oaks, CA: Sage Publications.

Eisner, E. W. 1984. "Can Educational Research Inform Educational Practice?" *Phi Delta Kappan* 65: 447.

Eisner, E. W. 1985a. *The Art of Educational Evaluation*. London; Philadelphia: The Falmer Press.

Eisner, E. W. 1985b. "Creative Education in American Schools Today." *Educational Horizons* 63: 12.

Finlay, L. 2008. *An Introduction to Phenomenology.* Available for download at: http://www.lindafinlay.co.uk/publications.htm.

Finlay, L. 2006. "Rigour, Ethical Integrity or Artistry? Reflexively Reviewing Criteria for Evaluating Qualitative Research." *British Journal of Occupational Therapy* 69 (7): 319–26.

Gombrich, E. H. 2000. *Art and Illusion: A Study in the Psychology of Pictorial Representation.* 11th ed. Princeton, NJ: Princeton University Press.

Guba, E. G., and Y. S. Lincoln. 1989. *Fourth Generation Evaluation.* Newbury Park, CA: Sage Publications.

Haack, P. A., and R. E. Radocy. 1981. "A Case Study of a Chromesthetic." *Journal of Research in Music Education* 29 (2): 85–90.

Kerlinger, F. 1979. "Behavioral Research." New York: Holt, Rinehart and Winston.

Koza, J. E. 2002. "A Realm without Angels: MENC's Partnerships with Disney and Other Major Corporations." *Philosophy of Music Education Review* 10 (2): 72–79.

Krueger, P. J. 1987. "Ethnographic Research Methodology in Music Education." *Journal of Research in Music Education* 35 (2): 69–77.

LeCompte, M. D., and J. P. Goetz. 1982. "Problems of Reliability and Validity in Ethnographic Research." *Review of Educational Research* 52 (1): 31–60.

LeCompte, M. D., and J. Preissle. 1993. *Ethnography and Qualitative Design in Educational Research.* San Diego, CA: Academic Press.

Lincoln, Y., and E. Guba. 1985. *Naturalistic Inquiry.* Thousand Oaks, CA: Sage Publications.

Patton, M. Q. 2002. "Two Decades of Developments in Qualitative Inquiry: A Personal, Experiential Perspective." *Qualitative Social Work* 1: 261–83.

Polkinghorne, D. E. 1983. *Methodology for the Human Sciences.* Albany, NY: State University of New York Press.

Polkinghorne, D. E. 1984. "Further Extensions of Methodological Diversity for Counseling Psychology. *Journal of Counseling Psychology* 31 (4): 416–429.

Richardson, L. 1992. "The Consequences of Poetic Representation." In *Investigating Subjectivity*, edited by C. Ellis and M. Flaherty, 125–37. Thousand Oaks, CA: Sage Publications.

Robinson, M. 2008. "From Competition to Collaboration: Lessons from the 'Second Chair.'" *Research Studies in Music Education* 30 (2): 202–08.

Saldaña, J. 2008. "Second Chair: An Autoethnodrama." *Research Studies in Music Education* 30 (2): 177–191.

Schleuter, L. 1991. "Student Teachers' Preactive and Postactive Curricular Thinking." *Journal of Research in Music Education* 39 (1): 46–63.

Smith, J. K., and D. K. Deemer. 2000. "The Problem of Criteria in the Age of Relativism." In *Handbook of Qualitative Research*, 2nd ed., edited by N. K. Denzin and Y. S. Lincoln, 877–96. Thousand Oaks, CA: Sage Publications.

Smith, M. L. 1987. "Publishing Qualitative Research." *American Educational Research Journal* 24 (2): 173–83.

Swanwick, K. 1996. "Theory, Data and Educational Relevance." *Research Studies in Music Education* 6: 18–26.

Wiggins, J. 1994. "Children's Strategies for Solving Compositional Problems with Peers." *Journal of Research in Music Education* 42 (3): 232–52.

Wiggins, J., and K. Bodoin. 1998. "Painting a Big Soup: Teaching and Learning in a Second-Grade General Music Classroom." *Journal of Research in Music Education* 46 (2): 281–30.

Yarbrough, C. 1996. "The Future of Scholarly Inquiry in Music Education: 1996 Senior Researcher Award Acceptance Address." *Journal of Research in Music Education* 44 (3): 190–203.

Yarbrough, C., and H. E. Price. 1981. "Prediction of Performer Attentiveness Based on Rehearsal Activity and Teacher Behavior." *Journal of Research in Music Education* 29 (3): 209–17.

CHAPTER 9

THE POLITICS OF PUBLICATION

Voices, Venues, and Ethics

MITCHELL ROBINSON

PUBLISH or perish. These words have become an unquestioned fact of life for academics as we navigate the often thorny path toward tenure and promotion. For music and music education researchers, notions of what constitutes scholarship, or creative activity, are too often contentious and confusing. Questions have come from our colleagues outside of music as to what forms of activity "count" as research, as have queries regarding the boundaries between research, teaching, and service. For qualitative scholars in music education, these challenges have come both from outside our discipline and from within, as colleagues who hold different assumptions about the nature and structure of research in music education have questioned the very tenets of qualitative inquiry. The purpose of this chapter is to examine the issues surrounding the publication enterprise in music education, with particular attention to the dissemination of scholarship to our multiple constituent audiences. The first section will discuss the issue of finding and developing our scholarly "voice," and will suggest new forms of delivering and presenting our research findings. The second section will address how authors can choose the appropriate venues to present their work, and will make the case for a broader conceptualization of what constitutes the dissemination of scholarly work. The chapter will conclude with a discussion of ethical considerations in respect to the publication of qualitative work.

9.1. FINDING OUR VOICES

Learning how to write for academic publications is a study in contradictions. As young students, we are encouraged to seek clarity in our writing; as academics, we are fascinated with the allure of impenetrable prose and jargon. As writers, we dream that our words and thoughts will be shared with millions of eager readers; as scholars, we become resigned to the knowledge that our work has a disappointingly small impact on those we seek to influence. The research community has become adept at "preaching to the choir," at the very time when our message most needs to be heard beyond the pews.

9.1.1. Developing Our Voice

As graduate students we are "socialized" to write in an academic style. This style, based on the type of writing found in traditional scientific journals, is often characterized by a reliance on citation, dense prose, and a parsimonious approach to writing. Brevity is favored over clarity, and the detailed explanation of methodology is valued over literary exposition. Our most prestigious music education research journals reinforce these values with guidelines that privilege page numbers over content, and equate length with quality. They ask for "clear and readable English," but warn against the use of "excessive words" (*CRME*, "Instructions to Contributors," 2012, no. 191). This may make sense when the "data" we are dealing with comes in the form of numbers, but for qualitative authors the glass slipper is an awkward fit.

Think of the difference between reading a recipe and a restaurant review. One is an orderly, sequential outline of ingredients, preparation, and method, but provides no sensory information other than temperatures and measurements. There is an assumption that the reader's context (i.e., access to and quality of ingredients, season of the year, proximity to the market, sharpness of knives, layout of the kitchen, time of day, whether or not guests are expected) has little or nothing to do with the successful replication of the recipe.

A well-written restaurant review, on the other hand, is a story. It welcomes the reader into the reviewer's world, and invites us to vicariously experience the meal along with the reviewer. We "see" the décor of the space, "smell" the aromas wafting from the plates that pass us by, and "hear" the rattles and bangs of the kitchen as the chefs prepare "our" food. Vivid descriptions of each dish help us "taste" the flavors and textures of the food, tripping memories of meals enjoyed in the past and enticing us to recreate these dishes in our own kitchens.

The point of this exercise is not to favor one form of writing over the other. Clearly, both have a place at the table. But it also seems clear that each form of writing is governed by a different set of expectations, traditions, and needs. Requiring a recipe writer to include a literary narrative for each dish makes as much sense as limiting the restaurant reviewer to a list of ingredients and 200 words. It also seems clear that some dishes (scrambled eggs) may require only a recipe for one to recreate them at home, while others (a paella enjoyed on one's holiday at a seaside bistro in Valencia) lend themselves to a more descriptive treatment.

As scholars, our research questions should drive the choice of paradigm, methodology, and writing style. As we discover our research interests and passions, we should develop the commensurate skills and dispositions to pursue our goals. For some this will mean learning about an array of advanced statistical procedures and knowing how and when to apply particular measurement tools appropriately. For others it will mean becoming better storytellers, and becoming adept at transforming interview transcripts into compelling vignettes and narratives that draw the reader into the world of the participants.

For research advisors, our task is to help our advisees find their voices as scholars. We must nudge, cajole, and prod our students to think deeply about what they want to know, to make them uncomfortable about critical issues in their teaching and in our profession, and to inspire them to follow their passion in scholarly ways. We must also work to make sure that there are places and spaces in which our students' voices can be heard, and to advocate for greater inclusion of underrepresented and marginalized voices in our collective discourse as a research community.

9.1.2. New Voices

As a scholarly community, we may wish to consider other means for welcoming more voices into our discussions. While the "solo" journal article has traditionally been the "coin of the realm" in music education research, our discourse in the "real world" is more varied and nuanced. We work with classmates and colleagues in classes, ensembles, committees, and professional organizations to produce work that would be impossible to accomplish on our own. It stands to reason that collaborative scholarly writing offers a mechanism for groups of researchers to work together in investigating a problem or line of inquiry.

This notion is not without its detractors. The idea of collaborative writing creates anxiety regarding issues of authorship. Some academics are concerned with determining who wrote specific sections of a work and ascribing credit for various ideas and particular aspects of the finished product to individual authors. As collaboration scholars Ede and Lunsford note, "everyday practices in the humanities continue to ignore, or even to punish, collaboration while authorizing work attributed to (autonomous) individuals" (2001, 354). Yet as musicians, we value the ability to play with others (i.e., ensemble performance, chamber music) as much as, if not more than, playing alone. The panel presentation is also an accepted part of our academic conference "culture," with participants understanding that each individual brings something special and unique to the group's collective work.

Collaborative writing should not be seen as taking the "easy way out": "Collaboration is not always the best, or easiest, or fastest way to accomplish learning goals. Collaboration is often messy, inefficient, time consuming and difficult. Consider the following apparent contradictions that characterize collaborations:

- We intuitively know that working together is preferable to working separately, but also understand that producing tangible results via teamwork can be harder and more time consuming than going it alone.

- Collaborators know that differences in opinion and approach provide the creative energy and tension that fuels [sic] sustainable relationships, but are equally aware that these relationships must be built on a foundation of shared visions, missions, and goals.
- The equitable allocation of resources from each partner is a prerequisite for effective collaboration, yet. . . partners are rarely equals in issues of power, prestige, or resources." (Robinson 2006, 149)

Indeed, the promise of sharing power with one's participants and partners throughout the research process is one of the most intriguing attractions of collaborative writing. For scholars committed to an egalitarian stance as researchers, collaborative writing offers an avenue for pursuing this work in interesting ways.

Another form of writing that holds promise for qualitative authors is web-based writing. Hypertext is text displayed electronically with embedded references to other forms of information, typically accessed by a mouse click or keyboard command. In addition to offering links to additional text, hypertext may also provide immediate access to figures, tables, graphics, and audio and video files. This kind of rich text is familiar to anyone who uses the Internet to browse for information, and offers authors the opportunity to imbue deeper context and alternative forms of information to their writing. Using hypertext also disrupts the linear, sequential presentation of the written form in favor of a webbed, non-hierarchical organizational structure that allows the reader to exert a measure of control over the navigation of information.

Hypertext is also a natural device for reinforcing the postmodern approach to research embraced by qualitative scholars; rather than creating a narrative along a single path, which may imply a particular perspective or interpretation, using hypertext as a narrative device allows the reader to follow any number of multiple tracks or possible interpretations by simply clicking a link. While there are obvious obstacles in terms of the adoption of hypertext in mainstream publishing, the proliferation of online journals should reduce these challenges and increase the acceptance of this form of research presentation.

The use of video in presenting qualitative research is another underutilized delivery system. To paraphrase the old saying, "writing about music education qualitative research is like dancing about architecture." While language can carry a multitude of emotions, expressions, and meanings, it is, at its core, a relatively "flat" medium. The power of video is that it conveys events as they happen, with less reliance on the observer's interpretive lens, and gives the viewer the power to make her or his own interpretive judgments.

Video can also tell the story of an event or case in the participants' own words and actions, eliminating—or camouflaging—the role of the researcher. Where a narrative tells the story in a series of vignettes or "snapshots," a video plays out more seamlessly, showing the arc of the story in broad strokes and sweeping lines.

These alternative forms of scholarly expression hold great promise for transforming the art of qualitative research in music education, and in bringing new voices and means of expression into our professional discourse. As with any new forms, there will be challenges and struggles in finding ways to bring these approaches "online" with our current practices (i.e., journal publication requirements, graduate school guidelines, conference submission formats), but the advantages of working and writing together in new ways and utilizing new technologies far outweigh these obstacles. If our goal is to share our knowledge with the community of music educators, and to blur the boundaries between researchers and practitioners, then welcoming these new voices and means of expression is not just our obligation; it is our privilege.

9.2. CHOOSING OUR VENUES

One of the most challenging aspects of becoming a scholar is figuring out how to get our work "out there." For scholars interested in sharing their work with multiple and diverse constituent audiences, "publication" really means "dissemination." Successful music education researchers are not just writers, scholars, and presenters; they are also entrepreneurs. Scholars must be aware of how to write for and speak to specific audiences, must understand the differences between and among the various journals, conferences, and professional organizations to which they will submit their work, and how to work with editors, reviewers, and conference planners during this process. We also need to consider the best ways to share our work with various audiences, and understand how these ways of sharing are valued by our multiple constituencies. As traditional dissemination patterns continue to adapt and evolve in response to technological innovations, we must also respond in innovative and entrepreneurial ways.

9.2.1. Understanding Our Audience

It is important for authors to review the submission guidelines for any particular journal very carefully. For example, the *Journal of Music Teacher Education* is interested primarily in studies that pertain to teacher education, and the journal is less likely to accept articles on other topics. The journal *Update: Applications of Research in Music Education* requires that authors use terminology that is approachable to practitioners and discourages the use of statistical terms and research jargon that could be distracting to a non-researcher audience.

Authors submitting to international journals should be aware of the questions that may be raised by an international audience regarding the topic of the manuscript and understand the differences between the music education enterprise in North America and other parts of the world. Be sure that the manuscript provides sufficient detail such that someone who knows little about the topic will be able to understand what has been done. Ask a colleague—or better yet, several colleagues—to read the manuscript before it is submitted to provide an "outsider's" view of the work. Finally, a reminder about the importance of adhering to the style requirements (i.e., APA, Chicago, MLA) as outlined in the intended journal's "instructions to contributors."

9.2.2. Title and Consistency of Purpose

The title of a manuscript can provide the reader with key details regarding the topic, participants, and design. Titles can also serve to draw in a prospective reader through the use of evocative language and imagery. With advances in search technology and computer databases it is no longer necessary to "load" one's title with as many descriptive terms as possible, allowing authors to be creative without ignoring their literary inclinations.

Consider the following titles from two articles on the same general research topic:

- "Composing with Computers: Meg Makes Music." (Sandra Stauffer, 2001, *Bulletin of the Council for Research in Music Education*)
- "A Study of the Relationship of Composition/Improvisation to Selected Personal Variables Differences in the Relationship to Selected Variables: An Experimental Study." (Marianne Hassler and Arnold Feil, 1986, *Bulletin of the Council for Research in Music Education*)

Both titles are descriptive, but in very different ways. Each title provides clues as to the author's approach to the investigation, and possible tips as to the study's methodology and paradigm choice. Neither is better or worse than the other; they are different, and appropriate to the choice of design, theoretical foundations, and worldview of the researcher.

I regularly suggest changes in title as a reviewer (and have often been asked to change my titles as an author). Look carefully at your title, the purpose statement, and then the key findings of your investigation to be sure there is consistency in the language in all these sections of the paper.

It is also important that the language of the purpose statement appear consistently throughout the manuscript. The crafting of one's purpose statement is an exacting procedure, and each reiteration of the statement in the paper must be identical. Some papers include a restatement of the purpose in the method section and the conclusion of the paper. Variations in wording in the purpose statement may create confusion for the reader and can distract from the content of the writing. This is not the time to indulge one's writerly instincts; keep the purpose statement consistent.

9.2.3. Responding to Reviewers/Tone of Response

Authors need to understand that they should feel encouraged when they are asked to revise a manuscript. Most journals use variations on a three-point scale (i.e., Accept without revision, Accept pending revision, Decline) for evaluating manuscripts, so a request for revisions is a very positive response.

Journal editors typically ask authors to respond to each suggestion made by reviewers in a formal "Response to Reviewers." As an author, it is difficult to take criticism on a paper you have worked on for an extended time period and it is important to avoid reflecting this frustration in your response to the reviewer. Always approach the review process as a learning experience and an opportunity to make the paper better. Most published authors will acknowledge that the review process invariably improves the finished product and that the benefits of thoughtful comments from reviewers and careful copyediting are extraordinarily helpful.

It is sometimes tempting to try to "teach" a reviewer something that you think they may have misunderstood about your design or analysis. Unless you are adding citations to the paper in response to a reviewer's suggestion for clarification I would suggest avoiding additional citations in the response to reviewers. For example, if a reviewer has questioned a sampling procedure, a good way for the author to respond might be:

The following sentence has been added to the method section of the paper: *"Criteria sampling was used to select participants. Patton (2002b) defines 'Criteria sampling' as . . .".* Keep in mind that if a reviewer was confused, or appeared "un-informed," a reader might have the same reaction and a clarification is warranted to address the concern.

While it is not necessary to make every specific change requested by the reviewers, it is recommended that authors make an effort to provide a response to each of the reviewers' comments. Strive for a positive, collaborative tone in your remarks, acknowledge the helpfulness of the suggestions, and thank the reviewers for their assistance in improving the paper.

Although authors do not always welcome the initial comments from reviewers in any manuscript, the review process does result in stronger manuscripts. Sometimes it becomes clear in the process that the manuscript was not meant for the particular journal to which it was submitted. That does not mean that the manuscript might not be welcomed by another journal. Far too many music education researchers "give up" after one rejection or do not take the time to re-submit when asked to revise. If one can learn to consider criticism and not to take any reviewers' comments personally, the process of publication can offer a satisfying end to any important music education project.

9.2.4. Toward a "Kinder" Review Process

Serving on an editorial board is not a glamorous task. One is asked to dedicate considerable time, expertise, and effort to reviewing the work of others, often on short turnaround schedules, and with little in the way of compensation or professional "value." Being a reviewer is, however, a noble endeavor. Providing advice and commentary regarding an author's methodological choices, design strategies, and writing style can greatly improve the final quality of the published product and help authors gain a more comprehensive understanding of how their work "fits in" to the professional literature.

The very nature of the review process, however, can sometimes work against the potential helpfulness of the reviewers' contributions. Limited by time and space, many reviewers tend to dwell on the more critical aspects of the reviewing process. These reviews may be characterized by a focus on design or method choices, unintentionally rude or even hurtful comments, and a dismissive or negative tone. The author is left angry and defensive about her work, and disillusioned with the peer review process.

I recently had an experience writing for a book project "outside" of music education, and was struck by the difference in the review process as compared to what I've become familiar with in our discipline; specifically, the nature of the reviewers' comments. As this was my first attempt at submitting a book chapter in general education (Robinson 2012), I was apprehensive about the reviewers' perceptions of my writing; would it be "good enough" for this audience, understandable by non-music educators, and make a strong enough contribution to the book? I opened the e-mail attachment with the reviewers' responses, steeling myself for the worst—and was pleasantly surprised to read a series of mostly positive and encouraging comments: "I like how you use this phrase, to draw the reader in"; "This section is very well done! And very interesting"; "Fascinating! This is so well written."

While there were a number of editorial requests and suggestions for changes included among the comments, the prevailing tone of the review was supportive, complimentary, and encouraging. As I finished reading the reviewers' comments, I felt as though I had just had a helpful conversation about my writing with a group of supportive colleagues. Perhaps more importantly, I came away feeling good about my work, confident about making a strong contribution to the book, and excited about using the reviewers' suggestions to improve the chapter.

I believe there are several lessons that we can learn as reviewers from this anecdote. First, reviewers should approach the editorial process as a collegial exchange, not as a critical investigation. Just as good teachers and research advisors work in a gentle fashion with their students to help them find their "voices" as educators and writers, reviewers should enter the editorial process thinking about how they can "kindly" help authors to tell their story more clearly, and to encourage authors to let their voice come through in their writing.

Second, if reviewers are truly interested in having their comments be used to improve the quality of the author's submission, they should understand that an author is much more likely to listen to suggestions that are offered in a supportive, constructive manner than to criticisms and negative comments. While it may be easier to focus one's critique on what the author needs to change or do differently, it is more helpful to the author when these suggestions are conveyed in an encouraging way. This does not mean that there is no place in a review for a critique of the author's writing style or methodological procedure—there are, after all, legitimate issues that should be addressed in every review. Rather, the issue here is more about style than substance. Just as a well-written concert review can convey less than successful aspects of a performance while maintaining a generally positive impression of the performer or group's efforts, a thoughtfully crafted editorial review can point out design flaws and writing errors in a kind, encouraging manner.

Finally, just as I came away from the editorial process described in the preceding feeling confident and positive about my work, reviewers should approach their task with the same goal in mind; to use the review process as a way to encourage and support aspiring scholars and authors. We often decry the lack of submissions to our scholarly journals and bemoan the preponderance of "one and done" studies in music education research; could the nature of the review process itself be a factor in these issues? Are authors who receive unnecessarily harsh critiques from reviewers dissuaded from pursuing further publication opportunities? Do negative comments from reviewers lead to a lack of confidence for some writers that precludes them from submitting additional articles to these journals?

For me, the positive nature of the editorial review process that I have described was an empowering, invigorating experience. Being treated in such a kind, compassionate way was a revelation for me as an author, teacher, and researcher. It has influenced how I respond to authors as a reviewer, and how I work with my students as an advisor. The end result was a renewed passion for writing, and a rekindled confidence in pursuing my scholarly interests. We should hope for nothing less for our colleagues who bravely submit their work for our review.

9.2.5. Journal-Article Formatting and Space

One of the most pressing problems for qualitative writers is how to take a project that may have taken multiple years to complete and may have involved in-depth interviews and observations resulting in mountains of data, and turning that mountain into a 20-page article. In discussions with students and colleagues I have likened this process to a parent trying to decide which of his children he likes better. Inevitably, something has to be cut in order to trim the length to acceptable standards. The question is, how much can be cut without destroying the whole?

Although there is some freedom in terms of formatting for articles that come from varying empirical traditions and styles, there has been somewhat of a common template for traditional journal-article reports. In the sciences, the most prominent format for journal-length articles is referred to by the acronym IMRAD, which stands for *Introduction, Methods, Results*, and *Discussion*. This structure follows from the linear sequence of the traditional scientific model, and is thought to be a "direct reflection of the process of scientific discovery" (International Committee of Medical Journal Editors 2010).

Due to the diverse array of topics and research styles found in the music education literature, it is not uncommon to find more variation in article formatting in our journals. There are some common elements in most published articles, however. Most journal-length research reports in music education include an introduction and rationale for the topic, a purpose statement, and research questions. The literature review section of most journal-length articles is between four and seven paragraphs in length, and synthesizes the most relevant points from the past literature; given the length required in a qualitative report to include interview transcripts and interpretive analysis, some authors truncate their literature reviews even further.

For authors determined to adhere to the traditional format, it can be a challenge to "fit" their work within journal page limits. APA style requires double-spacing for all sections of a manuscript (including block quotes and references). Many authors ignore this, and editors may assume they are doing so in an effort to save space. A better way to save space is to examine the document carefully for repetition. Journal-length articles do not need the same sort of repetitious introductions and conclusions that thesis and dissertation documents typically have (with the possible exception of the purpose statement).

A general rule in trying to format a 20-page qualitative paper is to be sure that the findings section is introduced by around page nine or so. Otherwise, the manuscript becomes too focused on design and analysis and does not highlight the importance of the findings in the study. Although the method and analysis sections of papers may differ significantly, most papers include a return to past literature after the presentation of results or findings, as well as a section on implications for future research and/or teaching practice.

Another "space-saving" strategy is to ruthlessly search each sentence and paragraph for unnecessary words. Search the entire paper for information that the reader may not need to know or for instances where writing is wordy and not "to the point." Creating graphics, tables, or grids to describe participants and/or present findings may also help to cut down on text in the paper while clarifying information for the reader.

It is particularly challenging to create a 20-page journal-length article from a large dissertation or thesis. The conclusion chapter of the dissertation often includes a scaled-down version of the literature review, method, analysis, and findings. In long qualitative studies, it may be necessary to report on only a limited number of research questions due to space limitations.

Another useful strategy is to look at the major themes present in the completed dissertation or thesis, and extract one or more of the most salient themes to focus upon in a single article, keeping in mind issues of audience and journal mission (e.g., choose a theme related to teacher preparation for a *JMTE* article, or a practice-oriented theme for an *MEJ* piece). In mixed methods presentations, the author may need to report on mixed method analysis only.

9.2.6. Choosing the Right Venue: Publication as Dissemination

Journals differ greatly in terms of mission, purpose, and intended audiences, and authors must consider these characteristics carefully when developing their publication agenda. The major types of journals in our profession can be grouped broadly into two categories: research journals and professional journals. The mission for a research journal is to present peer-reviewed reports of research on issues related to music teaching and learning. The audience for these reports is typically the community of music education researchers, and a "broad spectrum of other individuals with interest in music education" (*JRME* 2012). The mission for professional journals, on the other hand, is less focused on the research methodology or design of the report and more on its application to practice.

Historically, research journals have held a privileged place in our profession's value system, in spite of the fact that these journals have had a somewhat limited circulation among practitioners, and, as a result, a relatively limited impact on practice (Fung 2008). By way of comparison, the *Music Educators Journal*, a leading professional journal in music education, is circulated to roughly 65,000 homes and libraries, while the circulation for the *Journal of Research in Music Education*, one of our most prestigious research journals, is just over 4,400 (E. Wilcox, personal communication, June 18, 2012).

If the dissemination of scholarship to practicing music teachers is one of our primary goals as researchers, then perhaps we need to reconceptualize the notion of "publication." The current promotion and tenure system in place at many universities, for example, places a primary or even singular emphasis on published articles accepted by a small subset of limited-circulation research journals. If dissemination of our work is truly a desired outcome of the research enterprise, we need to embrace a broader view of scholarship that embraces publication in multiple journal types, presentations at research and professional conferences and meetings, in-service sessions provided for practicing music teachers, podcasts, webinars, and other ways to share our findings with the music education community.

Scholars should be encouraged to develop professional trajectories that include submitting their work to research and professional journals, and presenting their scholarship at professional development conferences and in-service meetings. Our value structures for these different venues must be adjusted accordingly as well. We need to consider not just the prestige factor of having an article accepted for publication at a high-status research journal, but the dissemination value of sharing this information with teachers at a state music education association conference, with colleagues at a national meeting of a professional organization, or by posting our findings on a web page for post-publication review and comment.

Further, if we are interested in having our scholarship influence music education policy and practice more broadly, we must also focus our efforts on sharing our work beyond our own disciplinary borders. As gratifying as it is to have our work accepted by our peers in our own discipline, the impact of our inquiry must also be shared with those who make the decisions regarding school policies, curriculums, and reform initiatives. By increasing our efforts at publishing and presenting our scholarship in venues in general education, we can exert a stronger influence on policymaking in the educational arena, and contribute our voices to the dialogue surrounding important issues in educational policy and practice. Establishing a more visible presence with professional organizations such as the American Educational Research Association, National Association of Secondary School Principals, Association for Supervision and Curriculum Development, and journals such as *Arts Education Policy Review, American School Board Journal,* and *American Educational Research Journal,* will bring the conversation to new audiences, and add our voice to the discussion at the policy level.

Just as there is no "best" university or college, there is no "best" scholarly profile. Music teacher educators and researchers must be strategic and entrepreneurial in crafting personal research agendas and portfolios that "fit" their scholarly interests and the particular academic setting in which they work. As a scholarly community, we should embrace the dissemination and accessibility of our work through multiple delivery systems and venues, and continue our efforts at bridging the divide between theory and practice. We must also work with our colleagues and administrators to promote the diversity of scholarly expression in music education research, to demonstrate the recognition and value of these forms of dissemination appropriately in the promotion and tenure process within our institutions, and to help our students and peers navigate and negotiate the path toward the full realization of their scholarly potential.

9.3. The Ethics of Publishing

Given the differences among the various forms of scholarship in music education, it is little wonder that authors conceive of publication strategies for their work differently. What all scholars agree on, however, are the beliefs that music education research is critical to advancing our understanding of the music teaching and learning process, that our research initiatives must be conducted ethically, and that the results of our inquiries must be reported clearly and appropriately given the methodological and epistemological choices we make as researchers.

9.3.1. Definitions

Several terms are commonly used to describe a varied set of conditions surrounding the issue of piecemeal publication. While these terms may be related, there are nuanced variations among the meanings of these terms, and the following section is provided in an effort to promote further clarity.

9.3.1.1. *Duplicate Publication*

While "duplicate" and "redundant" publications are often mentioned together, they are actually different phenomena. Generally, duplicate publication refers to the attempted simultaneous submission of a research report to multiple journals. Changes between the versions may be only cosmetic, including variations in title, abstract, and minor textual alterations.

As research advisors and journal reviewers, we find it difficult to think of circumstances that would rationalize such actions. Though some journals operate on frustratingly long backlogs, and can take months, if not years, for submissions to move from receipt to publication, this is not sufficient justification for sending the same article for consideration to more than one journal at the same time. In addition to being unethical, duplicate publication also puts journal editors and reviewers in untenable situations, and could create unnecessary confusion should the same article appear in multiple journals. Furthering the case against duplicate publication, secondary analyses and meta-analyses, though somewhat rare in music education research, could be compromised should identical findings be included more than once in these sophisticated forms of data analyses, giving unwarranted increased significance to the same set of results.

9.3.1.2. *Redundant Publication*

Redundant publication is often described as "reporting (publishing or attempting to publish) substantially the same work more than once, without attribution of the original source(s)" (CBE Views 1996, 76–77). Identifying characteristics of redundant publications include:

a. at least one of the authors must be common to all reports (if there are no common authors, it is more likely plagiarism than redundant publication),
b. the subject or study populations are often the same or similar,
c. the methodology is typically identical or nearly so, and
d. the results and their interpretation generally vary little, if at all (CBE Views 1996, 76–77).

A common practice of qualitative authors is the separation of multiple themes from a large-scale project into separate articles or other publications, often for different audiences, venues, or journals. While this sort of publication pattern may resemble items (b) and (c) from the preceding list, the decision to present individual themes, or groups of themes, in separate articles would appear to disqualify this practice from the preceding definition of redundant publication.

9.3.1.3. *"Piecemeal" Publication*

Piecemeal publication has traditionally been defined as "the unnecessary submission of findings from the same study, in piece-by-piece fashion, rather than as an integrated single report or a smaller number of integrated reports" (Drotar 2010, 225). Another related term, the "least publishable unit," is defined as the smallest unit of results from a study that can be published separately, and reflects the parsing of findings from one research project into several smaller publications (Stossel 1985, 123).

Historically, the objections to piecemeal publication have been concerned with notions of parsimony, or economy of writing, and the belief that the significance of a study's results could be diminished through publication redundancy. The basic notions surrounding piecemeal publication are based on a scientific, positivist view of the world, and of data—a view that is less understanding of postmodern paradigms, and can pose special problems for qualitative or narrative inquiry.

Take, for example, the notion of parsimony. A lean, sparse writing style is often seen as a strength in technical writing, and comes in handy when communicating the results of an experimental investigation. Knowing how to convey the relationship of a complicated statistical procedure to one's analysis of a data set in a clear, economical way is a valuable skill for a quantitative author.

The qualitative author, on the other hand, needs a different "toolbox" at her disposal. Consider the following excerpt from Clifford Geertz, the "father" of thick description, reproduced at length here:

> Consider, he says, two boys rapidly contracting the eyelids of their right eyes. In one, this is an involuntary twitch; in the other, a conspiratorial signal to a friend. The two movements are, as movements, identical; from an I-am-a-camera, "phenomenalistic" observation of them alone, one could not tell which was twitch and which was wink, or indeed whether both or either was twitch or wink. Yet the difference, however unphotographable, between a twitch and a wink is vast; as anyone unfortunate enough to have had the first taken for the second knows. The winker is communicating, and indeed communicating in a quite precise and special way: (1) deliberately, (2) to someone in particular, (3) to impart a particular message, (4) according to a socially established code, and (5) without cognizance of the rest of the company. As Ryle points out, the winker has not done two things, contracted his eyelids and winked, while the twitcher has done only one, contracted his eyelids. Contracting your eyelids on purpose when there exists a public code in which so doing counts as a conspiratorial signal is winking. That's all there is to it: a speck of behavior, a fleck of culture, and—*voilà!*—a gesture. (Geertz 1973, 5)

It is hard to imagine how parsimoniousness could improve this vignette. The excerpt is characterized by several of the elements of good thick description: rich, evocative prose (i.e., "I-am-a-camera," "twitcher," "*voilà*"); the use of sensory cues (i.e., "rapidly contracting the eyelids"); an accessible, conversational writing style that brings the reader "in" to the setting (i.e., "Yet the difference, however unphotographable, between a twitch and a wink is vast; as anyone unfortunate enough to have had the first taken for the second knows"). It is Geertz's use of literary conventions, word choices, and narrative writing style that distinguish this passage, not an overriding concern with word count.

The issue of "piecemeal publication" has become a difficult and controversial subject for many persons in our profession. At the core of this complicated topic may be differing conceptions of what research is, how it should be conducted, and what our goals as scholars should be. Traditionally, definitions and notions regarding piecemeal publication have been based on understandings derived from experimental scientific inquiry, including positivist assumptions such as:

- There is one "correct" or valid interpretation of a set of data.
- Research questions are best when tightly focused on observable, measurable behaviors.

- Data collection is best done at a "distance," and by individuals unconnected to the experiment—or better yet, via non-human means (i.e., a test, survey or other sort of measurement tool).
- In order to be most easily understood, data must be reduced or converted to numerical form, and subjected to statistical methods of analysis.

Qualitative researchers, on the other hand, operate on a different set of understandings concerning the research enterprise:

- There are often multiple interpretations of the data, depending on one's perspective, role, or background—and reanalyzing one's data can result in different interpretations.
- We avoid research questions that can be answered with a "yes" or "no," and favor questions that lead to more questions.
- Data collection is not an "objective" process, and is often best conducted by a participant-observer who is fully immersed in the research setting.
- Reductionist approaches to data analysis are avoided in favor of a more inductive stance toward understanding what our data means.

I have often encouraged my doctoral students to fashion multiple work products (i.e., research journal articles, professional journal articles, conference presentations) from a single large-scale study in an effort to disseminate particular research findings to specific audiences and venues. This sort of publication pattern appears to make sense when one is dealing with large amounts of disparate data, in the form of interview transcripts, videotaped observations, and archival documents, each analyzed in multiple ways.

That being said, so-called piecemeal publication is explicitly addressed in the APA's publication manual (2001). The manual states, "data that can be meaningfully combined within a single publication should be presented together to enhance effective communication" (352), and that whether the publication of two or more reports based on the same dataset constitutes piecemeal publication is a matter of editorial judgment.

9.3.2. The Issue of "Rigor"

For many qualitative authors, the issue of "rigor" has become a problematic notion. Usually associated with the positivist construct of validity, rigor often becomes a catch-all term for critiques of qualitative methods from a quantitative perspective. For example, most quantitative data analysis choices, such as the decision to represent the results of a survey using means and standard deviations, rarely require descriptions of the theoretical reasons behind choosing these techniques. It is common, on the other hand, for a qualitative author to receive the following reviewer request: "I found the presentation of themes and subthemes very helpful and artistic and think this is a promising mode of representation for your findings, but you need to substantiate the decisions that went into the creation of this visual scheme."

Given the limited page constraints for most research journals, the qualitative author must then decide whether to include lengthy detailed justifications of common qualitative techniques (i.e., in vivo coding, constant comparative method of data analysis, member checks, peer review, etc.) in lieu of excerpts of dialogue or quotes from participants. According to Sandelowski, "four factors complicate the debate about the scientific merits of qualitative research: the varieties of qualitative methods, the lack of clear boundaries between quantitative and qualitative research, the tendency to evaluate qualitative research against conventional scientific criteria of rigor, and the artistic features of qualitative inquiry" (1993, 27).

Qualitative scholars have established an assortment of positions in response to editors' and reviewers' requests for "more rigorous" methodological provisions. Sparkes (2001) defines four perspectives on validity: the *replication perspective* (which asserts that validity is appropriate for both paradigms, but is assessed differently in each); the *parallel perspective* (that a separate set of criteria must be developed for qualitative inquiry, paralleling those in quantitative work); the *diversification of meanings perspective* (establishing new forms of validity that do not have reference points in quantitative research); and the *letting-go-of-validity perspective* (which advocates a total abandonment of the concept of validity). Earlier in this volume, in chapter 8, I suggest a set of alternative evaluative criteria for establishing quality based on the work of Patton (2002a).

As research advisors, my colleagues and I have stopped asking our students to include lengthy justifications for the choice to use qualitative methods in their theses and dissertations. We found that such explanations were unnecessary, and were more distracting than useful in terms of students' ability to tell the story of their research. While I understand the need for qualitative researchers—indeed, all researchers—to "show their work" in the reporting of their work, there must also be an acknowledgment of the disproportionate impact of such requests on the quality of much qualitative inquiry. Requiring qualitative writers to devote significant space to lengthy explanations of common design choices and analytical techniques, in the name of rigor, betrays a fundamental misunderstanding about the nature of qualitative work, and an intention for this form of inquiry to adhere to evaluative standards that are ill-fitting and inappropriate.

I want to make a critical distinction here: I am not advocating for lower standards of rigor in qualitative research. Quite the opposite. What I am arguing for is an understanding of the differences between paradigms; of the inherent uniqueness of each form of inquiry, and the values that each espouses; and of the unfairness of holding one paradigm to the same methodological standards as the other, when doing so requires a wholesale abandonment of that approach's worth and appropriateness. Rigor in qualitative research is not demonstrated by a detailed explanation of one's coding choices, it is illustrated by the poignancy of an excerpt, or the richness of a vignette. Rigor in qualitative work is shown by the nuance of the author's interpretation, not by the justification of one's theoretical underpinnings with obscure citations.

The question becomes one of style over substance. As Sandelowski (1993) cautions, "We can preserve or kill the spirit of qualitative work; we can soften our notion of rigor to include playfulness, soulfulness, imagination, and technique we associate with more artistic endeavors, or we can further harden it by the uncritical application of rules. The choice is ours: rigor or rigor mortis" (8).

References

Drotar, D. 2010. "Editorial: Guidance for Submission and Review of Multiple Publications Derived from the Same Study." *Journal of Pediatric Psychology* 35 (3): 225–30.

Ede, L., and A. A. Lunsford. 2001. "Collaboration and Concepts of Authorship." *Publications of the Modern Language Association of America* 116 (2): 354–69.

Fung, C. V. 2008. "In Search of Important Music Education Research Questions: The Case of the United States." *Bulletin of the Council for Research in Music Education* 176: 31–43.

Geertz, C. 1973. *The Interpretation of Cultures: Selected Essays*. New York: Basic Books.

Hassler, M., and H. Feil. 1986. "A Study of the Relationship of Composition/Improvisation to Selected Personal Variables Differences in the Relationship to Selected Variables: An Experimental Study." *Bulletin of the Council for Research in Music Education* 87: 26–34.

International Committee of Medical Journal Editors. 2010. "Uniform Requirements for Manuscripts Submitted to Biomedical Journals: Writing and Editing for Biomedical Publication." http://www.icmje.org/urm_full.pdf.

Patton, M. Q. 2002a. *Qualitative Research and Evaluation Methods*. 3rd ed. Thousand Oaks, CA: Sage Publications.

Patton, M. Q. 2002b. "Two Decades of Developments in Qualitative Inquiry: A Personal, Experiential Perspective." *Qualitative Social Work* 1 (3): 261–83. doi:10.1177/1473325002001003636.

Robinson, M. 2006. "Issues Contributing to the Creation and Sustainability of Educational Collaborations." In *Teaching Music in the Urban Classroom*, vol. 2: *A Guide To Survival, Success, and Reform*, edited by C. Frierson-Campbell. Lanham, MD: Rowman and Littlefield Education.

Robinson, M. 2012. "Music Teaching and Learning in a Time of Reform." In *What Every Principal Needs to Know to Create Equitable and Excellent Schools*, edited by G, 89–109. Theoharis and J. Brooks. New York: Teachers College Press.

Sandelowski, M. 1993. "Rigor or Rigor Mortis: The Problem of Rigor in Qualitative Research Revisited." *ANS: Advances in Nursing Science* 16 (2): 1–8.

Sparkes, A. C. 2001. "Myth 94: Qualitative Health Researchers Will Agree about Validity." *Qualitative Health Research* 11 (4): 538–52. doi:10.1177/104973230101100409

Stauffer, S. L. 2001. "Composing with Computers: Meg Makes Music." *Bulletin of the Council for Research in Music Education* 150: 1–20.

Stossel, T. P. 1985. "Speed: An Essay on Biomedical Communication." *New England Journal of Medicine* 313: 123–26.

Index

Tables and boxes are indicated by *t* and *b* following the page number. Numbers followed by "n" indicate notes.

ABER (Arts-Based Educational Research), 56, 100–104
ABR (Arts-Based Research), 100
ABS (American Boychoir School) (Princeton, NJ), 47
Academic journals, 27–28. *See also specific journals by title*
   choosing your venue for publication, 152–159
Academic research. *See* Research
Accuracy, 136
Active participation, 23
AEPR (Arts Education Policy Review), 159
AERA (American Educational Research Association), 3, 100, 159
AERJ (American Educational Research Journal), 144, 159
Aesthetics, 140
American Boychoir School (ABS) (Princeton, NJ), 47
American Educational Research Association (AERA), 3, 100, 159
American Educational Research Journal (AERJ), 144, 159
American Folklife Center, 47
American Psychological Association (APA), 162
   APA Style, 157, 162
   Ethical Principles of Psychologists and Code of Conduct (2010 Amendments), 3
American School Board Journal, 159
Analog artifacts and data, 86–87
APA (American Psychological Association) Style, 157, 162

Arizona State University, 124
Art-based inquiry, 56
Art education, 136
Artifacts, 28
   analog, 86–87
   visual, 88
Artistic criteria, 140–141
A/r/tography, 56
Arts-Based Educational Research (ABER), 56, 100–104
Arts-Based Educational Research SIG (AERA), 100
Arts-Based Research (ABR), 100
Arts Education Policy Review (AEPR), 159
Art works, 88–89
Asking questions, 51–53
Association for Supervision and Curriculum Development, 159
ATLAS.ti, 121–123, 122*t*, 125
Audacity, 126
Audio data
   generating through recording, 82
   participant-generated, 87–89
   time-stamping, 85, 86
Audit trails, 133
Authenticity, 133, 140–141

Bare identification, 20
Barone, Tom, 141
Barrett, Margaret, 56–57
BCRME (Bulletin of the Council for Research in Music Education), 149, 153
Belmont Report, 2
Bias dump, 141

Bricolage, 93–94
Bulletin of the Council for Research in Music Education (BCRME or CRME), 149, 153

Camtasia, 85
CAQDAS (Computer Assisted Qualitative Data Analysis) software, 55, 118
Children, 135
Choir, community, 12
Classroom culture, 136
Classroom research
  academic research, 11, 13–14
  combined qualitative and quantitative studies, 14–15
  student teachers, 10
Classrooms, 136
CMC (computer-mediated communication), 48
Code books, 55
Code dictionaries, 55
Code of Ethics (American Educational Research Association), 3
Codes
  data codes, 31–32, 55, 74–75
  for music-making data, 113
  refining, 32–33
Code Table (Norgaard), 31
Collaborations, 24
  academic, 11
  in classroom research, 11
  in writing, 150–151
Collaborative participants, 26
Combined nonverbal, verbal, musical, and nonmusical analysis, 111
Combined verbal and nonverbal data analysis, 110
Common Rule
  45 CFR 46, 2–3, 4, 10–11
  exempt research, 10–12
  requirements of, 2–3, 4
Communication
  computer-mediated (CMC), 48
  conversational interviews, 43
  nonverbal, 71
Community choir, 12
Composition, 105

Computer Assisted Qualitative Data Analysis (CAQDAS) software, 55, 118
Computer-mediated communication (CMC), 48
Computer use, on-site participant, 84–85
Concept maps, 88
Conceptual models, 91
Confidentiality, 14–15, 67–68
Confirmability, 133
Connoisseurship, 20
Consistency, 133
Constructivist studies, 139–140
Content logs, 91
Conversational interviews, 44
Corporate welfare, 141
Cox, Gordon, 47
Credibility, 132, 133, 135
Critical change criteria, 141–142
Critical feminism, 141
CRME (Bulletin of the Council for Research in Music Education), 149, 153
Culture, classroom, 136

Data
  meanings-of-music-making, 106, 108*b*, 110, 113
  music-making as, 99–116
  process-of-music-making, 104–106, 108*b*, 113
  product-of-music-making, 104–106, 113
Data analysis. *See* Data collection and analysis
Data audits, 133
Databases, large-scale, 94
Data codes, 31–32, 55, 74–75
  for music-making data, 113
  refining, 33–334
Data collection and analysis, 6–7
  of analog artifacts and data, 86–87
  through audio recording, 82
  through bricolage, 93–94
  broadening analysis categories, 112–113
  combined nonverbal, verbal, musical, and nonmusical analysis, 111
  combined verbal and nonverbal data analysis, 110

coordination and synchronization of data, 85–86
criteria for, viii
from data, 89–90
of focus group data, 63–79
future directions, 94–95
interrogation of data, 119
of interview data, 54–55
of multimodal and multimedia data, 80–98
of music-making data, 99–116, 108b
of observational data, 20–42
paradigmatic approach, 56
of participant-generated data, 87–89
preliminary data analysis, 30–31
preparing interview data for, 54–55
with QDAS programs, 119, 120t
software for, 117–128
traditional, 138–139
transcription, 54, 74–75
triangulation of data, 136
through video and audio recording, 82
with web-based data, 94
Data management. *See* Data collection and analysis
Data records, 31–32
Data triangulation, 136
Decision-making "in-flight," 123
Dedoose, 123
Dependability, 133
Descriptions of observational data, 34–35
Descriptive observation, 27
DEVONThinkPro, 126
Dewey, John, 20
Dialogic interviews, 47
Digital devices, 84–85
Digital media, 94
Digital records, 31
Digitization, 86–87
Discourse analysis, ix
The Discovery of Grounded Theory: Strategies for Qualitative Research (Glaser and Strauss), 55
Dissemination, 158–159
Diversification of meanings perspective, 163
Documentation
  data records, 30

digital records, 31
media records, 85
Draves, Tami, 50
Drawings, 88–89
Duplicate publication, 160

Education. *See* Music education
Educational misconception, 7
Educational research
  arts-based (ABER), 56, 99, 100–104
  site permissions, 6
Educational story-sharing, emancipatory, 141
Elegance, 136
Emancipatory educational story-sharing, 141
Emerson, Ralph Waldo, vii
Etherington, Kim, 51
Ethical Principles of Psychologists and Code of Conduct (2010 Amendments) (American Psychological Association), 3
Ethics
  core principles for human participant research, 2
  in music education, 1–19
  in observational studies, 37–38
  in publishing, 159–164
  regulatory review, 3–5
Ethnographic interviews, 44–48
Ethnography, new, 144
Evaluative criteria, 144–145
  alternative sets of, 138
  artistic, 140
  constructivist, 139
  critical change criteria, 141
  establishing and selecting, 137–142
  evocative, 140–141
  traditional scientific research criteria, 138–139
Evaluative terminology, 131–134, 136–137
Evocative criteria, 140–141
Exempt research, 10–12
Express Scribe, 54
External reliability, 132

Facebook, 94
Federal research regulations, 17

Federalwide Assurance (FWA), 2–3
Feminist interviews, 46–47
Field notes, 28–29
    labeling, 31
    time-stamping, 86
Field research, 132
Fieldwork, 94
Final Cut Pro X, 86
Finlay, Linda, 51
Fittingness, viii
Flip video, 105
Focused observation, 27
Focus group data, 63–79
    analysis of, 74–77
Focus group interviews, 63–64
    defining characteristics, 64
    definition of, 64
    group dynamics, 68–69
    guidelines for, 69–70
    history of, 63–64
    informed consent for, 67–68
    logistics, 69
    moderation of, 70, 71
    in music education, 65–67
    opening, 71
    posing questions during, 72–73
    preparation for, 69–70
    process, 70–73
    protocol for, 69–70
    rationale for, 65
    recording, 69
    regulations for, 67–68
    researcher role during, 69–70
    selection of participants, 68–69
Follow-up questions, 53
Formatting journal articles, 156–157
Freire, Paulo, 141
Future directions
    for interviewing, 57–58
    for qualitative research, 94–95
Fuzzy search, 121

The Gambia, 26
Geertz, Clifford, 161
Gender Research in Music Education, 47
Generalizability, 131, 134, 135
Generalizable knowledge, 7

Generalization, 36–37
Glaser, Barney, 55
Good fit, viii
Goodness criteria, viii, 130, 134, 137
Goodrich, Andrew, 47
Gouzouasis, Peter, 56
Grand tour questions, 46
Grounded theory, 55–56
Group dynamics, 68–69
Group interviews. *See* Focus group interviews

Human subjects
    core principles for research with, 2
    proposals for studies involving, 49
    requirements for research with, 17, 58n1
HyperRESEARCH, 121, 122t, 125, 126
Hypertext, 151

Identification, bare, 20
iMovie, 126
IMRAD (Introduction, Methods, Results, and Discussion) format, 156
Indexing, 29
Individual interviews, 43–62
Individual responses, 113
Informal interviews, 46
Informants, 136
Informed consent, 14, 15
    for focus group interviews, 67–68
    requirements for, 67–68
Inquiry. *See also* Research
    art-based, 56
Institutional Review Boards (IRBs), 1–3, 15–17, 21–22
    activities outside IRB oversight, 8–10
    regulations for focus group interviews, 67–68
    research regulated by, 13–15
    review by, 13–15
    vignettes, 8–10, 13–15
Internet
    online interviews, 49
    web-based data, 94
    web-based writing, 151
Interpretation, 34–35
Interview guides, 49

Interview questions
  asking, 51–53
  beginning, 51
  follow-up, 53
  types of, 51, 52t
Interviews
  conversational, 44
  dialogic, 48
  ethnographic, 45–48
  excerpts, 53b
  feminist, 47–48
  focus group, 63–64, 65–70, 70–73
  future directions, 57–58
  individual, 43–62
  informal, 46
  life history, 47
  modes of interacting with
      interviewees, 48–49
  in music education research, 57–58
  online, 49
  oral, 47
  phenomenological, 44–45
  preparing data for analysis, 54–55
  protocols for, 49, 69–70
  qualitative, 12
  semi-structured, 44
  standardized, 44
  studies with, 49–51
  think-aloud, 107
  types of, 44–48
  unstructured, 44
Interview transcripts, 53, 54, 74–75
iPads, 123
IRBs. *See* Institutional Review Boards
Irwin, Rita, 56

Journal of Music Teacher Education (JMTE),
    152, 157
*Journal of Research in Music Education
    (JRME)*, 117, 131, 132, 158
Journal review, 153–156
Journals. *See also specific journals by title*
  choosing for publication in, 157–159
  consistency of purpose, 153
  formatting articles, 156–157
  "instructions to contributors," 153
  researcher, 29

  review process, 154–156
  space constraints, 156–157
  style requirements, 153, 157
  titles of articles, 153
*JRME (Journal of Research in Music
    Education)*, 117, 131, 132, 158

Kennedy, Mary, 47, 50
Knowledge, generalizable, 7

Labeling field notes, 31
Lather, Patti, 141
Leggo, Carl, 56
Letting-go-of-validity perspective, 163
Life history interviews, 47
Listening maps, 88–89
Logistics, 69
Lomax, Alan, 47

The Maud Powell Society for Music and
    Education, 47
MAXQDA, 121, 122t
Meaning, 163
Meanings-of-music-making data,
    106–108, 113
Media Educators Journal (MEJ), 157
Media records, 85, 86
MEJ (Music Educators Journal), 157, 158
MENC (Music Educators National
    Conference), 141
Microsoft Word, 124
MIDI (musical instrument digital interface)
    data, 84, 85, 86
MindManager, 118, 126
Mind maps, 88
Mindmeister, 118
Mini-tour questions, 45
Montage, 93
Mr. Holland's Opus, 141
MUDs (Multi-user domains), 49
Multimodal and multimedia data, 80–98
  analysis of, 90–94
  generation and collection of, 81–90
  preparation and processing of, 91–93
  transformation and transcription
      of, 92–93
Multimodality, 80

Multi-user domains (MUDs), 49
Music. *See also specific types, instruments*
    and ABER, 100–102
    audible aspects of, 101–102
    in the moment, 104–108
    at moment of articulation, 101
    subjective experiences of, 101
    visual representation of, 88–89
Musical instrument digital interface (MIDI) data, 84, 85, 86
Musical interactions, 112
Musical performance, 103–104
Musical responses, 110–111, 113
Music education, 1–18
Music education journals. *See* Journals; *specific journals by title*
Music education research
    and ABER, 102–104
    designing projects for educational settings, 5–8
    focus group interviews, 65–66
    interviews, 43–62
    observational, 20–42
    QDAS programs used in, 123–126
    qualitative, vii–viii, viii–ix, 1–18
Music Educators Journal (MEJ), 157
Music Educators National Conference (MENC), 141
Music-making data, 99–116
    analysis of, 109–113
    coding of, 113
    collection of, 104–108, 108*b*
    meanings-of-music-making data, 106–108, 108*b*, 113
    process-of-music-making data, 104–106, 108*b*, 113
    product-of-music-making data, 104–106, 113
    research topics that may benefit from, 113
Music teachers. *See* Teachers
Music teaching. *See* Music education
Music therapy, 113

NAfME (National Association for Music Education), 141
Narrative(s)
    configuration of, 56
    "turn" in qualitative inquiry, 135–136

National Association for Music Education (NAfME), 141
National Association of Music Merchants, 46
National Association of Secondary School Principals, 159
National Commission for the Protection of Human Subjects of Biomedical and Behavioral Research, 2
National Museum of American History, 47
Naturalistic generalizations, 36
Naturalistic research, 132–133
New ethnography, 144
Nonmusical responses, 110–111, 113
Non-participation, 22
Nonverbal communication, 72
Nonverbal interactions, 109–112, 113
Nonverbal, verbal, musical, and nonmusical analysis, 111
Notes
    field notes, 28–29
    labeling, 31–32
    time-stamping, 86
NVIVO, 74, 125

Observation
    descriptive, 27
    ethical issues in, 37–38
    focused, 26
    modes of, 20
    in music teaching and learning, 20–42
    participant, 24, 26
    participant-observer continuum, 23–24
    preparing for, 21–23
    qualitative, 20
    researcher role in, 23–25
    selective, 27
Observation data
    analysis of, 32–34
    collection of, 25–31
    writing about, 34–37
    writing descriptions of, 34–35
    writing interpretations of, 35–36
Office of Human Research Protections (OHRP), 10, 58n1
OmniFocus, 126
Online interviews, 49
Opening questions, 45
Open sound control (OSC) data, 85

Oppressed: pedagogy of the, 141
Oral interviews, 47
Organizational systems research, 8–9
OSC (Open sound control) data, 85
OSCulator, 85

Paradigmatic approach, 59
Parallel perspective, 163
Participant-generated data, 87–89
Participant observation, 24, 26
Participant-observer continuum, 23–24
Participation
  active, 23
  complete, 23–24
  moderate, 23
  non-participation, 23
  passive, 23
  researcher, 23
  voluntary, 13
Passive participation, 23
Patton, Michael Quinn, 50
Pearson intercorrelation, 132
Pedagogy of the oppressed, 141
Perception, 20
Performance, 103–104
Permissions, site, 6
Phenomenological research, 44–45
Photo elicitation, 89
Piecemeal publication, 160–162
PluralEyes, 86
Poetic representation, 56
Polkinghorne, Donald, 56
Pragmatic utilitarianism, 142
Prendergast, Monica, 56
Privacy, 13–14
Private information, identifiable, 9
Procedures, 134
Process-of-music-making data, 104–106, 113
Product-of-music-making data, 104–106, 113
Proportionate reason, 38
Propositional generalizations, 37
ProQuest database, 117
Publication(s), 148–164
  choosing venues for, 152–159
  as dissemination, 158–159
  duplicate, 159
  ethics of, 159–164
  piecemeal, 160–162

  redundant, 160
  style requirements, 153
  writing for, 148–152

QDAMiner, 121, 122t
QDAS. *See* Qualitative Data Analysis Software
QSRNVivo, 121–123, 122t, 124–125
Qualitative comparisons, 132
Qualitative Conference in Music Education
  (University of Illinois), 117
Qualitative Data Analysis Software (QDAS),
  118–119
  decision to use, 126–127
  main tasks of analysis with, 119, 120t
  major programs, 121–123, 122t
  programs used by music education
    researchers, 123–126
  use and special features of, 121–123
Qualitative interviews, 12
Qualitative observation, 20
Qualitative research
  assumptions of, 161
  criteria for, 137
  ethics and, 1–19
  evaluative criteria for, 131, 137–145
  future directions, 94–95
  guidelines for, 134
  key criteria for, viii–ix
  in music education, vii–viii, viii–ix, 1–19,
    102–104
  "narrative turn" in, 135–136
  quality in, 130–147
  questions to consider, 144–145
  regulatory ethical review of, 3–5
  software for, 117–129
  special qualities of, 137
  suggestions for, 134
  techniques and strategies for ensuring
    "goodness," 134
Quality
  criteria for, viii–ix, 130
  in music education qualitative research,
    130–147
Qualrus, 121, 122t
Questions
  asking, 51–53
  beginning, 51
  closed, 51, 52

Questions (*cont.*)
  follow-up, 53, 54
  grand tour questions, 46
  mini-tour, 46
  open, 51–52, 53
  opening, 45
  posing, 72–73
  types of, 51, 52*t*

Rapport, 68–69
Realism, 140–141, 143
Reason, proportionate, 38
Recall, stimulated, 89
Recognition, 20
Recording, video and audio, 151–152
  choosing and operating devices for, 82–84
  of focus group interviews, 69
  generating data through, 82
  time-stamping, 85, 86
Records. *See also* Data collection and analysis
  data, 30–31
  digital, 31
  media records, 85, 86
Redundant publication, 160
Reflection, shared, 89, 90
Reflexivity, 51, 137
Regulatory ethical review, 3–5
Reliability, 131, 132, 133
Replication perspective, 163
Reporting. *See* Publication(s)
Research. *See also* Qualitative research
  academic, 13–14
  activities outside IRB oversight, 8–10
  art-based inquiry, 56
  arts-based educational research (ABER), 56, 99, 100–104
  classroom, 13–15
  combined qualitative and quantitative studies, 14–15
  designing projects for educational settings, 5–8
  exempt, 10–12
  future directions, 94–95
  goal of, 143
  with interviews, 48–50
  musical performance as, 103–104
  in music education, 102–104
  naturalistic, 132–133
  on organizational systems, 8–9
  proposals for studies involving human subjects, 49
  qualitative, vii–ix, 1–19, 94–95, 101–103, 117–129, 130–147, 162
  regulated by IRBs, 13–15
  software for, 117–129
  subjectivity of, 50
  topics that may benefit from music-making data, 114
Researchers, 136
  as collaborative participants, 26
  during focus group interviews, 69–70
  as interviewers, 69–70
  as moderators, 69–70
  as observers, 23–25
  participation of, 21–24
  relationships with participants, 24–25
  as research instruments, 24
  selective inattention of, 24
  teachers as, 7–8
Research interviews, 43, 44. *See also* Interviews
Research journals, 29–30. *See also specific journals by title*
Research participants
  collaborative, 26
  data generated by, 87–89
  relationships with, 23–24
  selection of, 68–69, 135
  use of computers and digital devices on-site, 84–85
Research subjects. *See* Research participants
Responses
  individual, 113
  musical, 110–111, 113
  nonmusical, 110–111, 113
  to reviewers, 154
"Response to Reviewers," 154
Responsivity, 110
Reviewers, 154
Review process, 154–156
Richness, 136
Rigor, 163–164

Samples, 133
Sampling, 21

Saturate, 123
Scholarship. *See* Publication(s); Research
Scientific research, traditional, 138–139
Screencasting software, 85
ScreenFlow, 85, 126
Selective observation, 25
Self-portraits, 88–89
Shakuhachi music, 31
Shared music focus, 112
Shared music interactions, 112
Shared music understandings, 112
Shared reflection, video-based (VBSR), 89, 90
Signature: Women in Music, 47
Site permissions, 6
Skype, 49, 76
Smithsonian Jazz Oral History Program, 47
Smithsonian Museum, 47
SMV (synchronous multiple video) systems, 86
Social construction, 139–140
Social context, 111
Social influence, 112
Social interactions/connections, 111–112, 113
Software, 117–129
Stauffer, Sandra, 56–57
Storytelling, 141
Strauss, Anselm, 55
Students, 5–6
Student teachers, 10
Style requirements, 153
Style vs substance, 164
Subjectivity, 50, 101
Synchronization of data, 86–87
Synchronous multiple video (SMV) systems, 86

Target children, 135
Teacher-researchers, 7–8
Teachers
 as participants, 8
 as researchers, 7–8
 student teachers, 10
Teachers College, Columbia, 124
Teaching. *See* Education
Technology
 focus group interviews with, 76–77
 web-based, 94

Terkel, Studs, 46
Terminology
 choosing our words, 138–143
 evaluative, 131–134
 music therapy, 113
 new vocabulary, 136–137
Think-aloud interviews, 107
Think-aloud protocols, 136
Timelines, 31
Time-stamping field notes, 86
Time-stamping media records, 85
Titles, 153
Traditional scientific research criteria, 138–139
Transana, 122*t*, 126
Transcription
 of field notes, 30–31
 of focus group interview data, 74–75
 of individual interview data, 54, 55
 linguistic-focused frameworks, 92–93
 of multimedia data, 92–93
Transcripts, 54, 55, 73–74
Transferability, viii, 133
Triangulation
 of data, 136
 as state of mind, 27
Tuskegee Syphilis Study, 2
Twitter, 94

United Kingdom, 48
University of Illinois, 117
Update: Applications of Research in Music Education, 152
Utilitarianism, pragmatic, 142

Validity, 131, 132, 134, 163
VBSR (video-based shared reflection), 89, 90
Verbal and nonverbal data analysis, 110
Verbal and nonverbal interactions, 109–112, 113
Video and audio recording, 151–152
 choosing and operating devices for, 82–84
 of focus group interviews, 69
 generating data through, 82
 time-stamping, 85, 86
Video-based shared reflection (VBSR), 89, 90
Videoconferencing, 76

Video confessionals, 88
Video data or footage, 82
    content logs of, 91
    participant-generated, 87–89
    transformation and transcription of, 91–93
Video diaries, 88
Video elicitation, 89
Visual artifacts, 88
Visual data, participant-generated, 88–89
Vividness, 136
Vocabulary, 136–137, 138–142
Vocal events, 110
Voice over Internet Protocol (VoIP), 49
Voice, writer's, 34–35, 140–141, 148–152
Voluntary participation, 13

Walt Disney Company, 141
Web-based data, 94
Web-based writing, 151
Wolof language, 25
Writer's voice
    development of, 149–150
    establishing, 36–37, 148–152
    new voices, 150–152
Writing
    for academic publication, 148–152
    collaborative, 150–151
    descriptions of observation data, 34–35
    goals in, 35
    in hypertext, 151
    IMRAD (Introduction, Methods, Results, and Discussion) format, 156
    interpretations of observation data, 34–35
    about observation data, 34–37
    space-saving strategies, 157
    style requirements, 152–153, 157
    web-based, 151

Yarbrough, Cornelia, 142
YouTube, 94, 123

Zone of proximal development (ZPD), 109

www.ingramcontent.com/pod-product-compliance
Ingram Content Group UK Ltd.
Pitfield, Milton Keynes, MK11 3LW, UK
UKHW051250180426
11947UKWH00020B/1636